Donated by the

WEST MIDLANDS POLICE AUTHORITY

October 1990

POLICING BIRMINGHAM

POLICING BIRMINGHAM

AN ACCOUNT OF
150 YEARS OF POLICE IN BIRMINGHAM

By JOHN W REILLY
Chief Inspector

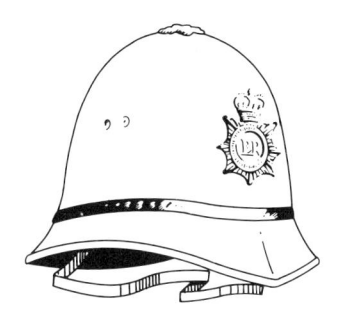

WEST MIDLANDS POLICE

© THE CHIEF CONSTABLE
West Midlands Police
Lloyd House, Colmore Circus
Birmingham

ISBN 0 9515152 0 9

All rights reserved. No part of this publication may be reproduced, stored in a retrieval system or transmitted, in any form or by any means, electronic, mechanical photocopying, recording or otherwise, without the prior permission of the West Midlands Police.

Made and printed in England by
Renault Printing Co. Ltd., Birmingham B44 8BS, England

To the memory of every Police Officer who ever walked the streets of Birmingham in the freezing cold of a winters night; especially to every such policeman who shinned up a gas street lamp to warm a flask of tea; or who sheltered out of the rain for a smoke; or who used every uncharted alleyway, passage or cutting to make a 'point' on time, and never got caught by the Sergeant, this book is dedicated.

Acknowledgements

The City of Birmingham Central Reference Library
The Birmingham Evening Mail
The City of Birmingham Polytechnic
(Faculty of Government)
The West Midlands Police Law Research Unit and
Force Museum

Foreword

In any organisation the arrival at the milestone of one hundred and fifty years of continuous service is a worthy celebration. When such a celebration coincides with the centennial of a great City then there is good reason to pause and reflect on policing in Birmingham. Over the years the methods and organisation of the system of policing have undergone radical change to respond to the demands of the times. However the ethos of policing this City and of service to the public and the equitable enforcement of the law, has remained a constant.

The Police are a rock upon which the constitution of this country is built. This book records the history of how part of that rock has grown in durability. It records the development of a Borough Police Force, into a City Police Force, and into a Force which covers the largest conurbation in the provinces.

Birmingham
August 1989

G J DEAR

Contents

Introduction   xi

1 In the Beginning   1
THE CHARTIST RIOTS; BUILDING A POLICE FORCE; THE NEW BIRMINGHAM BOROUGH POLICE; GROWTH AND REORGANISATION; FIRST AND LAST COMMISSIONER RESIGNS

2 Early Days   18
THE MURPHY RIOTS; EARLY COMPLAINTS OF BEHAVIOUR; POLICE DUTIES EXPLAINED IN 1878; JOHN THOMAS WILSON, MISSIONARY TO BIRMINGHAM POLICE; MAJOR BOND VS. THE WATCH COMMITTEE; THE IRISH TROUBLES COME TO BIRMINGHAM; EXPANSION OF BIRMINGHAM AND ITS POLICE FORCE; THE BEGINNING OF AN ERA-CHARLES HAUGHTON RAFTER; THE MURDER OF PC SNIPE; CRIME IN THIS PERIOD

3 Edwardian Days   45
THE TOWN HALL RIOT; BIRMINGHAM'S FIRST FINGERPRINT PROSECUTION; HAWKERS AND TRADERS; THE FIRST KING'S POLICE MEDALS FOR GALLANTRY; THE GREAT WAR; ZEPPELIN RAIDS; THE SPECIAL CONSTABULARY; OTHER WARTIME POLICE DUTIES; REBUILDING THE BIRMINGHAM CITY POLICE; BIRMINGHAM'S FIRST WOMEN POLICE; CRIME AND DETECTIVES; POST WAR TRAINING; THE 1919 POLICE STRIKE; IMPROVED CONDITIONS; POOR PC CAPEWELL; THE HOCKLEY BROOK DISASTER; MODERN TIMES; THE THIRTIES; STEELHOUSE LANE POLICE STATION; PAY AND CONDITIONS IN THE 1930's

4 End of an Era   90
THE BOMBERS RETURN; THE SECOND WORLD WAR; ADJUSTING TO WARTIME DUTIES; AIR RAIDS ON THE CITY; MR MORIARTY RETIRES; DEVELOPMENTS ON THE HOME FRONT; CHANGES IN PERSONNEL; WARTIME CONDITIONS AND CRIME

5 The Very Thin Blue Line   113
THE SEARCH FOR EFFICIENCY; RECRUITING AND RECRUITS; BACK ON THE ROAD; POST WAR AUSTERITY; THE RECRUITING PROBLEM; THE SEARCH FOR AN ANSWER; LAW AND ORDER IN THE 1950's; BIRMINGHAM'S POLICE DOGS; POLICE MOTORCYCLES; OLD AND NEW POLICE STATIONS; MODERNISATION

6 All Change   145
THE CRIME WAVE; TACKLING THE CRIME PROBLEM; TRAFFIC CONGESTION AND CITY CENTRE RECONSTRUCTION; EASING THE CONGESTION; THE CONTINUING SEARCH FOR RECRUITS; BIRMINGHAM'S POLICE CADETS; INTRODUCTION OF PERSONAL RADIOS; UNIT BEAT POLICING, 'PANDAS'; PRAISE AND CRITICISM OF 'PANDAS'; THE CHANGING ROLE OF POLICEWOMEN; THE BUILDING OF TALLY HO!; NEW POLICE STATIONS; MR DODD DEPARTS; THE APPOINTMENT OF MR CAPPER AND HIS DEPUTY; CHERRYWOOD ATTENDANCE CENTRE; THE ORIGINS OF THE SPECIAL PATROL GROUP; IMPROVING CONDITIONS IN THE 1960's

7 The Beginning of the End   182
LOCAL GOVERNMENT REORGANISATION; HUNTING FOR A NEW FORCE HEADQUARTERS; THE FINAL BUILDING PROGRAMME; MOTORWAY POLICING; POLICING CITY TRAFFIC; THE RECRUITING SAGA CONTINUES; COMMUNITY RELATIONS; THE COMPUTER AGE; COMMAND AND CONTROL; THE MINERS' STRIKE OF 1972; THE BATTLE OF SALTLEY GATE; THE IRA RETURNS; THE END OF A SEPARATE BIRMINGHAM POLICE; SPORTS AND SOCIAL ACTIVITIES; THE LAST DAYS

Postscript   209
'B' TO 'F' DIVISIONS WEST MIDLANDS POLICE; THE BOMBS BEGIN IN EARNEST; SIR DERRICK CAPPER TAKES LEAVE OF THE FORCE; THE MURDER OF PC GREEN; OLD BUILDINGS FOR NEW; STREET DISORDERS; RESTRUCTURING AND REORGANISING; LOZELLS ROAD DISORDERS; THE CONTINUITY OF POLICING

Appendix   220

Bibliography   226

Index   227

List of Illustrations

Charge Office at Holyhead Road Police Station, 1929	10
Kenyon Street Police Station in 1950's	20
Police Sergeant's day uniform 1930's	26
Digbeth Police Station 1912	32
Police Constable's night helmet and greatcoat 1930's	38
Sir Charles Haughton Rafter, whilst Sub Inspector of the Royal Irish Constabulary	41
'Before and After' for the Aided Association	44
Bloomsbury Street Police Station 1960's	47
Ladywood Police Station c.1950	55
The Ladies of the Policewomen Department 1930's	62
Point duty at the junction of Bull Street 1930's	67
Results are posted at Digbeth Police School in 1930's	70
September 1939: Sand bagging at Steelhouse Lane	84
Marching to their beats, Steelhouse Lane 1935	86
Mr CCH Moriarty, Chief Constable, Sept. 1935 – Sept. 1941	91
PS C24 Christie and PC C601 Grills together with PC C114 Leslie Thomas: all recipients of BEM's for air raid bravery	94
An exhibition at Lewis's Ltd to publicise the new radio area cars in 1943	103
Mr William Clarence Johnson, Chief Constable, Sept. 1941 – Oct. 1945	105
One of the first area cars fitted with radio in 1940's	106
Mr E J Dodd, Chief Constable, Oct. 1945 – Sept. 1963	109
Bomb damage repairs to the Chief Constable's office, Newton Street	114
Victory Celebrations: Special Constabulary March Past, 1945	122
PC A30 uses a Police Pillar in Dale End, 1949	124
Recruits in training at Digbeth Police School c.1940's	131
Austin Mini Cooper 'S' on Traffic Patrol in 1968	152
Police Constable's uniform and equipment 1970	161
The ubiquitous Panda car at Tally Ho! in 1970	166
Detective Sergeant Charles Elworthy lectures on the art of fingerprint identification	170
A sylvan setting for a Police Vespa, 1956	173
Mr William Derrick Capper, Chief Constable, Sept. 1963 – Aug. 1975	174
Command and Control goes live in the Information Room 1972	194
'The Battle of Saltley Gate' February 1972	197
An empty Selly Oak Police Station 1976	204
Mr Philip D Knights, Chief Constable, August 1975 – April 1985	210
The old Stechford Police Station with the new building at the rear 1975	214
Mr Geoffrey J Dear, Chief Constable, 8 April 1985	216

Introduction

The streets of Birmingham have been policed in what may be termed as the recognisable modern sense for 150 years. During that time policemen have been visible by day going about their duty either on foot, or more recently, by car. At night their presence has not always been so obvious, but over the years the quiet footfall of the patrolling constables along the back-streets, courts and alleyways of the industrial capital of the nation has been a reassurance to the majority and a fear to the wrongdoer.

To write a history of Policing in Birmingham is a challenge. Where does one draw the line? What item should be included and which should be excluded? In an historical tapestry as rich as that of 150 years of social control in Birmingham incidents and developments are legion. Every member of Birmingham Borough, and later City, Police played a part in that development.

Policing in Birmingham was born as a result of Chartist disorders and rioting. As the City grew in size and population so did its Police Force. Through two World Wars when the City was attacked by air raids the police were, in the words of Sir Winston Churchill, 'In it everywhere.' In four bombing capaigns by Irish Republicans, Birmingham police never wavered in their hunt for the guilty. Supported by the Birmingham public they have always succeeded in arresting those terrorists. From the Chartist Riots onwards there have been incidents of serious disorder on the streets of Birmingham at irregular intervals. The Police were always on hand to maintain the King's or Queen's peace.

Outside of the Metropolitan there is arguably no other police force, whose development and growth can be taken as a yardstick for the development of a local police force, better than Birmingham. The Metropolitan Police have no police authority in the sense of locally elected politicians controlling 'Citizens locally appointed as constables.' To read the Watch Committee minutes spanning 150 years of Birmingham history is an illumination of what is meant by the localised control of policing in England and Wales. The Watch Committees have seemingly always taken the professional advice of their Chief Officers. After the Second World War the Watch Committees fought battles with the Home Office for the benefit of Birmingham policemen and their Force, as well as for the good of the public.

The Police of Birmingham have always been proud of their City and this has been the essence of policing in Birmingham. Those police officers who joined the City of Birmingham Police prior to 1974, and those members of the West Midlands Police who currently police the streets of Birmingham, jealously guard their heritage. In the course of researching this work I have met many men and women whose knowledge and interest in the history of the Birmingham Police is more than received knowledge or canteen gossip, but a genuine historical fascination. I spent a particularly interesting morning at Solihull Hospital in April 1989 listening to the reminiscences of Mr Cyril Mansell one time police constable of Birmingham City Police. Mr Mansell was the driver for four chief constables in Birmingham, having joined the service in 1919. He retains an appearance suggesting that if he were to put on a police uniform could still fearlessly walk a beat. But in a history of policing in Birmingham if one man should be particularly remembered it is Mr Charles Elworthy. Ex Detective Sergeant Elworthy, by hard work, dedication and unrelenting effort, started and built up the Police Museum which is currently situated at Tally Ho! Training Centre. Although retired he continues to give his own time improving our knowledge of Birmingham Police history.

Thanks to 'Charlie' generations of policemen in Birmingham and the West Midlands can gain a glimpse of the life and times of their forebears. A visit to the museum is an educational experience. One thing that becomes clear is that times change, appearances change and political environments change but police work stays the same. That work is getting people to do what they would rather not do or getting people to stop what they would rather be doing. The history of Birmingham Police is a history of how that was achieved within a framework of cheerfulness, kindliness and the law.

I wish to take this opportunity of thanking Assistant Chief Constable Mr Francis Wilkinson for his support and guidance in the preparation of this work. I also wish to thank Chief Superintendent Derek Williams and Detective Superintendent Frank Rawlings for proof reading the book and the advice and corrections they volunteered to the author.

1
In the Beginning

History records that Birmingham Borough Police first commenced duty on 20 November 1839. However, different forms of policing had existed long before that. In common with the rest of the nation, responsibility for the 'Maintenance of the Peace' was imposed upon the Hundred or Tything. For the nascent town of Birmingham, this was the 'Hemlingford Hundred' and the Court Leet of the Manor.

In the year 1789, a Mr Thomas Lee, the Steward of the Manor of Birmingham had cause to prepare a list of duties of 'the respective officers appointed by the Court Leet of the Manor.' The Court Leet was an ancient body consisting of the High Bailiff and Court Leet Jury, who were all members of the local 'great and good' upon whom the responsibility of the Peace rested. Thomas Lee reported that in relation to the Office of the Constable

> 'The Jury find and present, that these Officers are annually elected by the Jury; and their Duty is to suppress all Riots and Affrays within the Manor, to arrest all Felons, Night Walkers and suspicious Persons, which they may do of their own Authority: and they may charge and command any Person, to assist them in the Execution of their Office, if needs require, and they are to be attendant upon the Justices of the Peace, and to execute their Warrants: and they have a power, by virtue of their Office, of Billeting the Officers and Soldiers, which they are to do fairly and impartially.'

Lee also recorded that for the Office of Headborough:

> 'The Jury find and present that this Officer is annually elected by the Jury, and is a Secondary Constable, in the Absence or on the Death of the Constable, it is his Business to do and execute the Duties of the Constable, and when required, he is personally to assist the Constable in preserving the Public Peace.'

As many commentators have recorded the Office of Constable was unpopular because of the demands made upon the time of the men elected. Usually, they paid someone else to undertake their duties. These souls were often of the character of Shakespeare's Constable, Dogberry, inasmuch as they were lazy and incompetent rogues.

Birmingham Public-Office.

AT a very numerous and refpectable Meeting of the Inhabitants of the Town, held this Day, it was refolved *nem. con.* to enter into an Affociation for profecuting every Species of Rogues, and that the Inhabitants of the Town be waited on for their Signatures to Articles for that Purpofe.

The Subfcribers are refolved to exert their utmoft Endeavours in bringing to Conviction every Offender. And fuch poor Perfons as may happen to be robbed, and cannot defray the Expences of a Profecution, are requefted to give immediate Notice to Mr. Parker, Attorney, on Snow-hill.

SEPTEMBER 9; 1785-

Fig. I — Handbill for Felons Society, 1785

In Birmingham the constables were paid £400 a year for expenses and were provided annually with a 'Constables Feast.' The antiquarian, Hutton, mentions that in 1773 he found 'great resentment aroused locally at this extravagance.' From 1820 onwards the Feast was replaced by the gift of a pair of cased pistols presented to the retiring officers. Of the pistols presented, it is known that two sets are now in the United States and one remains in the Birmingham City collection. To execute their duty the constables were assisted by watchmen in the town. Under the Streets Act of 1769, the Street Commissioners for Birmingham appointed street keepers and night watchmen to deal with traffic and the general protection of persons and property. These men were provided with clothing, tall hats and cloaks, and equipment in the form of long staves and lanterns. They were popularly known as 'Charlies.' The expression 'a right Charley' is thought to derive from this, meaning a person of little commonsense and foresight. The watchmen were sworn in as constables by the Justices, upon whom fell the ultimate authority in Birmingham, for the enforcement of the law. The Justices in Birmingham were housed in public offices in Moor Street and were also responsible for the small prison cells in Peck Lane. At times of necessity the Justices also swore in special constables.

The system was archaic and inefficient and did not meet the needs of a town, like Birmingham, as it progressed into the Industrial Revolution. The inhabitants of the town were clearly fearful for their property and persons. On 9 September 1785 a meeting was held at the public offices by concerned townspeople to consider the situation of crime in Birmingham. A handbill exists for this meeting *(Fig. I)* and it shows that those present resolved to form an Association for the Prosecution of Felons and to aid those who could not afford to prosecute to do so. These associations were common at this time and several still exist in parts of the country, such as Derbyshire. They are now dining/debating societies. As previously mentioned, difficulties arose in obtaining the services of people of standing and the following letter remains to confirm this:—

> Mr Kempson
> Sir
> At a General Meeting on Friday last at the Public Office I observe that I was nominated one of yr. Committee to assist in soliciting Subscriptions for a General Association for prosecuting felons etc....
> I am Sorry to Inform You that at this time I cannot Render the Essential services I cou'd with having some Particular Business of my Own in Hand. Add to these Others of my Late Brother in Law, Mr Wm Hall Whose

family I am left in Trust for Engages my Attention at the Present so far that my Business must be Neglected were I to Engage in Other Concerns that Really it is not in my Power to pay that due attention I cou'd wish in Public Matters therefore hope that my Worthy Friends will Constitue some Other Person. When I am more at Leisure shall then think it an indisspensible Duty to Render every Aid & Assistance in my power in Promoting so laudable a scheme or any other good cause tending to the Interest of Ye Town of Birm. to the utmost of my abilities and In the Present Case will contribute wth Chearfulness to the support of ye Plan now Establishing I remain wth all due Respect to the Gentlemen Concerned & to Self.

Yo.r most Hble Servt
Birm. September 13th 1785. Tho Martson.

The Association was all well and good for ensuring the prosecuting of felons and rogues but first they had to be efficiently caught. The only answer was private police and *Aris's Gazette* for 15 December 1789 reports from The Bell Inn, New Road, 'At a numerous and respectable meeting of inhabitants held in pursuance of a circular letter; Mr William Smith was in the Chair. The meeting passed unanimously: That it is highly expedient for the protection of our persons and property to form an association for establishing a night patrol.' Private patrols were set up but mainly in notable thoroughfares such as New Street, Colmore Row and Moor Street. At a meeting of the Moor Street Patrol Association on 5 January 1831, held at the Wool Pack Inn, it was reported that the Moor Street Nightwatch employed eight night patrol constables, who were in possession of handcuffs and truncheons.

The Municipal Corporatións Act of 1835 which introduced enabling powers for the establishment of Incorporated Boroughs, to raise a Police Force, did not include Birmingham, Bolton, or Manchester. Eventually on 31 October 1838 Birmingham was granted a Charter of Incorporation under the Act of 1835. However this statute was not enacted primarily for the purposes of promoting police forces. It was a sequel to the Reform Act of 1832 and was seen as bringing fresh blood to local government. As T A Critchley claims in *A History of Police in England and Wales 900-1966,* 'Dissenters and tradesmen once and for all ousted the last generations of Tory lawyers, churchmen and noblemen's agents who had long ruled the Courts Leet and instituted the age of municipal enterprise and local self-government.' This was obviously true of the town of Birmingham which had grown through industry and through tolerance towards Non-Conformists. A writer in the *Birmingham Journal,* of the 21 October 1837, denounces the existing system by claiming, 'We have our Court Leet and our bailiffs, chosen by themselves; our Street Commissioners, chosen by themselves, our Town Hall Commissioner, chosen by themselves: all working in the dark unseen by the public eye and irresponsible to the public voice, appointing their own officers, levying taxes at their pleasure and distributing them without check or control.'

Once the Charter of Incorporation had been granted and a Town Council had been elected the Council were required to form a Watch Committee from among their own number, with the Mayor as an ex-officio member. Within three weeks the Watch Committee was to appoint a 'sufficient number of fit men' sworn in as constables for the preservation of the peace by day and night and the prevention of robberies. As many of the early constables found out, the Watch Committee was empowered to dismiss as well as appoint constables.

In Birmingham a Watch Rate to raise the requisite funds for the new Police was put before the Council on 12 April 1839. The Old Guard found legal doubts for the Council as to their powers to levy the rate and this led to a failure to appoint a Watch Committee and thereby establish a Police force. However as so often happens in Police matters the Council were overtaken by events.

THE CHARTIST RIOTS

Those events were the political agitation surrounding the 'People's Charter'. Following a depression in trade in 1837 and 1838 a new political awareness arose in the working classes and they made their demands in the Charter, and became known as Chartists. The Charter called for universal suffrage, vote by ballot, equal electoral districts, annual parliaments, abolition of an MP's property qualification and the payment of MPs. In support of the Charter meetings were held in Birmingham every Monday evening on Holloway Head. On 13 August 1838 a 'monster' demonstration which was held there was believed to be of 10,000 persons. On the 1 and 9 April 1839 Feargus O'Connor and other Chartist leaders held meetings in Birmingham and made 'violent and inflammatory speeches'. The unemployed and poorly paid workmen of the town supported Chartism.

Sensing disorder the Justices appointed over 2,000 special constables and they were organised by Wards. If one considers the size of the population of Birmingham in 1839, which was approximately 150,000, a body of 2,000 special constables was a substantial proportion. On 13 May 1839 the National Convention of the Chartist Movement moved from London to Birmingham. There were two reasons for this. Firstly it was due to increased activity from the Metropolitan Police against the seditious speeches by Chartists and secondly from the support which was obvious in Birmingham. It was said that the

Convention would be, 'safer under the guns of Manchester and Birmingham'. Birmingham was of course even then the centre of firearms trade in the country.

By the end of June special constables together with members of the military were posted in various parts of the town. The military were made up of members of four troops of the 4th Dragoon Guards and a Company of the Rifle Brigade who were stationed in Duddeston where Barrack Street stands to this day.

On Monday 1 July Feargus O'Connor addressed a meeting in the Bull Ring. On hearing that several of the other Chartist leaders had been taken from the town by the military, he led his audience to Gosta Green in order to deliver his speech from outside the town boundaries where the Specials had no powers. On finishing his address O'Connor had the crowd march back to the Bull Ring to 'take' their usual meeting place. This was the pattern that was set for the next few days. The crowd would meet and march off, flags flying, banners waving, cheering and shouting to 'take' some other place. With such large numbers in such a mood the worst happened to a nation of small shopkeepers, trade was affected. The Mayor, Mr William Schofield, and two magistrates went to London for help.

On the 4 July at the request of Birmingham Magistrates, 60 Metropolitan Police officers were brought from London. They were sworn in as Special Constables and on the same night turned out to a riot in the Bull Ring. After an hour of being subjected to attack they were rescued by the Dragoons who dispersed the mob. The following day 40 more Metropolitan officers arrived and for three days together with the military they dispersed meetings by the Chartists in the Bull Ring and Holloway Head. On 9 July the Magistrates approached the Council and asked them to form an efficient Police Force under the Act. The Council passed a resolution to do so when funds were available.

On the 10 July the superintendent in charge, believing the worst of the problems to be over, returned 40 officers to London. On 15 July there were only 50 Metropolitan Police officers left in Birmingham.

At about 7 pm on that day, a crowd again gathered in the Bull Ring, made up for the greater part of those attracted by curiosity. Initially their conduct was orderly and no attempt was made to disperse them. Pressure from the numbers present led to the shopkeepers closing their premises at 8 pm. Shortly after this a mob, estimated at about 500, were seen coming from the direction of Digbeth. They were armed with pieces of iron, wooden railings and other weapons. The mob made its way to Moor Street and headed for the Public Office and commenced to attack the building. They smashed nearly all the windows and the policemen inside closed the gates. It is believed that they were under orders not to confront the rioters without instructions from the Magistrates. The mob taunted the Police without success and then moved off to attack nearby shops. They split into parties and demolished several shops. This would have been at about 8.45 pm. As so often with mobs acting under the righteous indignation of social disadvantage they turned to looting. From the shop of Messrs Leggat, an upholsterer, a large quantity of bed ticking was stolen. This was then spread like carpeting around the Bull Ring. It was set light to by the mob who used a lamp from on top of Nelson's monument for a flame. When alight it was rolled up and parts of the fire carried into different shops. Within moments the buildings were in flames.

The intent of the rioters was now very clear. The gullible and curious fled the scene. The Nelson Hotel was next attacked and fired. The actions of the mob continued until 9.40 pm when the Police, together with the military, turned out. The rioters fled and engaged in sporadic outbreaks of stone throwing as they were pursued by the cavalry. Initially several boys and men had been arrested but after the arrival of the military the prison in Moor Street was literally filled with offenders.

The following day the town was heavily patrolled by the cavalry. The remaining Police were occupied searching houses for stolen property and the lanes and courts for any weapons, such as pikes. Eventually some of the rioters were tried at Warwick Summer Assizes and were sentenced to terms of imprisonment. Three men and a boy were condemned to death but were reprieved and suffered transportation to the colony in New South Wales, Australia. Compensation was paid to those whose property was damaged. The cost of this was borne by the Hundred of Hemlingford and amounted to some £15,000.

Critchley states that the Magistrates believed that the intervention of London Police had exacerbated any danger there might have been. This is of course a claim we have heard on many occasions subsequently, especially at the time of the miners' strike in 1984/85.

A degree of normality returned to the streets of Birmingham and on 16 August the Magistrates requested the two constables to take immediate measures for the establishment of a night horse patrol, to be paid for by voluntary subscription.

A Parliamentary debate about the riots and state of affairs in the town was held. One of the last words on the subject was by the Duke of Wellington who told the House of Lords that, 'I have been in many towns taken by storm, but never have such outrages occurred in them as had been committed in

ANNO SECUNDO & TERTIO

VICTORIÆ REGINÆ.

****

C A P. LXXXVIII.

An Act for improving the Police in *Birmingham* for Two Years, and from thence until the End of the then next Session of Parliament.
[26th *August* 1839.]

WHEREAS Questions are pending as to the Powers of the Mayor, Aldermen, and Burgesses of the Borough of *Birmingham* to levy Rates under the Authority of their Charter of Incorporation; and it is expedient to make Provision for the Police of the said Borough until such Questions shall be determined: Be it enacted by the Queen's most Excellent Majesty, by and with the Advice and Consent of the Lords Spiritual and Temporal, and Commons, in this present Parliament assembled, and by the Authority of the same, That it shall be lawful for Her Majesty to establish a Police Office in the Borough of *Birmingham*, and by Warrant under Her Sign Manual to appoint a fit Person to be Chief Commissioner of Police for the said Borough. *Her Majesty may establish a Police Office in Birmingham, and appoint a Chief Commissioner of Police.*

II. And be it enacted, That it shall be lawful for Her Majesty to appoint the said Chief Commissioner so appointed to be a Justice of the Peace of the said Borough, and of the Counties of *Warwick*, *Worcester*, *Salop*, and *Stafford*, and of all Liberties therein, to execute the Duties of a Justice of the Peace at the said Office, together with *Commissioner so appointed to be a Justice.*

10 A such

Fig. II — The Enabling Act for the Birmingham Borough Police

Birmingham!' On 26 August 1839 an Act for Improving the Police in Birmingham was placed on the Statute Book.

This Act acknowledged the problem of town council's powers to levy rates and to circumvent this the Crown was empowered to establish a Police Office and appoint a Chief Commissioner of Police. Under directions of the Secretary of State he was to appoint a sufficient number of fit and able men as a Police Force and swear them in as constables. For the time that the Act remained in force all the powers of the Metropolitan Police Act 1829 were to apply in Birmingham. Necessity has always been the mother of invention and by a typical parliamentary sleight of hand the Treasury was empowered to lend money to the Commissioner for Police purposes. The capital was to be repaid from the town's rates. Here was the embryo City of Birmingham Police.

BUILDING A POLICE FORCE

On 1 September 1839 the Government appointed Mr Francis Burgess as Chief Commissioner of Birmingham Police. Burgess was a barrister who practised at Warwick Sessions. He had seen service in the 54th Regiment, from 1812 to 1817 and had been a captain with that regiment at the battle of Waterloo. At that time no better mixture than that of law and military service could possibly have been found for the new Police. It is of interest that when the Metropolitan Police had been formed in London ten years earlier it had two commissioners, one a soldier and the other a lawyer.

Burgess arrived in Birmingham on 23 September 1839. He rented the Branch Bank House in Union Street and took up residence with his family. It was also here that he established the first Police office in Birmingham. Burgess set about his work swiftly. A Major John Shaw was appointed as his deputy, and Mr Henry Shaw the Borough Treasurer as the Receiver for the Force. It is a matter of record that Chief Commissioner Burgess received much assistance from Superintendent May, the officer in charge of the Metropolitan Police detachment who were still in town.

The enabling Act gave the new Birmingham Police all the powers and privileges of the Metropolitan Police Act of 1829. In fact the Birmingham Act states that, 'An Act for Improving the Police in and near the Metropolis, shall apply to the Borough of Birmingham'. Also that, 'all things done under the Authority of that Act shall apply as if the said Act had been made applicable to the Borough of Birmingham instead of the Metropolitan Police District'. The Birmingham Act also allowed the constables, 'all such powers, authorities, privileges and advantages', in the counties of Warwick, Worcester, Shropshire

Charge Office at Holyhead Road Police Station, 1929

and Stafford. Clearly the new Force had powers based upon those of the Metropolitan Police but they were also organised along the same lines. This is not surprising when one remembers that at that time most areas and Forces turned to the Metropolis for help and guidance in forming their new police.

On 26 September Burgess held a parade of serving constables and watchmen at Bindley's Repository. He was obviously disheartened by what he saw and selected comparatively few for his Force. One man who did catch his eye, was William Hall, described to him as a most meritorious officer. Burgess appointed him as inspector. The first pay sheet for the Force is dated from 24 to 29 September 1839 and shows one inspector at 38s 6d weekly, one inspector at 29s 2d, four sergeants at 21s and two constables at 17s 1d.

Undeterred Burgess advertised in the *Birmingham Advertiser* on 3 October 1839 inviting applications for the new Force from 'Young men, not over 36 or under 5' 8", able to read, write and produce testimonials of exceptional character'. Applications are said to have been numerous and candidates were examined daily at the Town Hall by Mr Charles Gem, the new Police surgeon and Inspector Harris of the Metropolitan Police. The first man recruited to the Birmingham Borough Police on 23 September 1839 was George Anthony Howick, 26 years of age. His description is given as 5' 8¼" tall, a fair complexion, hazel eyes with dark brown hair, no distinguishing marks and a proper figure. Howick had been born in Sidmouth, Devon and was a farmer by trade being a single man with no children. It was stated that he could read and write and at that time was residing in Edgbaston Street, City. He had served in the 6th Regiment of Scots Grenadiers for three years and had been discharged with a gratuity of £200 on 10 June 1838. His last employer was shown as 'C' Division, Metropolitan Police, 10 Vine Street, Piccadilly, London. Howick was certified as fit. By the 1 November 1839 the strength of the force had risen to 260.

Burgess planned the force to be made up of four sub-divisions, policed in total by: one superintendent, four inspectors, eight sub-inspectors, 26 sergeants, and 250 constables. 'Policing by Objectives' is not new and Burgess caused a 61 page booklet to be printed of Instructions and Orders. These were issued to every member of the Force. The booklet informed the Police of their powers and duties; their principle objective being the prevention of crime. Each man was to devote his whole time to the Police service, to serve and reside where ever he was appointed, to obey all lawful orders and at all time appear in complete uniform, on or off duty.

The pay of a constable was stated to be 17s 1d per week and he was to be supplied with clothing. If lodgings were found for the officer he was to be deducted 1s. Every constable was to wear a letter and a number on his collar in order that, 'He might be known to the public.'

On 25 October 1839 the Court Leet re-appointed Mr John Bolton and Mr Thomas Clive as constables and George Redfern as headborough. Bolton and Clive declined to serve and on 1 November 1839 Mr William Corbett of New Street together with Thomas Weston of High Street were appointed constables. They were the last police officials appointed in Birmingham by the Court Leet. Nineteen days later they were superseded by the new Police Force. On 30 October the Metropolitan Police Officers began to return to London.

On 4 November 1839 Burgess issued his first general order to the force from the Police Office in Union Street. The order concerned warrant cards, daily sick parades and instruction books. The constables were placed into sections and were practised daily by their sergeants on their beats in accordance with beat cards. Burgess ordered that men who were off duty were to remain in the locality of their Police Station so as to be on call for emergencies.

By the 8 November 1839 Beardsworth's Repository in Moseley Street, close to the present Bradford Street Police Station, was rented as the Principal Police Station. Other Police Stations were established in Bath Row, near the site of the present Davenport's Brewery, in Deritend, in Sandpits, leading to Dudley Road, and Staniforth Street, beside the present Council Offices at Lancaster Circus. Later stations were established in Crooked Lane, the site of the present Martineau Way and Square, and in Cardigan Street next to Curzon Street Railway Station. These buildings were not Police Stations but either large warehouses like Beardsworths or ordinary dwelling houses or commercial premises.

On 17 November Commissioner Burgess had the whole force parade at Beardsworths where they were fitted with hats, stocks and capes. After an inspection the men were drilled and practised on their beats by their sergeants. These parades continued daily and *Aris's Gazette* reports that on the night of 19 November, 'the men rendered good service at a fire'.

THE NEW BIRMINGHAM BOROUGH POLICE

On 20 November 1839 the new Birmingham Police Force took over the policing of the town. The old Police system was suspended. Those Metropolitan Police officers remaining who had been in the town since July returned to London.

The new Police were initially welcomed by the populace, unlike in London where 'Peels bloody lobsters' were not at first received wholeheartedly. Burgess soon reported to the Home Secretary that his men 'cut a very good figure and seem to have made a good impression'. In January 1840 he reported that he had heard, 'nothing from all quarters but expressions of approval of the new Force'.

The development of the Force and policing in Birmingham continued at a rapid pace. On 25 November the Magistrates arranged to sit daily at the Public Office at 10 am to hear Police cases. On 29 November handcuffs were issued to the Force and those constables patrolling outbeats in the suburbs were issued with cutlasses due to the number of 'desperate characters' committing burglaries. From 30 November onwards Police Orders were regularly issued from Beardsworths in Moseley Street. Here Superintendent Shaw was delegated with disciplinary matters, suspending defaulters 'until the pleasure of the Commissioner was known'. On 1 December the pay sheet shows that the Force was now made up of 304 men. On 16 December 1839 each sub-division was allowed to have a clerk constable who could work from 8 am to 7 pm. Administration was therefore born on this day.

On 23 December of that year orders permitted that lists of stolen property could be circulated to all pawnbrokers. In the view of subsequent generations of policemen this merely helped the pawnbrokers to know what to buy or take in hock at better personal terms. On 24 December, Christmas Eve, six of the best officers resigned as constables only to join Worcestershire County as superintendents at £80 per annum.

The conditions at that time were arduous, as documented in many police histories. Superintendents and inspectors in Birmingham were obliged to provide their uniforms at their own cost. These consisted of a double breasted dress coat, trousers, hat and greatcoat of the approved pattern. Sub-inspectors were issued with uniform similar to a sergeants but wore inspectors' badges and were allowed silver buttons at their own expense. Sergeants and constables were supplied with two hats, a stock, two blue coats with white lace collar numbers, two pairs of blue trousers, a belt, two pairs of boots, a greatcoat and a cape. At their own expense they had to provide armlets, two pairs of white gloves and two pairs of white trousers which could be worn on fine summer days. The officers' appointments consisted of handcuffs, truncheon, rattle and a lamp. The purpose of the rattle was for summoning aid and for warnings. Its use was, 'not to be sprung save only when necessary' and a constable had to make report to his sergeant any use of it. Kit and clothing was inspected once per week and plain clothes could not be worn except by special permission. The Chief Commissioner at first ordered that men were to be clean shaven but soon allowed the wearing of whiskers. Nothing changes in this world as often as fashion, clothes, or opinion and especially hair styles. In 1858 the Force

Surgeon Mr J V Solomon wrote to the Chief of Police, 'Those members of the Police Force who discharge street duty shall be required to allow the hair to grow on the chin and neck. The beard is great protection against sore throats and affections of the air tubes. I therefore anticipate if this regulation be carried out there will be a diminution in the number of officers and men on the sick list.'

However, all members of the Force were to parade once a month to have their hair and whiskers trimmed in the prescribed manner. No constable could marry without permission of the Commissioner. Those men not on duty on Sunday afternoons paraded at their respective stations and were marched to their places of worship. Every night at 11 pm a roll call was made at the stations.

Recruits were initially attached to the 1st Sub-division covered by Beardsworths. They were drilled every morning by a drill sergeant and marched to the Public Office where they would learn the rules of evidence listening to court cases. The afternoon consisted of more drill and from 6 pm to 8 pm they had to learn Police duties from instruction books. After successful examination in drill and Police duty they were posted to sub-divisions. This was not the end of instruction for the younger constables who were obliged to continue to attend court in felony proceedings for experience. In April 1840 an experienced and competent officer in each division was appointed to act as a tutor to instruct constables in their duty. The Training Department was therefore born unwittingly in this month. Drill instruction was also continued by the requirement that all officers and men not on duty undertook drill for an hour once a week at Beardsworths, Sandpits and Staniforth Street. Men on night duty were drilled at Beardsworths for an hour every second afternoon!! Drill instruction books were issued in June 1840 and sword exercises were practised at drill.

Growth and Reorganisation

In 1840 the size of the town was over 15 square miles and had a circumference greater than 21 miles and was growing. The Commissioner reported to the Home Secretary that an increase in establishment was an absolute necessity, as he could not give protection to all as the town beats were too extended. He complained that the borough was full of crime and on 14 January nearly 60 prisoners were taken before the magistrate. He asked that the Force should be made up of 400 men. Burgess was allowed to add 50 men to his establishment.

On 3 April 1840 the force was reorganised, with the sub-divisions becoming divisions as follows:

1st Division — Headquarters at Beardsworths', covering the market, Pershore Street, Sun Street, Holloway Head and Five Ways.

2nd Division — Headquarters at Sandpits, covering Broad Street, Congreve Street, Colmore Row, Warstone Lane, Ninevah, Albion Street and Livery Street.

3rd Division — Headquarters at Staniforth Street, covering Wheeler Street, Summer Lane, Gosta Green and the Old Square.

4th Division — Headquarters at Deritend, covering Bordesley, Dale End, Coleshill Street and Nechells.

A section station at Crooked Lane was opened on 11 June 1840. This station was in an ideal location for the Town Hall and had an establishment of nine sergeants and 25 constables. On 16 June the Chief Commissioner, Mr Burgess moved the Police office from Union Street to Waterloo Street where he again took up residence with his family. In August of that year Mr W A Palmer was appointed Chief Clerk of the Force. It is his name that can be seen on Force Orders for that time. Clearly civilian support to the Police is not an exclusivity of the 1980's.

By 15 September 1840 the strength of the force was 376 men. The Home Secretary consented to an increase to 396, allowing seven constables to be horse police, the forerunner of the Mounted Branch. The horse patrol was attached to the 1st Division, and were required to patrol from 5.30 pm to 10.30 pm daily. New scales of pay came into operation on 5 October but the 340 constables remained on 17s weekly. However it was not all bad news, because on 29 October 1840 the Home Secretary made a gratuity of £10 to ex-PC Clows who had been brutally attacked whilst on duty and consequently medically discharged. This must have given some comfort to the rank and file, as no superannuation fund was in existence. Additionally from May 1841 onwards the Chief Commissioner made monetary rewards for good police duty. He directed that every day one constable from each division should attend his office to receive a gratuity for good conduct and efficiency.

The establishment at this time consisted of the commissioner, the receiver, a surgeon, a chief superintendent, five superintendents, nine inspectors, ten sub-inspectors, ten superior sergeants, 20 sergeants and 340 constables.

Force Orders for 31 October 1840 directed that beats should be patrolled at 2½ miles per hour and premises be examined frequently. Lamps were directed to be used for the examination of premises at night. If a burglary or robbery were committed, the constable on the beat was to be suspended and dismissed if negligence were proved.

Force Orders up to 4 July 1841 show that 358 men had been dismissed, 273 had resigned, died or been medically discharged. Out of a total of 1,019 men who had been recruited since the inception of the force, only 388 remained. Being a constable was not a sinecure and by December 1841 Burgess insisted that the Police in Birmingham must always consider themselves on duty and act and assist on occasions when their services were required. This applied particularly in relation to fires, as it was a Police responsibility to assist the fire office companies. In May 1841 Messrs Bolton, a timber merchants, caught fire and despite the efforts of over 200 Police and the 6th Inniskilling Dragoons the wood yard was destroyed.

It appears that at this time 74 constables worked the day beats and 215 worked from 9 pm to 6 am together with the horse patrol. These officers policed a population in Birmingham of 182,698. Within the town there were 577 public houses, 573 beer houses and 83 pawnbrokers. During 1841 a total of 5,556 persons were arrested, of whom 594 were committed for trial at Warwick Assizes for indictable offences. Records show that there were 469 robberies by day and 417 by night. A total of 844 premises were found insecure and there were 74 fires. On two occasions Birmingham Police detachments were sent to Bilston and Dudley, an early form of aid to the local authority in just the same way as the Police from London assisted the Birmingham authority in 1839, at the time of Chartist meetings.

On 27 August 1842 a Superintendent Stephens was given exclusive responsibility for a Detective Department. His orders were to work from the Commissioners Office in Waterloo Street and select four intelligent men to assist him. They were attached to the Crooked Lane section station. These men were the forerunners of the Criminal Investigation Department.

The First and Last Commissioner Resigns

On 1 October 1842 the Act for Improving the Police of Birmingham was due to expire and those men who wished to remain members of the Force had been sworn in at the Town Hall on 24 September. The legal problems surrounding the Charter of Incorporation had been settled in August and the Town Council appointed a Watch Committee to take charge of the force as from 1 October 1842.

As Commissioner Burgess only held a commission under the Act he resigned on 30 September 1842. In Police Orders of that day he sent the following message to his force:

> 'The Commissioner in taking his leave of the force, the Act under which that force was constituted expiring today and with it the commission he has

the honour to hold from her Majesty, begs to offer to the officers and men his sincere thanks for their excellent conduct on all occasions, but more particularly so for that which was so prominently displayed during their duties in the late disturbances, when their patience, temper, firmness and strict obedience to orders was above all praise. He hopes that under their new rulers they will continue to show the same disposition and endeavour to maintain that high character they have so deservedly attained.'

There seems to be confusion about the actual date that Burgess resigned his commission. From 1 October 1842 Force Orders were signed by Superintendent R Atkins as 'Officer Commanding.' However Council minutes show that a letter was received from Mr Burgess on 11 November announcing the termination of his powers and authority.

What is clear however is that on 2 December the Town Council appointed Superintendent R A Stephens, who had been responsible for prosecutions and the detective branch, as Chief Superintendent in charge of the Force. His salary was fixed at £250 a year. Superintendent G Maturin of the 2nd Division was appointed the deputy to the new Chief Superintendent, at a salary of £150 and made responsible for the discipline of the force. It is worth considering the difference in salary between Messrs Burgess and Stephens. By the Act of 1839 Burgess was to be paid an annual salary not exceeding £800. When the Watch Committee took responsibility for such payment, the salary dropped by 70%.

2

Early Days

A reorganisation of the force followed the appointment of Mr Stephens. Seventy three men who had enrolled prior to 31 October 1839 still served and ten of these retired on pension. Two superintendents, several inspectors and sub-inspectors were required to resign in the interests of efficiency. Twenty one of the sergeants were re-appointed and the remainder were offered posts as constables. One of the sergeants retained was Sergeant George Glossop who subsequently became Chief Officer. The rank of superintendent was replaced by that of inspector. The reorganisation was completed by reducing the number of divisions to three and the Detective Force was established under Inspector William Hall and three constables. Inspector Hall was one of the few remaining 'Street Commissioners' Constables in Birmingham and had been promoted to inspector on joining the new force on 26 October 1839. The Birmingham Police were then apparently on a good footing.

In 1844 and 1845 a Mr Joseph Sturge wrote letters of complaint to the Town Council about the carrying of arms by the Police. He bewailed the fact that they 'were armed with mortal weapons'. No doubt he was referring to the use of cutlasses. These weapons were carried by men on night duty especially in the suburbs. Sturge's complaint did little as the weapons were still carried in 1863. Major General Cartwright, the Inspector of Constabulary for the Midlands area, wrote in that year, 'In some cases I consider the cutlass to be necessary for the protection of constables, such for instance as in the outskirts of Birmingham'. In 1847 Police Stations were established in Duke Street and, the principal station, in New Street. It is said that the cells of New Street Police Station reached back to Waterloo Street, some fifty yards, therefore the station must have been very large for its time. The Duke Street Station remained in Police use as an operational Police Station and subsequently traffic patrol garage and workshop until the land reverted to Aston University in the 1980's. On removal to the new traffic complex at Park Lane, a City of Birmingham street sign of 'Duke Street' was installed there as a reminder of the long connection between the Police and Duke Street.

In 1847 Mr Stephen's salary was raised to £450 per annum, but not without protestations by several ratepayers who complained because taxation in the borough was 'too heavy'. By 1848 the Force was reported to the Watch

Committee to be 282 officers, which was 76 fewer than the previous report. No details can be found as to why this is so but it is fair to assume that the discipline and arduous life in the Force took its toll. Records show that in 1850 a Police Station was opened in Alcester Street. Clearly Beardsworth's Repository had reached the end of its use as the Alcester Street Police Station was soon moved to Moseley Street and the basement of the Town Hall was used as a drill room for the Police. Also in 1850 Council minutes show that many complaints were received about the discipline of the force. However this was reciprocal as many complaints were made about the conditions of service and a report of July 1853 mentions numerous resignations. In order to stem this the Council approved higher rates of pay.

In 1856 Parliament passed the Boroughs and Counties Police Act. This Act enabled the Treasury to pay one quarter of the cost of a Police Force after a satisfactory inspection. This was at first objected to by the Town Council as 'Containing objectionable provisions.' It is fair to assume that the Council saw this as an attempt by Government to have some control of local Police forces but their subsequent acceptance of the Act saw it as 'reasonable and proper.' This is the foundation of the modern tri-partite agreement between the Home Office, the Chief Constable and the Local Authority. However the force failed an inspection by Major General Cartwright, the Inspector of the Constabulary for the district and it was not until 8 December 1857 that he reported favourably upon the Birmingham Police. Nonetheless the Corporation accounts do not show any income from the Treasury until 1860 when £5,328 was received as one fourth of the cost of pay and clothing. This continued until 1874 when a further statute increased the government grant to one half of salaries and outfits. This level of 50% grant by Central Government remains a principle to this day, as the Government now pays 51% of policing costs.

A little local difficulty occurred in 1857 when the Watch Committee announced on 4 August that, 'The Chief Superintendent can no longer possess the confidence of the Committee, nor command the respect of the officers and men under his authority, and that his continuance in office must therefore prove detrimental to the Police force and injurous to the public interest.' His conduct was described as 'very irregular and improper'. Eventually Stephens resigned from office at the end of 1859 on the grounds of ill health. He was replaced as Chief Officer by Mr George Glossop in February 1860 at a reduced salary of £350 per annum. Mr Glossop had originally joined the Force as a constable on 5 November 1839.

A letter remains from Glossop in which he makes application to transfer to the Detective Branch. It remains as a testament to his eloquence and ambition

Kenyon Street Police Station in 1950's

and reads:—

> Worshipful Sir, Gentlemen,
> A vacancy having occurred in the Detective Force I trust it will not be considered an act of presumption on my part in offering myself for appointment. In so doing I beg most respectfully to lay before you my pretentions to the same. I beg to state that I was appointed as a police constable in the Birmingham Police Force on its first formation in 1839. In 1840 I was promoted to the rank of sergeant and in 1843 I had the distinguished honour of receiving at your hands the appointment that I now hold of sub-inspector. I beg leave to state that during the whole period of my servitude I have never been reported.
> Gentlemen, from the nature of my duties at the principal station (New Street). I have had the opportunity of making observations of the various characters and cases apprehended and detected not only by the detectives but by officers and constables belonging to the Division. In addition to this I have been almost daily in attendance at the public office by which means. I not only became acquainted with the persons of the thieves taken into custody by the constables of other divisions, but also obtained the necessary requisite information detective officers ought to possess to fill the important situation I now seek at your hands.
> Gentlemen, I beg to lay before you the recommendations of several magistrates and other gentlemen who have had the personal opportunity of observing my conduct, and can with confidence refer you to my officers under whom I have served.
> In conclusion if you should be pleased to confer on me the honour I now solicit I will by diligent discharge of my duty strive to merit your entire approbation.
> I have the honour to be, Gentlemen your most humble obedient servant.
> Geo Glossop
> Sub-Inspector

He was successful and transferred duties on 1 April 1845. In October 1970 several personal items such as a cutlass, tip staff and badges belonging to Glossop were bought at auction by the Birmingham City Police Social and Athletic Club and presented to the Force Museum.

THE MURPHY RIOTS

A serious riot broke out in Birmingham on 16 July 1867 and has passed into history as 'The Murphy Riots.' On that date a Mr William Murphy had arrived in the borough to deliver a series of anti-Papist lectures in the Town. He was refused the use of the Town Hall and therefore erected a wooden tabernacle in

Carrs Lane, the centre of Non-Conformist worship in the area. As he was preaching he was barracked and jeered by a group of Irishmen who were the worse for drink. One of their number was arrested and a general disorder broke out. Stones were thrown and several more arrests were made. An English mob led by a well known local prize fighter retaliated by attacking the Irish quarters around Park Street, Digbeth. The fronts of most houses were destroyed and several were unroofed. Two long days of rioting followed and the hard pressed police were aided by the military who were quartered in the Bull Ring to be on hand. Murphy continued his inflamatory lectures and was himself arrested. He then brought an action against the Mayor, Mr Holland and Mr Glossop, the Chief of Police, for false imprisonment and recovered damages at the Warwick Assizes.

In 1865 a request for extra pay was made by the members of the force and this was granted. This happened again in 1872. On 25 February 1873 the Watch Committee made a report to the Council recommending a 'considerable increase in pay, and increase of establishment by 50 to raise the strength to 450. The basis for the demands was said to be caused by 'the number of robberies and other offences committed in the Borough', and by the extra duties, 'cast on the Police by recent legislation' and, 'by the increase in the population, mileage, houses, shops and so forth.'

The Watch Committee's report also records that the Chief Superintendent, Mr Glossop had 'laid before your committee (themselves) the photographic likeness of 717 returned convicts, or ticket of leave men, discharged from different gaols, who have selected Birmingham for their residence; and 103 discharged convicts, all of whom require Police surveillance. Your committee, however, are pleased to report that they are informed that a large majority of these convicts are honestly earning their living. Nevertheless, the proper surveillance of so large a number of criminals, and the usual proportion of thieves found in all large towns, is a great and increasing tax upon the strength of the Police force.' The Watch Committee had little success. The increase in pay was refused and over a year later on 12 May 1874 an increase of only 15 men was allowed. Pay was enhanced however on 9 February 1875 and on 3 August of that year the authorised establishment was raised by 50 men.

EARLY COMPLAINTS OF BEHAVIOUR

By now Birmingham was well established as the leading industrial centre of the nation. The town continued to grow at a rapid rate with all the attendant social problems that such growth entailed. Drunkenness was a particular problem. A report by the Watch Committee in 1876 bemoans the increase in drunkenness in the borough 'as shown by proceedings in the Police courts, by street disturbances, and the frequency of crimes of violence.' Unfortunately, the report also makes mention of the 'intemperance in the Police force itself.' The Watch Committee laid the blame for this squarely on the 'illegal treating in public houses of police constables whilst on duty'. To reinforce this claim they showed that in 1875, 1,792 persons had been fined for drunkenness, and only six publicans were prosecuted for permitting drunkenness, and only two of those were fined. The Committee was therefore at pains to point out that an inspection of public and beer houses could not be left to constables on their beat. They proposed a novel system whereby five Inspectors were selected from amongst the Force, to be paid £3 per week to enforce the licensing law. These men were to be, 'picked and intelligent men, whose sobriety, integrity and firmness can be confidently relied upon and, who being better paid, will be open to fewer temptations than the ordinary constable.' The system was vehemently opposed by the Town's publicans but was approved by the Council. The five inspectors were appointed from the uniform branch.

After 36 years service, 16 as Chief Officer, Mr Glossop offered his resignation to the Council on 4 April 1876. The Council minutes record that as Glossop had 'Always discharged his duties to the best of his abilities', he was awarded a pension of £400 per annum, a remarkable sum. They also show that his successor was to be advertised for at a salary of £700. This was not the end of Glossop's appearance in the public eye. On 5 March 1878 a serious complaint was made by a Mr W H Hart on behalf of a group of ratepayers. The complaint concerned an allegation of lack of diligence and neglect of duty by the Police in the matter of Henry Stephenson, a man who had recently been convicted for fraudulently obtaining goods. The Watch Committee was instructed by the Council to investigate the complaint. On 4 June 1878 the committee reported that their investigations had heard evidence against the Police of a 'very serious nature' which 'at various times during the last 20 years had embraced charges against their zeal, their want of skill and their honesty.' The allegations were that due to a friendship between Mr Glossop and Alderman Mr Brindley, and the latter gentleman and Stephenson, there was an 'absence of active interference with Stephenson's criminal conduct.' The Watch Committee guarded their words and concluded that their investigation had resulted in the 'entire exculpation of the present members of the Birmingham Police Force from all blame.' Brindley admitted trading with Stephenson in the normal course of business. He denied knowledge of Stephenson's character and denied that any alleged friendship between them had influenced the actions of the

Police. However he resigned his position. Glossop retained his pension but the question mark remains over the matter inasmuch as it was not until after his retirement that Stephenson was prosecuted.

This was not the only serious complaint laid against the Police in 1878. In October of that year a complaint was made concerning a fatal fire at the premises of Joseph Dennison, a confectioner, in Digbeth. On 26 August 1878, his wife, child and two servants perished. Allegations made by the Coroners jury concerned the conduct of the Police and their deficiency of life saving and fire extinguishing equipment. The jury laid the blame fairly on the shoulders of the Chief Officer. They alleged that even though he had known the fire escape equipment to be defective he had misled the Watch Committee as to its serviceability and was responsible for poor organisation whereby no reserve of men for firefighting was kept at the central Police Station on that night. The outcome was that the Watch Committee exonerated the Police and importantly recommended that firefighting should be removed from Police duty. On 1 April 1879 Mr A B Tozer was appointed Superintendent of the new Birmingham Fire Brigade.

The Chief Officer at the time of the fire was Major Edwin E Bond who had succeeded Glossop. Bond was the first officer to take the title of Chief Constable. No fewer than 96 candidates had applied for the post. Bond had served in the Crimean War and was at the time of his appointment Chief Constable of Cardiff.

On 3 July 1877 pay rates were revised by the Council. Superintendents' pay was set at £160-£180 per year, inspectors 50s to 42s per week, sergeants 38s to 32s, and constables from 23s for probationers to 30s after ten years. On the same date the scheme for licensing inspectors was abolished and the responsibility reverted to divisional superintendents, with a rider that other ranks were forbidden to enter public houses whilst on duty, except under special circumstances. Also at this meeting a new Police Station for Moseley Street was ordered at a cost of £4,800. Discussion was also held concerning a Police Station for Small Heath. The land had previously been bought in May of that year. This was for the Coventry Road Police Station which stood until the 1980's.

An interesting historical point occurred in October 1877 as to policing in the Borough's Aston Park, which although at that time in Warwickshire County, belonged to the Birmingham Corporation. A Birmingham constable was placed on duty there.

The Chief Constable of Warwick County, a Mr Kinchant took exception to this and demanded the removal of the constable claiming there was no right for this infringement. The Birmingham Watch Committee took legal opinion and were told that Mr Kinchant was in the wrong and had 'fallen into error in his construction of the Acts of Parliament' and the Borough Police were correct. Poor Mr Kinchant probably realised that one constable was the thin end of the wedge and over the next thirty odd years saw his chiefdom whittled further back. But this was not the first occasion that policing in Aston Park had caused problems. In June 1858, Queen Victoria and her Consort opened Aston Hall and men were drafted in from various Police Forces to assist. Amongst them were a detachment from the 'A' Division of the Metropolitan Police. The officer in charge of this detachment began using his stick to prod off the hats of members of the crowd, shouting at them to stand back, in order to relieve pressure on the Police lines. It did give temporary relief, but angered the crowd so much so that the Birmingham officers ordered the London officer to stop. It is reported that, 'The dilemma was met by using kind words and persuasion ... The London Police, however were decried and unfavourably spoken of.'

POLICE DUTIES EXPLAINED IN 1878

It is worth recording what the duties of the Birmingham Police were at this time and an 1878 Handbook issued to the Force shows them. The inspectors are said to be responsible for the general good order of the sergeants and men under them. They were expected to make themselves well acquainted with the general character of each member of the Force. The management tasks and requirements of an inspector can be found in the entry that, 'They will always be supported in a correct discharge of their office, but will not be allowed to be overbearing or tyrannical; on the other hand they are to be careful to avoid any familiarity with either sergeants or constables.'

The regular duty of the inspector ranks can be found to be that, 'The inspectors will always attend at the Station punctually at the hour appointed for duty, and call over the names of the men for duty and inspect them, ascertain that they are perfectly sober, correctly dressed, equipped, etc. They will then furnish each man with a card with the number of his beat and the streets constrained therein printed on it; the names of the men will then be inserted in a book kept for that purpose, and opposite names the numbers of their respective beats. The inspector will then read and explain (if necessary) the orders of the day; the men will then be marched regularly on their beats, in single file, taking the outward side of the flagging.'

During his tour of duty the inspector was expected to check every sergeant and constable on patrol, 'not permitting any section sergeant to accompany him

Police Sergeants' day uniform, 1930's

while doing so.' He was also to visit the cells during the night as often as he may consider necessary.

The reserve sergeant duty is the equivalent of the modern station sergeant, or custody officer. He was responsible for the acceptance of all charges brought to the station and was directed to enter such in the charge sheet. If not satisfied with the evidence he was obliged to enter such in a refused charge book. He was also responsible for property. The reserve sergeant was also responsible for ensuring that the reserve constable visited any prisoners, 'four times in every hour' and that such prisoners were provided with refreshment, 'either at the expense of the Borough or at their own expense, taking care that no beer or spiritous liquor is given them'. He was also required to 'inspect daily the rooms and cells of the Station, reporting any neglect in the matter of cleanliness and order to the superintendent; to keep all the books of the division accurately while he is on duty, making all alterations in such books not by erasure, but by drawing the pen neatly across the erroneous entry, and making the proper entry above it.'

The instructions of the reserve sergeant in relation to bail were that, 'In cases of petty misdemeanour, after taking the charge, he may admit the person accused to bail, taking and entering the names, addresses, and occupation of the surety or sureties; but in cases of aggravated assault, or of felony of any description, he must on no account admit to bail.'

The reserve sergeant had what may be termed, pastoral duties, in that he was expected to, 'visit every room in the barracks at 12 midnight, and report in the night book whether all the men were present, excepting those on leave of absence or temporary leave, and will, in addition, report to his superintendent, at the end of each month, that the mess has been carried on in accordance with the chief superintendent's order, and that the bills have been countersigned by the inspector, and are all paid.'

The sergeant also had the task of keeping a beady eye on the 'slower' officers as we are told, 'He is to give over to every Man who may have a case before the Courts, the foil of an absence ticket, properly filled up, which the officer is to deliver to the summoning superintendent, at roll call, at 10.45 am. The reserve sergeant will also be careful to enter in the counterfoil the exact time of the return of the officer at the Station. In due time the foil will be returned by the summoning superintendent, who will have caused to be therein entered the time of the completion of the case in Court. Any unreasonable delay thus discovered on the part of the officer will be duly reported.'

The section sergeant's main duty was the supervision of constables and they were to be, 'responsible for the good discipline and general efficiency of every constable on the section of which they have charge. They must, therefore, make themselves thoroughly acquainted with the character and temper of their men; enforce the necessity of paying proper attention to the instructions to constables contained in this book; and by their own alacrity, skill, attention, and civility, set a good example to all placed under their charge.'

Each sergeant to be at the Station before the hour fixed by his orders; to form his section into rank and inspect them; to fall in for the superintendent or inspector's inspection; to march his men to his section and distribute them to their beats; to remain on duty from adjoining beats the place of any constable who may be absent from his beat, and, ascertain the cause of such absence, to report it, if irregular, to the inspector; to see that every constable in his section is acquainted with the residences of the firemen, volunteer fire brigade, and turncocks, and also with the situation of all the fire-plugs on their respective beats; to visit at uncertain hours such constables on the sick list as may reside in his section, and report those who are absent from home. He was required to give all assistance in his power to persons applying to him, and act upon the instructions to constables in making arrests, entering houses, and taking possession of property; to send to the nearest Station for assistance in cases requiring it; and, in case of fire, to act until the arrival of the superintendent or inspector, in accordance with the instructions previously laid down for the guidance of those officers; to pay particular attention in the night time to such vehicles as may appear to him to be employed in the conveyance of suspicious persons or things; to make note of the manner in which all public houses and beer houses on his section are conducted.

The sergeant was warned, 'not to take any undue advantage of constables, by endeavouring to entrap them into the commission of an offence,' and 'not to make himself familiar with constables, but he is to instruct them in the duties they have to perform, and so conduct himself as to secure the respect of those over whom he is placed to command.'

The reserve constables who were the equivalent of the modern office PC had the following duties, 'The reserve constables on duty will attend to the fires in barracks, and prepare the coffee supplied to the men during the inclement weather'. Also, 'They will keep clean and in good order the cells and out-offices, and will have immediate charge of the lamps of the men, which they are to clean and keep in order'. Further, 'They will also take the notices of routes and other written communications in a leather despatch case to and from headquarters, at 9 am; 1 pm; 5 pm and 8 pm.'

The duties of the constables state that a constable was required to reside within the division to which he was appointed, and as near to it as possible; but he could not live either in a public house, a beer house, or the house of an officer of the Force; nor could his residence be in a disorderly street. He was to devote the whole of his time and abilities to the service, and not carry on any trade or calling. If single he was not allowed to marry until he had been in the Force 12 months, and then only with the permission of the chief superintendent.

The handbook made a constables' duties clear and in the main they were that, 'his demeanour must invariably be respectful towards his superiors; he must be civil and attentive to all who apply to him for information or assistance; and conform to all regulations made for the good government of the Force; and obey all the instructions of his officers, doing what he is told first, and, if it appears to him to be wrong, reserving complaint for the chief superintendent afterwards'.

The constable was warned that, 'He is liable to be ordered on duty at all times, and when called upon at unreasonable hours, must lose no time in dressing and hurrying to the rendezvous. When for ordinary duty he should be at the Station a few minutes before the stated hour. Thence he will be marched to his beat, of which he is to take charge, and for due care of which he will be held accountable.'

He was instructed to make himself thoroughly acquainted with all the streets, thoroughfares, and courts in his beat and its vicinity, and to possess himself such knowledge of the inhabitants as will enable him to recognise their persons; and he is to walk through every part of his beat at and within the time stated on his card, unless, when in the due performance of his duty, he is required to make a stand, in which case he must report the fact to his sergeant. He is not to leave his beat, excepting under special circumstances herein specified, not to enter any house unless in the exercise of his duty, and then only with great caution. Nor is he to stop or loiter on his round to talk with other constables, or any person whatever, excepting in the strict performance of duty. He is not to take any refreshment at a public house or beer house, nor, on any account, to receive liquor or refreshment of any sort from a publican. Nor is he, on any pretence whatever, to receive money by way of donation or gratuity, directly or indirectly, for anything done in the execution of his duty, without reporting the same, and asking permission to retain it, nor to drink beer or spirits offered to him by any person, such beer being often drugged for a purpose, and, if not drugged, the drinking of it being an infringement of the regulations of the Force.

The Handbook continues that, 'When a constable is on duty at night he is to see, from time to time, that all premises on his beat are safely closed; and if they are not, and there is no person in charge, he is to pass the word for another constable, and place him there until the owner or occupier, or the servants of either, can be called up. If all is secure, he is to arrange the padlock, if there is one, or to so place something in the keyhole, or otherwise, as that he may on his next inspection be able to see whether the fastenings of the premises have in the interval been tampered with. When going on early morning duty, he is, in like manner, to see that the constable who was on night duty has left all safe; and on Sundays, and particularly on Sunday evening he is to pay special attention to warehouses and other business premises, and to private houses whose inmates may have gone to Church.'

Moreover the instructions were that, 'He is also to remove all orange peel from the footpath; to take note of and obliterate in the night time all obscene writing on walls; to impound stray cattle in the nearest pound; to report and hand over to the inspector or officer on duty at the Station, all articles he may find; to report all cases of violent or sudden death at his Police Station; to return a ready and civil answer to all enquiries that may be made of him, referring persons who ask him questions concerning his instructions to his superior officers, and in no case refusing to give his number to any person who may demand it. He must be careful so to use his lamp as not to startle horses. He must not smoke while on duty, nor carry a stick or an umbrella; nor must he wear medals on his breast unless with the permission of his officers. He must take no notice whatever of ridicule, nor suffer himself to lose his temper in consequence of any opprobrious epithets or threats that may be applied to him.'

A constable was warned that, 'He must use every form of persuasion, in the case of disorderly assemblies or disorderly persons, before resorting to arrest; and, in the case of disorderly soldiers, he must display peculiar delicacy in his course of action. He must also be careful in his dealings with street musicians and street singers, there being no power of arresting them unless they become disorderly. When obstructed in the execution of his duty, he should refrain from taking the offenders into custody if he knows where they may be found afterwards; and he should be careful to enter no disorderly house, if he can possibly avoid it, without another constable as a witness. He is not to search any house without a warrant, except in cases previously mentioned, unless he has asked and obtained permission of the occupier, and then, unless the case be a very urgent one, he should rather apply for a warrant. When he has a warrant he must produce it when called upon; and when he is doing duty in plain clothes, he must give all persons concerned notice of the nature of his office, after all possibility of the ends of justice being frustrated by his so doing has passed away. He may act off the beat when called upon to do so, but should return as soon as possible.'

The constable had to take notice that, 'In taking persons into custody he is to be careful not to use any unnecessary violence. Unless resisted and that seriously, he is not to use his staff; and in the case of drunkards he is under no circumstances to use his staff. If he requires assistance he is to call for it, and see that he or she does not throw away any article which might otherwise be used in evidence. He is always to tell his prisoner the offence with which he or she is charged; to listen to and take note of any statement the prisoner may make; but on no account to question him or her with the view of extracting any admission of guilt. He is to take with him to the Station the complainant, except in cases of felony, when he knows the complainant to be a responsible man, in which case he may dispense with the complainant's attendance, but he must still have the complainant's name entered in the charge sheet. Persons who have accompanied the prisoner's favour, are not to be taken into custody, either if they are known and can be found, or if responsible persons are prepared to answer for their appearance. In conveying to the Station persons who are insensibly drunk, care should be taken to carry them with the head well raised.

A constable who has brought in a case must warn all necessary witnesses to attend at the Police Court next morning, and must attend himself at 10.45 and answer to his name at roll call, delivering at the same time his absence ticket to the summoning superintendent; and he must give his evidence with clearness and precision, using no slang terms in doing so, and not mentioning any previous conviction against the prisoner, unless called upon to do so.

As to public houses and beer houses, no constable must enter them except when called upon to quell a disturbance or eject a troublesome customer. He must report this to his sergeant.'

The young constables, or probationers, duties are shown as that, 'for the first fortnight, are to be placed on the following duties: He will attend every morning at 9.30 am for squad drill. He will attend the Police Courts at 11 am, and will be present during the sitting of the Magistrates in Court till 12.30 pm to enable him to have an insight into the Court proceedings and learn how to conduct himself in the witness box when called upon to give evidence. He will attend drill for one hour in the afternoon, from 2.30 till 3.30, and will fall in with the first night watch, and will be relieved at 10 pm.

Before promotion to the fourth class, the young constable must pass a satisfactory examination in reading, writing and in his general duties.'

'A constable going on the sick list was told that he must bring, or send in by some member of his family, or by another constable, to the officer on duty, his beat card, at least three hours before the time fixed for his going on duty. When requiring medicine the instructions were that he must send for it to the police surgeon, taking care to send also a half-pint bottle and such other vessels as may

Digbeth Police Station 1912

be required. No constable, while on the sick list, is to be absent from his quarters unless to visit the police surgeon.'

JOHN THOMAS WILSON, MISSIONARY TO BIRMINGHAM POLICE

The work of the members of the Birmingham Force was hard and hours were long, but there were those who cared for their welfare and at the request of the Honourable Mrs Feinnes, Mr John Thomas Wilson, who had been a school master in India, came to Birmingham in 1878 to undertake evangelical work amongst the Borough Police. His early days were a trial for this reverend gentleman. On 30 September 1878 he wrote in his journal,

'Their spiritual condition I found to be at a very low ebb, and except in about ten cases, I am unable to say there is any real earnest regard for Godly things and the soul's eternal welfare. The Reverends Messrs Lee and Winter of Edgbaston and Ladywood have for a considerable time past conducted a religious meeting at the Police Station. At the latter place on every alternate Friday afternoon. I have not thought it necessary to see the gentlemen at present as I am unable to be there on Fridays that being my afternoon at Duke Street in another part of the town.'

Mr Wilson went about his tasks with missionary zeal and was soon writing,

'Another man of the 3rd Division, a PC, who lost his wife three years ago and was left with three little children and yet the first time I saw him he was under the influence of liquor. I have seen and spoke with him once since and hope 'ere long to make a lasting impression as God may direct one. I feel deeply for the young immortals he has been left with.'

The evil of drink and the Devil's work laid heavily upon Wilson for on 15 October 1878 he writes,

'They have a bowling alley at each place where they spend much of their spare time. They also keep cards and dominoes in the day rooms and from my observations during my brief sojourn here I am bound to pronounce them all evil. The men are not allowed to gamble with them. The Watch Committee have prohibited it. The sad fact is that they do and it causes a deal of unseemly wrangling. During my short time I have been here it has been painfully evident that the moral condition of the Police is greatly lowered by the free indulgence in intoxicating drinks. At the last fortnightly meeting of the Watch Committee six men were fined sums varying from 6s to 40s and dismissed from the force for drunkeness. I intend as soon as possible to inaugurate a total abstinence movement in the Force which if carried on successfully will no doubt prove a valuable pioneer to higher and nobler things.'

Mr Wilson became the founder and organiser of the Birmingham Police Total Abstinence Association.

It is only fair to say that Mr Wilson's ministrations to the Birmingham Police were not always welcomed by the rank and file. He confides in his journal on 2 December 1879 that he spoke to Detective Sergeant Mountford at Kenyon Street Police Station. Whether the detective sergeant was having 'one of those days' or did not welcome Wilson's solicitude is not recorded but a flavour of his attitude can be gauged from the entry. Detective Sergeant Mountford told him,

'Mr Wilson I am a man of this sort. I never wronged any man willingly. I never took what didn't belong to me from anyone. I don't owe a man a shilling in the world and I bear no malice to any man. If I have any enemies I don't know it and I try to do to everybody as I wish them to do to me and I don't think there can be much amiss with a chap who is like that.'

Unperturbed Wilson went on his way but records that on the same day,

'I also met PS Jeffins, a man of very queer notions regarding the eternal hopes of men. He told me he did not believe in religion of any sort and his opinion of those who did was that they were a parcel of hypocrites.'

John Thomas Wilson was not shaken in his Christian faith and it was a good thing for Birmingham City Police that he wasn't. In 1891 working with the Police authorities he obtained dilapidated premises in Easy Row which were then fitted out with a gymnasium, a refreshment room and a room for prayer meetings. Eight years later in 1899, as a result of generous public donations a new Police Institute was built at the corner of James Watt Street and Dalton Street. The Institute housed a Police school, a gymnasium, refreshment and prayer meeting rooms and bedrooms for policemen staying in Birmingham overnight. As could be expected alcohol was not allowed to be consumed on the premises. It is worth observing therefore that the Birmingham Police had their own equivalent of a West End club in the City, notwithstanding that it was 'dry'. Clearly Mr Wilson was the first welfare officer to Birmingham Police. In this work he was ably assisted by his wife. When he died a magnificent commemorative brass plaque was purchased by the Force in order that his work and name would live on. The plaque is now held by the Tally Ho! Police Museum. On the opening of Steelhouse Lane Police Station in 1933 the Police Institute was closed and sold off.

Major Bond vs The Watch Committee

The relationship between Major Bond and the Watch Committee began to deteriorate in 1880. It had been custom and practice in Birmingham that persons apparently drunk in the town's streets, who were not disorderly, and could make their way home were not arrested. Bond ordered that they should be arrested and taken before the Bench. The matter became a local cause célèbre and was known as the 'Arrest of the Quiet Drunkards'. Prosecutions soared and due to mistakes the law was brought into disrepute. The Watch Committee and Justices criticised the Chief Constable and he was forced to abandon this policy. However further problems were not long in coming for Mr Bond. In the early part of 1881 he undertook a prosecution of Day's Concert Hall for improper performances and performing stage plays without a licence. The prosecution failed and Bond was called before the Watch Committee to account for his action. He claimed an independent right to institute proceedings without Watch Committee consent as he was, 'the guardian of public morality and order'. The Committee ordered the he should only institute proceedings with their consent, (probably with an eye to the 'Quiet Drunkards' debacle). The Chief Constable refused and referred the matter to the Home Secretary. He found little support in that quarter and was referred by the Secretary of State to the Municipal Corporations Act whereby Watch Committees could make regulations for rendering constables efficient in their duty and the ability of two Justices to dismiss any negligent constable. Bond backed down and in a letter dated 21 August 1881 claimed to have 'misunderstood the meaning of the Committee's resolution and would acquiesce to their authority'. The Committee accepted this and did not call for his resignation.

However, Mr Bond again caused controversy by giving evidence at an appeal at Quarter Sessions in relation to the refusal by the Licensing Justices of the renewal of a licence of the Old Engine Public House in Dale End. The Licensing Justices and the Watch Committee later announced a resolution of lack of confidence in Bond, and after unsuccessfully requesting him to resign, announced their intention to dismiss him. On 3 January 1882 the Watch Committee informed the Council that they had received a letter from the Chief Constable offering to resign. His resignation was accepted as from 24 December of the previous year. Bond was awarded six months salary of £350 and his superannuation payments were returned to him.

The post of Chief Constable was then advertised at a salary of £700 and 'without allowances of any kind'. Ninety two applications were received and of these five were interviewed by the Watch Committee. The successful candidate was Mr Joseph Farndale, who, for ten years, had been the Chief Constable of Leicester. Mr Farndale took up his position on 14 February 1882.

Early in 1883 the Watch Committee again sought an increase of establishment from 520 to 570. They made the normal arguments of increase in population, the number of houses, greater value of property in the borough, the street mileage and 'the fact that at the present time there are between 20 and 30 beats not properly covered'. In a truly modern fashion the Committee planned their bid for 30 constables immediately, a further ten in 1884 and ten in 1885. On 17 April the Committee reported that the Home Office had approved an increase of 30 constables.

THE IRISH TROUBLES COME TO BIRMINGHAM

The same year of 1883 saw the trial in London of four Fenian Dynamiters, Whitehead, Gallagher, Wilson and Curtin for possession of explosives for an unlawful purpose. The circumstances of the case are that on 27 March 1882 Sergeant Price of Birmingham Police was given information by a Mr Gilbert Pritchard that a large quantity of glycerine had been sold to a man named Whitehead and delivered to his premises in Ledsam Street, Ladywood, close to Sandpits Police Station. Observations were kept on these premises and access was gained by an officer disguised as a painter. They were found to be used for manufacture of nitro-glycerine in large quantities. Whitehead's accomplices were followed to London where they were arrested in possession of the explosive. At the same time Whitehead was arrested. The remaining nitro-glycerine was seized, made into dynamite and then destroyed. The offenders were sentenced to penal servitude for life.

The trial judge was highly complimentary to the Birmingham Police and the Watch Committee commended the officers involved to the Council in these terms, 'The manner in which the Police conducted their investigation, the sagacity, patience and coolness displayed by them under circumstances of almost inconceivable danger and difficulty are highly appreciated by the Committee and have met with the approval and commendations of the Home Secretary'. The Council obviously agreed and rewarded the Chief Constable Mr Farndale with a salary raise from £700 to £800 per annum. Inspector Black was promoted to First Class Superintendent with an increase in pay from £130 to £180. Sergeant Price was promoted to First Class Inspector and pay raised from 34s per week to £130 per year. Sergeant George Rees was appointed Third Class Inspector at 42s per week. Mr Pritchard the original informant could not be rewarded by the Council as no facility existed for such payment. He was granted £30 by the Home Office which was regarded as niggardly by the Birmingham populace who contributed to a public subscription to increase his reward.

This was not the only encounter in Birmingham at that time between the Force and Fenian terrorists. In 1884 an Irish-American named John Daley was identified by an informant as living in Grafton Road, Sparkbrook under the alias of John Denham. As there was no evidence available to substantiate the belief that he had been responsible for bombings in London, he was kept under observation by Inspectors Stroud and Black of the Detective Branch. Initially observations were kept from rooms opposite Daley's lodgings but after a while Stroud moved into the same house. As time progressed the Detective and Daley became firm friends, the latter's suspicion never being aroused. On Good Friday, Daley was arrested at Birkenhead entering the mainland with three bombs in his luggage. Stroud had done his work well and the arrest was no speculative chance. Daley's landlord, James Egan, was then arrested as his principal accomplice. A search of the house revealed a large quantity of incriminating Fenian literature. Both men were tried at Warwick Assizes for treason. Daley was sentenced to penal servitude for life and Egan was sentenced to 20 years imprisonment. On this occasion however there were no promotions in the field for Stroud and Black or any sign of monetary reward. Perhaps the Watch Committee believed that hard work was its own reward.

Expansion of Birmingham and Its Police Force

The Town and its Police Force continued to grow throughout the 1880's and 90's. In the last 15 years of the century the establishment of the Force was increased three times. In 1889 at the time of the grant of Letters Patent raising the Borough to City status the authorised establishment and actual strength was 550 Officers. At the close of the century the establishment had risen to 700 and the strength to 685 respectively. The population of Birmingham continued to expand, the ratio of population to each constable remained in the region of 700 and the acreage per constable grew to 18. This was of course due to the extension of the City in 1891, which added a further acreage of nearly 50%, some 4,015 acres. It is difficult now to imagine a Birmingham which did not include Saltley, Little Bromwich, Balsall Heath or Harborne, but this was so as they only became part of the City in 1891.

Saltley and Little Bromwich were part of Warwickshire, Harborne was in Staffordshire and Balsall Heath in Worcestershire. Inducements were offered to these districts as the rates for Birmingham were higher, especially the levy for the Poor Rate. Amongst the inducements was an increase in Police strength. Saltley was promised 11 Birmingham officers instead of their own eight and Harborne was likewise promised nine instead of six Staffordshire officers who were presently engaged there. When the take over was finalised Birmingham

Police Constables' night helmet and greatcoat, 1930's

paid £2,800 for the Police Station in George Arthur Road, Saltley and £5,250 for the Edward Road Police Station in Balsall Heath.

In spite of the increases in establishment, an increase in Police duties and legislation reduced the numbers in real terms. The introduction of a monthly leave day in 1883 had to be compensated for by the employment of 15 extra men. The burgeoning Detective Department had grown by ten more officers. Six Officers were employed on duty at the new Art Gallery in Congreve Street. 16 officers were also transferred from the night watch to days to deal with the increased day time traffic. Interestingly 13 officers were employed in regulation of the new tramways. They were responsible for inspecting tramcars and regulating the traffic. These early tramways were horse-drawn, steam driven and cable-drawn. Eventually Birmingham City had probably the finest electric tramway system in the world.

Nonetheless Birmingham had one of the most overworked Forces. On a population ratio for 1883, Birmingham was 1:826, Liverpool 1:482 and Manchester 1:432. That difference has continued to the present day when Greater Manchester Police have a higher establishment but a lower population than that policed by the West Midlands Force.

Conditions at about this time improved for the officers of the Force. In 1890 constables pay was raised from 23s to 24s and the different periods of service lowered allowing a top pay of 30s after seven years. The maximum pay for sergeants was raised to 38s and inspectors' maximum pay raised to 50s. A rise in 1897 saw constables' maximum set at 32s after 15 years service and sergeants' 40s after nine years.

The Police Act of 1890 introduced a new Superannuation Fund for Police and removed the power of Watch Committees to control amounts of pension at their discretion. An officer was allowed to claim a pension after 25 years service or a medical pension after 18 years service if medically unfit for further duty. The Birmingham Watch Committee took exception to this as they claimed to use their discretion to reward diligent officers. Tradition has it though that they did the opposite. In fact on reporting to the Select Committee on Police Superannuation Funds in 1875 Birmingham's Chief Officer, Mr Glossop complained of the Watch Committee's attitude, by using the words 'As their money and not as the policeman's money, but as if they were doing it out of the ratepayers pocket'. The first Birmingham officer to receive a pension from the Watch Committee had been Constable Enoch Palmer, who on 18 June 1861 had been granted a pension of 7s a week for 19 years service.

The Birmingham Police operated a system of reward by merit stripes awarded for diligence, bravery and good Police work. A constable received 6d extra pay for the first stripe, a further 6d for a second and 1s for a third making an extra 2s per week pay. However, on promotion the stripes were lost. Regulations introduced in 1892 allowed for constables to retain their merit stripes on promotion and for sergeants to be awarded a maximum of two stripes at 1s each. However, the stripes were replaced on award of the third stripe for sergeants by an embroidered badge with the word 'merit.'

The Beginning of an Era – Charles Haughton Rafter

On 29 May 1899 Mr Joseph Farndale, the Chief Constable resigned, on the grounds of poor health. He was awarded a full pension of £600 a year. A search for a successor on this occasion saw 50 applicants, reduced to a short list, or 'short-leet' as it was known, of eight candidates. A unanimous decision was reached and Mr Charles Haughton Rafter was appointed Chief Constable on 6 August 1899 at a salary of £800, also 'without allowances of any kind'. On the same occasion Superintendent McManus was promoted to Deputy Chief Constable. Rafter was a district inspector in the Royal Irish Constabulary at the time of his appointment. He maintained his military bearing for the whole of his service.

Police buildings and stations of this time are dominated by the building of the Victoria Law Courts and the Central Lock-Up. This magnificent building was designed by the Victorian architects, Aston Webb and Ingress Bell, and built by John Bowen and Sons. The exterior red terracotta was brought from Ruabon, North Wales and the internal yellow terracotta from quarries in Tamworth. They were first used on 30 July 1891 and Lord Chief Justice Coleridge was first Judge to sit at the Assizes. This is commemorated by the existence of Coleridge Passage which runs between the courts and the Central Lock-Up. In 1891 the Watch Committee obtained land of 500 square yards in Newton Street alongside the courts for a proposed new central Police Station. This building was also designed by Webb and Bell and built by John Bowens to maintain architectural harmony with the Victoria Law Courts. The cost was £11,363.

A building was rented in 1887, for £37 per annum, in Wellington Road off the Bristol Road. Complaints had been received by the Watch Committee of disorderly behaviour by 'roughs' in Bristol Road. This building was extended in 1890 by the addition of two cells and an ambulance station. The same problem existed in the area of Bridge Street West where disorderly behaviour was concentrated in Moorsom Street. This sub-station was established by the rental of no less than five houses at £66. A further £666 was spent on adapting the buildings and the addition of cells.

Sir Charles Haughton Rafter, whilst Sub-Inspector of the Royal Irish Constabulary

The Birmingham Police Aided Association was founded in 1893 to provide clothing for destitute children and 'to foster friendly and humane relations with the poorest classes of the population.' The organisation was not of a purely philanthropic nature but born out of first hand knowledge and experience of the poverty of the worst sections of the City. The aim of this police charity was to provide boots and warm garments for the children. In 1893, the first year, 1,218 children were issued with 1,064 pairs of boots and nearly 4,000 garments. Money was raised from such sources as boxing tournaments, sports and athletic meetings of the City Police and by donations from organisations with a direct contact with the Police such as the Hall Green Greyhound Racing Association. Within time an annual flag day was held. The largest sum raised in one year was £4,048 4s 8d in 1931-32, at a time of the Association's greatest need. A 1928 pamphlet issued by the Association shows 'before' and 'after' pictures of children, where the benefits of the charity are clearly visible. After the Second World War the fruits of the Beveridge Report on social provision were had by all and the work of the Association declined. The Police Aided Association was wound up in 1968 and the remaining stock and responsibilities were handed over to the Women's Royal Voluntary Service. By then almost a quarter of a million, exactly 222,590, children were helped. The children were directed to the Association's Distribution Centre by teachers. The Centre was staffed by policewomen and a full time helper, a Mrs Harbridge. The memory of the Police Aided Association is a testament to the social responsibility of the City of Birmingham Police. It was an organisation which received little credit but did much for the good of Birmingham children.

A point of interest occurred in 1895 when a matron was appointed for duties in the Lock-Up in relation to prisoners. A deputation of ladies from the City approached the Watch Committee with a request that matrons should be appointed at all Police Stations. The Committee demured and pointed out that regulations whereby two police officers were to be present when females were in custody were adhered to. In cases of illness, it was pointed out, the services of the wife of a resident police officer were used.

THE MURDER OF POLICE CONSTABLE SNIPE

The *Birmingham Daily Mail* for Monday 19 July 1897 reports that PC 'C' George Snipe had died in the General Hospital as a result of injuries he had received quelling a disturbance in Bridge Street West with other policemen. The paper stated, 'Enquiries show clearly that the trouble originated in a row between persons who had had more liquor than was good for them and who were not disposed to take kindly to interference of the police on being turned from the public house at closing time.' A certain William Colrain was arrested by PC Snipe and PC Mead for being drunk and disorderly. A crowd gathered and tried to rescue Colrain whereupon PC Mead arrested a Charles Elvis. Stones were then thrown at the officers, one of whom blew his whistle attracting the attendance of PC Claydon. The officers were then attacked by a volley of stones, feet and fists. The police forced their way into the entrance of St Matthews Church. It was here that PC Snipe was struck on the temple by a thrown brick. He collapsed and Charles Elvis escaped. A member of the public ran to Kenyon Street Police Station, from where Bridge Street West Police Station, which was three miles away, was alerted. Several officers attended the scene. PC Snipe died four hours later in the hospital.

A woman came forward and informed Superintendent Monk of the identity of the person who had thrown the brick. This in fact was her boyfriend a James Franklin. He was later arrested in the locality by PC Belfield. Elvis was also recaptured.

The reporter from the *Mail* described Franklin on his appearance before the stipendiary as, 'An inoffensive looking man rather small in stature, pale in complexion with no whiskers'. He denied the offence but was later convicted at the Assizes for manslaughter and sentenced to penal servitude for life.

PC Snipe was 28 years old and left a widow and child. His general character was described as 'exemplary.' The helmet he wore on the night of his murder rests in the Force Museum. It bears the marks of the murderous attack upon him.

CRIME IN THIS PERIOD

In the last 15 years of the century the number of persons convicted rose from 9,284 to 18,744. An increase of over 100% appears to suggest an outbreak of criminality but in all likelihood the answer lies in the growth of the size of the City and increased legislation. It would be unfair to the then citizens of Birmingham if consideration was not given to the fact that these figures are not comparable to modern statistics. They contain such matters as muzzling orders, swine fever orders and attempted suicide. Offences against the person in 1899 amounts to only 62, but these are not just assaults as we presently class them but include bigamy and concealment of birth. In fact the largest group of offenders are found under Education Acts.

One series of offences that show a gradual decrease are those of prostitution. No evidence can be found of a change of Police policy in relation to prosecuting these offences but in a City of increasing population and wealth it could be expected that prostitution would increase.

'Before and After' for the Aided Association

3
Edwardian Days

In January of 1900 the authorised strength of the Birmingham City Police was 700. After the annual inspection of 1900, the HMI, Captain the Hon. C G Legge, announced that in his opinion the City was under policed and no less than an additional 220 officers were required. Notwithstanding that the Force was up to strength on the authorised establishment the beats were undermanned by about 200 officers and the detective department is said to have been understaffed and overworked requiring an increase of 25 officers. The Watch Committee accepted Captain Legge's argument but obviously being aware of the realities of local government approached the Council with a plan for incremental rises in numbers of the officers. On 5 February 1901 the Council gave permission for an immediate increase of 100 men with an annual increment of 20 men each year for six years. However, this did not alleviate the problems, as before the full figure was reached more officers were taken away from patrol work to specialised duty. Fourteen officers were used for the policing of the tramway terminal. Fifteen were used and paid for by the Baths and Parks Committee for patrolling the City's parks. Twenty six extra officers were also used so that each member of the Force could have two days holiday a month instead of one.

The year 1911 saw a further extension to the City when Aston Manor, Erdington, Yardley, Acocks Green, Hall Green, Sparkhill, Moseley, Kings Heath, Kings Norton, Northfield and Handsworth were brought within the boundaries. From this further extension the City gained Stirchley, Sparkhill, Acocks Green and Hay Mills Police Stations from Worcester County at a total cost of £18,193. The Hay Mills Police Station is now converted to a public house, titled the Old Bill and Bull. To this day the Worcester County Crest of a shield and three pears is displayed above the entrance door. Sparkhill and Acocks Green Police Stations are still in use. The County of Warwick ceded the police stations of Victoria Road, Aston together with its Police Court and Erdington Police Station in Wilton Road and police cottages for £25,229. Staffordshire County lost the present Thornhill Road Police Station and Police Court for the princely sum of £8,000. The City of Birmingham Police gained an extra 214 officers from the amalgamations.

This was a period of extension of police building within the City by the

Watch Committee. Before 1911 Bloomsbury Street, Nechells was built to replace an existing station in Nechells Park Road. On 5 December 1899 the Council paid £4,150 for 1,990 square yards of freehold land with frontages on Saltley Road, Lingard Street and Bloomsbury Street for the new police station and fire station. In January 1904 £7,000 was borrowed by the Council and the police station was built to include a house for an inspector and quarters for 17 single men. It was completed and occupied on 22 June 1905. A police station costing £9,771 was built at Bordesley Green in 1907 and land purchased from Saltley Reformatory for £1,000. The building included an inspector's house and accommodation for 22 single men. The station is in use to this day.

On 5 January 1909, the Council approved the purchase of 1,188 yards of land fronting Allison Street and Digbeth. The result was the building of the architecturally pleasing police station that still stands in Digbeth. The specification included accommodation for an inspector and 49 men and cost in the region of £20,000. This building was needed because the public office in Moor Street had been condemned as dilapidated by the Inspector of Constabulary. That old building was bought by the Great Western Railway for the building of Moor Street Railway Station, another pleasant structure which at the time of writing is due for demolition. The Police took possession of Digbeth Police Station on 1 July 1911.

In the same period 670 yards of land were purchased in Duke Street in 1904 for an extension to the police station. In 1906 further land was bought there for the provision of stables to replace those in Moor Street. In 1909 Ladywood Police Station, which stood beside the Children's Hospital and Lench's Almshouses in what is now Ladywood Middleway, was enlarged at a cost of £1,273.

In 1906 a loan was raised for the building of a public mortuary in Newton Street at the rear of a then existing fire station. Until this time mortuaries had been attached to police stations. The new mortuary could hold 11 bodies and had a post mortem room and other accommodation.

At the same time the Central Police Station was situated in Corporation Street as an adjunct to Victoria Law Courts. Space was cramped both in the Chief Constable's offices and Victoria Law Courts, so land was purchased from St Philip's School in Newton Street and further land was rented from the Estates Department also in Newton Street to build a new police headquarters. Probable cost of the new building was set at £12,850. The Council demured at this and suggested to the Justices Committee that they should make use of those police courts that had come into the City's possession in 1911. The justices replied that this would waste the time and cost of detectives, whose duty was

Bloomsbury Street Police Station, 1960's

said to be mainly at the Victoria Law Courts, if they had to travel to the old police courts to identify prisoners who had been charged with indictable offences. Arguments continued for some time until the price reached £29,295 without furniture and fixtures. On 28 July 1914 the Council voted the monies for the new building. But time and tide wait for no man and the hostilities of the First War broke out, causing the building work to be suspended.

THE TOWN HALL RIOT

One matter of great interest that occurred in this period was the 'Disturbance of 1901'. A meeting was held at the Town Hall on the evening of 18 December 1901 by the Birmingham Liberal Association. The main speaker was Mr David Lloyd-George MP who at that time was leader of a parliamentary group who disapproved of the conduct of the Boer War and the Government policy that led to it. He was critical of the conduct of the Government and its commanders in the field. Lloyd-George had been derided in the Birmingham press where it was suggested that his conduct gave succour to the rebellious Boers and thereby prolonged their resistance to British dominance in South Africa. Trouble was obviously anticipated and no less than 400 officers were on duty within the Town Hall and its environs. No sooner were the doors open than a crowd stormed the Town Hall platform and broke up the meeting. A larger crowd outside smashed windows of the Hall and street lamps in Victoria Square. The meeting was dispersed and Lloyd-George was smuggled out wearing a police helmet and cape belonging to PC Edward Taylor, for his safety. The diminutive 'Welsh Goat' escaped unnoticed amongst Birmingham's finest. A telegram later found in the pocket of the cape had been sent to Lloyd-George wishing him a quiet night. At about 10.40 pm the Chief Constable assured the crowd that the object of their hatred, Lloyd-George, had departed. The crowd disbelieved him and a scaffolding pole was used to break open door 'B'. Serious disorder then broke out. The exasperated police drew their truncheons and cleared Victoria Square. The mob scattered pursued by police along Colmore Row. At the far end just before Livery Street a young man named Harold Ernest Curtin was struck on the head and died.

At an inquest on 13 January 1902 the verdict of the coroner's jury was manslaughter by a police constable as yet unknown. The jury spoke for the City in censuring the Police. A rider to their verdict confirmed this censure, 'Because some policemen had been guilty of culpable excess of duty and importantly, because no evidence was forthcoming from policemen who knew who had struck the blow that killed Curtin.'

The Watch Committee had sensed that popular indignation and feeling was running against the Force and asked the Home Secretary to hold an enquiry. The Secretary of State declined. The Watch Committee in the search for an independent element then approached the City Council who in turn also declined to enquire into the incident but suggested that the Watch Committee should do so. They did, and took evidence from 48 police officers and 66 members of the public. Their findings were that no blame could be attached to police inside the Town Hall, that the police outside acted with forebearance and self control until the breaking of door 'B', and that the baton charge, though begun without orders, was justified by the aggressive temper of the crowd. They also decided that the Chief Constable who had assumed control of the charge tried to stop it when it had gone far enough; and that entirely innocent persons had been struck; also that certain officers of the Force had committed errors of judgement, but not such as to deserve censure. Their final conclusion was that no evidence had been obtained identifying, either by name or number, those policemen who had lost their self control and had committed unjustifiable homicide. Popular feeling was not satiated by this and the suspicion of the coroner's jury that the guilty policeman was being shielded by his colleagues continued. The second casualty in the affair was Mr Lancaster, the chairman of the Watch Committee who lost his seat in the following November election.

BIRMINGHAM'S FIRST FINGERPRINT PROSECUTION

The first successful prosecution by way of fingerprint evidence occurred in Birmingham in 1905. The circumstances of this case are that at 11.55 pm on 22 September 1905, Mrs Lily Shaw, the wife of the licensee of the Britannia Inn in Hampton Street, Newtown was in bed when she heard the sound of breaking glass below. Mrs Shaw blew hard on a whistle she kept for such purposes. This attracted the attention of PC C 538 Ollis who ran to the premises and arrested a well known criminal, George Eccles, close by. Eccles admitted smashing a kitchen window of the pub in order to burgle the premises. He implicated a Dennis Kennedy as his accomplice. Kennedy was arrested but he denied the offence, perhaps knowing that there was no other evidence to connect him other than the word of Eccles. The gods had failed to smile on Kennedy as the previous day PC Ollis and his inspector, Mr Parry, had attended a lecure at Kenyon Street Police Station on the new science of fingerprint impressions. Both officers went to the Britannia and found finger marks on the glass. They developed these latent prints by use of mercury, chalk and graphite. The evidence was sent to Scotland Yard for expert evidence which proved Kennedy's guilt. At the next Sessions he was sentenced to 18 months hard labour.

HAWKERS AND TRADERS

The Employment of Children Act 1905 added responsibility to Birmingham Police as the City streets were plagued by child street traders. Bye-laws enacted on 3 July 1904 forbade any child under the age of 16 to trade in the streets after 9.00 pm, neither could they trade without a licence, nor do so without wearing a badge that was issued with the licence. In the following March no less than 1,340 children made application for a licence to whom 777 were issued. To supervise this scheme a police sergeant and two constables together with three probation officers of the Children's Court reported to a sub-committee of the Watch Committee. Any offenders were cautioned or punished by temporary suspension of their licence. In the second year 2,390 children held a licence and by the third this fell to 1,955. It is reported that children's behaviour and school attendance actually improved. In 1908 the bye-law was amended whereby girls between 14 and 16 years were forbidden to trade unless accompanied by a parent or guardian. It is not hard to imagine why this amendment was made.

The crime statistics for this period show a fairly static nature of the number of indictable offences. However, in 1904 it can be seen from the Chief Constable's Report that offences against property virtually doubled. This was a strange phenomenon without apparent explanation as by 1905 they had stabilised noticeably. The extension of the City in 1911 did not make an impact on the total numbers recorded.

THE FIRST KING'S POLICE MEDALS FOR GALLANTRY

The first award to Birmingham officers of the King's Police Medal for Gallantry occurred on 23 February 1911 when King George V presented medals to Police Constables D 112 Patrick Clancy and D 41 George Smart. What makes the awards particularly interesting is that they were made retrospectively for actions four months before the establishment of the medal.

The circumstances surrounding the matter are that at about 11.15 pm on 9 March 1909 Clancy and Smart were on patrol and examining premises of the Standard Metal Company at the rear of 114 Coleshill Street in the City. The long monotony of checking premises must have suddenly been broken for the officers for they found the gate padlock had been broken off and a light was visible in an office. The officers stepped back into the darkness and waited for their quarry. A short while later two youths came up to the gates and on finally seeing Clancy and Smart each pulled out a revolver. There were cries of 'Hands Up', 'Blow their brains out' and 'Fire'. One youth ducked behind a handcart and shot at PC Clancy from only a few feet. PC Clancy popularly known as 'Pat', was a big brawny Irishman with a brogue to match. The youth would have done better to poke a hornets' nest with a short stick. The officer took his 'bulls-eye' lamp from his belt and threw it at the impetuous youth hitting him and causing him to fall. PC Clancy closed on him as he raised himself to his knees. The youth took aim with his revolver again and this time shot Clancy in the chest under the left armpit. The bullet passed through his shoulder blade and lodged under the surface of the skin. Out came Clancy's truncheon and down went the youth. Still the youth took aim and tried to shoot the officer. Three times the revolver misfired. A blow on the hand from a truncheon put paid to the young man's murderous attempts. The gun was later found to hold the three bullets that had misfired.

Meanwhile Police Constable Smart went after his man who pointed a revolver at him and pulled the trigger twice. At the same time the other youth's gun had been firing so PC Smart had no way of knowing, as was subsequently found, that his prisoner's revolver was unloaded. A single blow to the youth's face by Smart's fist put him to the ground and out of the contest.

The sound of gunfire brought Police Sergeant Husband to the scene and he assisted in having Clancy taken to hospital and the youths to Duke Street Police Station where they were both found in possession of further ammunition and stolen property. At Birmingham Assizes on 27 July 1909 they were both sentenced to Borstal Training.

On 24 February 1911 the *Birmingham Gazette* reported upon the previous day's investiture when the officers had received their medals. It is said that Police Constable Clancy, 'is a smart, popular and assiduous officer who since he has been connected with the City Force, has been instrumental in bringing several notorious burglars to justice. He has also been associated with many smart arrests.' The article continues that Police Constable Smart, 'Is a very familiar figure on the 'D' Division and is one hated by all the criminals. He first joined the City Force in November 1907, being stationed at Duke Street where he remained for three years before being transferred to the Jewellery Quarter. He has had several exciting adventures and is no stranger to the Assize Courts. From his exceptional height and bearing it is easy to credit him with his several years service in the Army.'

However Birmingham officers were not only winning the KPM in their own backyard but elsewhere. The courage of Police Constable E 44 Joseph Philips is also worth recording. It would appear that on Sunday 13 August 1911 a demonstration and meeting was called in Liverpool by the Transport Workers Strike Committee. The meeting was to be held at St George's Hall Plateau, Liverpool. The Chief Constable of that City anticipating trouble had requested aid in the form of 100 officers from Birmingham under the command of Superintendent Boulton. But this was Liverpool so the Chief Constable also had a detachment of 100 men of the Royal Warwickshire Regiment and two Royal Navy gunboats anchored in the Mersey. On the Sunday thousands of people converged on the Plateau. For an unknown reason a severe riot flared which spread throughout the crowd. One Liverpool newspaper reported, 'The Police used their truncheons mercilessly. It was a display of violence which horrified those who saw it.'

However the Police were being attacked on all sides, and a much different picture is given in the following letter from Sir Charles Rafter to Winston Churchill the Home Secretary which is testament enough to PC Philips brave actions:—

27th September 1911

Sir,

King's Police Medal

I have the honour to forward herewith a recommendation for the King's Police Medal in the case of Police Constable E 44 Joseph Philips of this Police Force for his gallantry and devotion to duty on the occasion of a riot in Liverpool on the 13th August 1911, when he risked his life by going to the rescue of Mr Superintendent Boulton who had been knocked down and was being kicked and jumped on by the crowd and was in danger of being killed.

The Constable himself was knocked down by the crowd, had his head cut open, and was severely kicked and injured. This officer has not yet quite recovered from his injuries.

I attach copies of reports from Mr Superintendent Boulton and from Police Constable E 44 Joseph Philips.

The circumstances are shortly as follows:

On the 10th August owing to the strike riot in Liverpool a detachment of 100 constables of this Force (of which Police Constable E 44 Joseph Philips was one) was sent to Liverpool under the command of Superintendent Boulton.

On the 13th August, a mass meeting of Trade Unionists was held in St George's Square, Liverpool. During the proceedings a serious riot took place and it became necessary for the Police to clear the square.

Superintendent Boulton with about 20 men was directed to clear Lime Street. He did so twice — the crowd having returned after the first clearance.

On the second occasion having dispersed the crowd he ordered his men to retire, but paused a moment himself to watch the crowd.

He was struck on the leg by some heavy missile which broke his leg and brought him to the ground. His men were still retiring and had their backs turned towards him, and were about 10 or 15 yards away.

When the Superintendent fell the crowd immediately rushed upon him, jumped upon him and kicked him all over, cutting his head badly, and bruising his face and body.

Police Constable Philips looked round and saw what was taking place. He said 'The Governor's down' and at once rushed back to his Superintendent's assistance. He was himself knocked down, and his head cut open and was very severely cut and beaten before the arrival of the others of the detachment.

Superintendent Boulton states, and I have no doubt he is correct, that the efforts of this Constable were instrumental in preserving his life.

The crowd was armed with bricks, bottles, iron bars, knives and other weapons.

The Superintendent sustained very severe injuries, having cuts on his head and being kicked in the face and about the body.

The Constable was also very severely injured.

A member of the public called John James Diamond, rendered yeoman service and his services are being recognised by this Police Force. It it were possible for an Albert Medal to be given to him I would strongly recommend it.

I have every confidence in recommending Police Constable E 44 Joseph Philips for the King's Police Medal.

He is an excellent officer, having joined this Police Force on 21st October 1901 and having a good character and records.

I am,
Sir,
Your obedient servant,
Chief Constable.

The Under Secretary of State,
Home Office,
Whitehall,
LONDON.

THE GREAT WAR

On 4 August 1914 war was declared against Germany and her allies of the

C

Austrian Empire. A shot from an assassin's pistol in Sarajevo led directly to the death of millions and was a watershed bringing rapid change between the old world and the new.

At the outbreak of war the authorised strength of the Force was 1,431 men, the actual establishment stood at 1,394. Pay for constables at this time ranged from 29s to 39s for constables and 41s to 46s for sergeants. Inspectors were paid between 50s to 58s compared to chief inspectors at £170 per annum.

Immediately 82 reservists were recalled to the Colours of whom four reserves returned to the Royal Navy. The Chief Constable and Watch Committee soon lent 149 men to the military as drill instructors. In keeping with the general patriotic fervour to enlist that swept the Kingdom at this time a number of officers requested release to join the Military Mounted Police and the Military Police. Some were permitted to enlist in the Army. At the same time the Watch Committee allowed the Chief Constable, Mr Rafter, to recruit the first Police Reserve to duty.

This was a body of some 300 police pensioners, and older men with military service, who had declared their availability for duty in the event of hostilities. Throughout the duration of the War the numbers of these men never exceeded 280 and by 1918 only 127 remained. When Birmingham Police Officers were released for military service there was keen competition by regimental recruiting officers to capture them. The first batch of 80 policemen were wooed by promises of joining crack regiments with good conditions of service and an attractive life. However an officer of a Welsh regiment promised immediate promotion to corporal and a week's extra leave. Whilst his competitors for this better class of recruit tried desperately to arrange the same conditions the bulk of the 80 men were enlisted into the Welsh unit.

It was also at this time (in common with most Police Forces), that the Birmingham City Police Special Constabulary made the transition from an ill-trained, ill-equipped anachronism to a formal police reserve. In the early days of the Force specials were sworn in when needed, were untrained, issued with a truncheon and disbanded when no longer required. By the end of the First War 8,005 special constables had been recruited and in the last year of hostilities 6,150 were still serving. Over 3,500 were employed on beat duty, 1,260 were engaged as volunteers for air raid duties and 935 as ward warners for air raids. The remainder were employed on guard and protection duties.

When the War started the City Police were given extra duties such as the arrest of enemy aliens, the guarding of vulnerable points, enforcement of light restrictions and dealing with air raids and their consequences.

Ladywood Police Station c.1950

ZEPPELIN RAIDS

One of the first acts by the Chief Constable Mr Rafter, was the issue on 23 November 1914 of a notice under the Defence of the Realm Act to reduce lights visible from above. Mr Rafter's orders were that external advertising lights, shop illuminations and skylights should be shaded and tram and omnibus lights should be reduced. The order was criticised locally at the time inasmuch as it had, 'An unnecessarily depressing effect and increased the danger of street accidents at night.' But when the first Zeppelin raids were experienced in London and on the East Coast, most of the citizens of Birmingham came round to the Chief Constable's way of thinking. It soon became evident that without a large number of anti-aircraft batteries the Zeppelins could roam at will over the country and they did so. On 27 January 1915 the Chief Constable announced a system of air raid warnings. The signal was to be given by the sound of factory steam whistles and hooters. It was to consist of five notes, the last being prolonged like a cock crow. Mr Rafter also announced that when an air raid warning was given the public were to quit the streets and go into cellars and lights were to be extinguished for the remaining hours of darkness. There was no 'All Clear' warning.

Before long the population of Birmingham was to be grateful for the Chief Constable's actions. On the night of 31 January 1916 people living in the north western suburbs heard heavy explosions in the distance. A few days later it was revealed that Zeppelins had tried to raid Birmingham but due to the success of the lighting restrictions had flown past attracted like moths to the glow of the Black Country furnaces. Walsall was bombed twice and several people killed. The next visit by the airships was on 19 October 1917 when a Zeppelin was reported flying over the City at 11 pm by several patrolling constables. It was clearly visible and the noise of the engines reverberated across the town. The 'black-out' had been intensified in the City Centre but the Austin works at Longbridge were brilliantly lit as production of munitions was now a 24 hour business. The Zeppelin dropped a bomb on the works hitting an outlying building and injuring two people. The Watch Committee and Chief Constable were justifiably annoyed that no warning of the approach of the airship over the coast had been given. However, Mr Rafter took small consolation as in the previous days there had been a concerted press attempt to have the lighting restrictions lifted. The final air attack took place on 12 April 1918. On this occasion intelligence was good and as soon as the Zeppelins had left their sheds the telephone exchange in Newhall Street were alerted that a raid was going to take place. At 9 pm five raiders crossed the coast and airship L60 detached itself and made course for Birmingham. On reaching Coventry it met the first anti-aircraft fire and the captain decided to make height. In order to do so he dropped bombs, some landing on Hockley Heath. At this point the craft was caught by a searchlight and subject to anti-aircraft fire. The pilot took fright on crossing the City boundary, circled over Hall Green dropped two large bombs on Robin Hood Golf Course and Manor Farm, Shirley, and then scuttled off home. Each of the bombs weighed a quarter of a ton but the only damage they did was to cause shattered windows in Hall Green. That was the last attack on Birmingham.

THE SPECIAL CONSTABULARY

When the Chief Constable first appealed to citizens over military age to enrol as special constables without pay, the urgency of his call was not realised by the public and only about 200 enrolled. By 1917 the Watch Committee realised they had to act as the police were released in great numbers for military services and the number of soldiers killed on the Western Front caused a devolution of responsibility for guarding strategic targets from the military to the police. Mr J Ernest Hill, the prosecuting solicitor, was appointed Head Special Constable and after a publicity campaign over 3,000 men were sworn in as specials within a month. They were issued with a great coat, peaked cap, truncheon, armlet and whistle and given a small allowance for boots. The special constables were obliged to undertake tours of duty of four hours, either on patrol or point duty. Duty during the day was undertaken alone but on night duty specials patrolled in pairs. Within time they were given training in drill and ambulance classes. It is recorded that the 'Volunteer' special constables turned out up to four times a week and were regarded as an asset by the inspectors and sergeants. Those specials who joined later, at the instigation of military tribunals, proved truculent and were held in much lower esteem. The Birmingham City Police were responsible for the guarding of the City's property at the waterworks in the Elan Valley and the Severn Bridge at Bewdley. They were seen as the two most vulnerable points in the City's water supply and competition amongst the specials to be posted there was intense. The fishing and other country sports were obviously a great attraction. From 17 July 1917, no less than 27 Birmingham police officers were on duty in the Elan Valley, a 24 hour guard being posted at the Foel Tower, the islet in the lake, and 17 were stationed by the bridge at Bewdley. The City's Water Committee were more than pleased with this 'free' service and provided board and lodgings together with railway fares for the Birmingham men.

From the wartime service of the special constables a volunteer motor transport service was organised. About 100 private cars belonging to specials were placed at the disposal of the Force. It was estimated that through the use of the vehicles between 700 and 800 men could be mobilised in an hour. The use of private cars on duty by special constables was retained until the demise of the City of Birmingham Police.

OTHER WARTIME POLICE DUTIES

The City Police were of course in the front line of the investigations of spy scares and the supervision of aliens. In 1914 the Police Aliens Office registered 1,200 enemy aliens and arrested 160 of those, who proved to be of military age, and saw them interned in camps. In September 1914, 21 young unmarried Germans who had been living in Harborne were arrested and interned as a precautionary measure. In May 1915 the City Police were requested to intern all German and Austrian subjects of possible military age, but on this occasion the action was taken to protect them due to the incidence of feelings running high after submarine and air attack outrages. It is a worthy record that there were never any attacks upon any naturalised Germans in the City during the course of the war.

For the Force as a whole, life and especially discipline, continued as normal. In Force Orders for 27 September 1914 it is reported that:

> '*PC E 266 Albert Owen* is fined 10/- and cautioned to be truthful, for being absent from duty without leave on Saturday 22 August 1914; also leaving the City without permission on the same date.
>
> This constable has told a tissue of falsehoods, stating that his mother was ill and that he was nursing her, whereas he did not sleep at his home at all while absent without leave. This is the second time he has played a somewhat similar trick.
>
> Should further complaint be made his services will be dispensed with.'

On the same date it is reported that:

> '*PC E 33 John Burke* is reinstated and finally cautioned for being under the influence of drink when parading for night duty at Sparkhill Station at 9.45 pm on Friday 21 August 1914 and being found asleep in the WC of the single men's quarters at 10.20 pm of the same date.'

From 1914 onwards Force Orders unfortunately show numerous discipline offences of constables being found asleep on Special Protection Duty or leaving this duty to congregate with other officers awaiting their reliefs. Time and again the instruction is given, 'Only reliable men are to be put on this duty.'

This was so because in the main the points were armed posts. Policemen are not fond of firearms and the majority are unfamiliar with them. Several incidents are recorded in Force Orders that, with hindsight, are humorous but at the time must have given cause for concern. In September 1914 men who were armed with Lee Metford rifles were warned that they were not to be carried loaded. Five rounds of ammunition were issued with instructions that they were to be carried safely and the rifle was to be loaded with one round at a time in case of dire necessity. On 29 October that year it was pointed out that a case had occurred where a revolver had been fired in a police station, 'With what might have been serious results.' Instructions were emphasised that the revolver should only be loaded in four chambers, the fifth being empty and on first firing this empty chamber should be the first to meet the hammer. An obviously nervous Chief Constable stated, 'It cannot be too firmly impressed on the minds of all men using revolvers that they must stop tampering with the arms, and that every care must be taken to prevent any misuse of firearms.' However, by 29 April 1915 Force Orders were stating:

> 'Referring to Orders of 4 and 17 August and 29 October last, a case has again occurred in which a revolver was accidentally discharged by meddling with it *and* the matter not reported by the officer. Superintendents will now issue instructions to all men in charge of revolvers in any case in which a barrel is discharged to forthwith report the occurrence.'

By 1916 special constables were also being armed on Special Protection Duty and a memorandum from the Chief Constable to all superintendents on 16 August makes it clear that:

> 'Special constables who carry firearms are to be instructed that these firearms are not to be used for the purposes of shooting suspicious persons, or persons whom they think suspicious, but they are provided only for their own self defence.'

The enthusiastic but largely untrained specials warranted many mentions in Force Orders of this type, as an order for 27 January 1916 says:

> 'There seems to be some misunderstanding among special constables as to the pocket best adapted to carry the staff.
> Superintendents will please show the specials the pocket made for the purpose of carrying the staff in constables' trousers, so that they may have an idea as to the best way to carry the staff.'

An earlier order of the same month gives directions for the supervision of special constables, amongst which are:

> 'They are to be advised not to be too ready to make arrests without sufficient cause, and to keep out of mischief.
> They should not interfere with matters between the sexes but leave that to the ordinary police, as it is of a very technical nature, and should not be dealt with except by police of experience.
> All special constables are personally responsible for their own acts.'

It was not only specials who appeared somewhat foolish to their more experienced colleagues. Unfortunately no record exists of what the 'rank and file' thought of this order dated 17 January 1916.

> 'An experiment has been successfully tried at the Five Ways with the policeman on point duty there at night. He was provided with two police lamps with red lens, one lamp being on the front and the other on the back of his belt. He could thus stop traffic by turning himself half round.
> I would suggest that you should try it in other places as it seems to work very well.'

The Police in Birmingham were also ordered to seize and destroy pamphlets and documents under Section 51 of the Defence of the Realm Act. A list of this seditious material was printed in Police Orders and included such works as, 'Peace at Once', 'Christianity and War', 'Letter to an ex-pacifist' and 'Socialism and War'. The City Police were warned that if they had any information that any of the documents were in any house then the information should be at once communicated to the Chief Constable. However the extra war time duties of the Birmingham Police were not all oppressive and the matter of 'Soldiers' Wives' gives proof to this. It became the practice of the War Office to withdraw allowances to the wives of serving soldiers if their conduct caused concern and thereby discontent for their husbands at the front. Conditions were abnormal for these women. There was tense anxiety for their husband's safety, unfamiliar freedom and the sudden change in life style on entering the labour market. Some of these women either took to drink or were suborned into drinking. In a memorandum to all superintendents in 1915 from the Chief Constable he points out that the War Office were withdrawing allowances of some Birmingham soldiers' wives. He expresses the hope that all constables on the beat coming to hear of misconduct by soldiers' wives will take steps to ensure that they are protected and safeguarded from moral danger. Mr Rafter states; 'It is a pity that women have gone so far as to lose their allowance and probably wreck their future. Perhaps some effort on the part of the Police may prevent further cases recurring.'

Life continued in the City virtually unchanged. In his annual report to the Watch Committee the Chief Constable appears to be surprised that no complaints had been received of misconduct by persons using the cabmen's shelters. These were structures placed for the refuge of cab drivers around the City. There were a total of 21 at one time and they were greatly appreciated as refuges from the elements by the cabbies. Amongst the sundry items of found property received during the year were six sets of false teeth, one artificial leg, a bag of horse shoes, a fire grate and one ear trumpet.

The War saw an increase in the number of motor vehicles on the Birmingham roads with attendant necessity for police intervention. The Motor Car Act 1903 placed the registration of cars and motor cycles under the Public Carriage Office. In 1915, 2,063 new cars and 2,502 new motor cycles were registered making a total of 20,605 such vehicles registered in the Birmingham area. By 1918 it is clear that the cost of increased car and motor bicycle traffic was recognised as being a drawback on its benefits. In that year there were 1,188 accidents involving motor cars in which 30 people were killed and 435 were injured. However, it appears though that motor cars had not been raised to the exalted position accorded them in modern society. In the Chief Constable's Report for 1918 there is a table showing the combined numbers of cattle and vehicles found in the streets and impounded by the Police. Perhaps it is worth remembering that motor cars are in reality beasts of burden.

REBUILDING THE BIRMINGHAM CITY POLICE

During the First War 536 members of the Force served in the Armed Services. Out of these 55 were killed or died on active service. Their names are recorded to this day on a memorial board at Lloyd House Police Headquarters. Some 80 men were wounded by the enemy and six were held captive as prisoners of war. Recruiting to the Regular Force was suspended during the course of the War. In 1914 the authorised establishment stood at 1,431, but this bore no relation to the wartime reality as the strength of the Force fell in 1917 to 999 and reached a low of 853 in 1918. With the end of the War recruiting was resumed. The first effect of this was a sudden outflow of time expired officers and First Police Reserve. In a memorandum to superintendents, on 21 January 1919, the Chief Constable refers to this outflow as a 'general stampede.' The second effect was the recruitment of 286 men and the return of 419 men from the Forces. The actual establishment then stood at 1,341, a shortfall of 90 officers. Problems

The Ladies of the Policewomen Department, 1930's

therefore remained which would be compounded for the City by the Police Regulations of August 1920 issued under the Police Act 1919. These regulations reduced working hours and increased periods of leave.

T A Critchley in his seminal work *The History of Police in England and Wales*, declares that the First War sent an impact on the police service, 'that led to the transformation of the Victorian police system, into something very much like the national institution we know today'. One of these changes is the increased centralisation of control by the Home Office which is inevitable in times of war. This control manifested itself in regulations, orders, advice, correspondence, Parliamentary Acts, in short a growing bureaucracy. In 1912 the 'R' Division of the City of Birmingham Police, the Headquarters Administration of the Chief Constable's office, had an establishment of 137. By 1920 it had grown to 187 and was still short of a proper establishment. The 'R' Division as a headquarters division continued into the West Midland Police to be changed to 'A' Division in 1978.

BIRMINGHAM'S FIRST WOMEN POLICE

The second and most important change was the evolution of the Women's Police Department. The First World War had seen the emergence of women in the workplace as men were replaced to go to the Western Front, and generally to die.

In common with society generally at this time the status of women in the police service changed. At the outset it is correct to say that the City of Birmingham Watch Committee, the Chief Constable, and the Force as a whole welcomed the role of women in the police service. This was not true for the rest of the country and especially the Metropolitan Police. Suspicion about the motives of those ladies who were advocating police work for women was grounded in their role in the women's suffrage movement. At that time feminism was interpreted as the 'sugar and spice and all things nice' variety and not the strident clamouring for equality. Chief Constables could see no place for women in their forces but could accept the need for work amongst women and children being undertaken by voluntary bodies. When one sees photographs of early founders and leaders of the 'Voluntary Women's Patrol' and the 'Woman's Public Service', sympathy for the leaders of the police force can be felt. With short cropped hair, monocles and jack boots these women looked as though they would strike fear in a Prussian general, let alone a common thief. Even when they saw fit to patrol the streets they were invariably followed by two constables at a short distance to ensure they came to no harm.

The First World War saw the massive employment of women in Birmingham's munitions and other manufacturing industries. Birmingham boasted the title 'The Small Arms Arsenal of the World' and so it was. Quite literally the smaller arms made small arms. Added to the cocktail of young women and women separated by the War, the City saw an influx of soldiers, especially Canadian soldiers.

Watch Committee minutes for 7 May 1917 record the receipt of a communication from the Women's Labour League and the Women's Cooperative Guard urging the appointment of women to perform police duties. The letter was acknowledged by the committee. Clearly a problem existed and the matter was at that time being considered by the judicial sub-committee of the Watch Committee. The sub-committee reported on 14 May 1917. They had received opinion from the Law Officers of the Crown that women could not be appointed as constables, and that 'Women police are servants of the Watch Committee.' The deputation to the Watch Committee had suggested that women police should patrol parks, railways and common lodging houses. The sub-committee pointed out that these areas were not within the responsibility of the Watch Committee so their servants could not patrol them.

It was pointed out to the committee that evidence had been heard of outrage and in-cest (sic) against women and children and this was ideal work for policewomen. However the committee did say they were satisfied with the system employed in the City where statements were only taken by an experienced inspector of detectives in the presence of a woman of experience. The sub-committee claimed that, 'the complaints which have been made that such statements were taken by an inexperienced young police officer do not apply in this City.'

However in an act of enlightenment the judicial sub-committee recommended that women might be experimentally employed in certain patrols in uniform on the streets. Accordingly on 1 June 1917, the Watch Committee appointed Mrs Rebecca Lipscombe and Mrs Evelyn Myles who were Lock-up matrons as Birmingham's first women police. These ladies, the figurative grandmothers of all policewomen in the City, were paid 35s per week.

At the start of the War a hostel existed in Corporation Street as temporary lodgings for women dealt with by the police. With the expansion in their numbers, brought about by the War, these premises proved inadequate. The matter was discussed at a meeting of the Watch Committee in March 1918. Alderman J H Sayer offered premises of his own at 67 Dale End for a nominal rent of £50 per annum. As a measure of his public spiritedness it is worth recording that he gave this income to the Police Aided Association for the relief of poor children.

On 2 January 1918 the committee voted £290 for alterations to the premises. On 21 January discussions were held in relation to the appointment of a matron for the hostel. The decision was made to offer £100 per annum plus board, coal, lighting and lodgings in order to attract the right person. On 25 January the Misses Rubery and Julian Osler together with Mrs Harrison Barrow accepted to be the Ladies Advisory Committee to the girls' hostel. Older readers will recognise the names Rubery from the Rubery Owen Company and Barrow from the Barrow Cadbury family. On 6 February 1918 a Miss Katie Short of Sutton, Surrey was interviewed and appointed matron at £80 per annum with uniform and 'all found'. The final appointment was Doctor Lena Walker, a female sugeon, as medical officer on 3 July 1918. The doctor received the sum of 10s 6d per case.

The hostel was officially opened by the Lord Mayor in June 1918. The work of the hostel was a measured success and is believed to be the first of its kind in the country. In 1928 the Dale End premises proved inadequate for the numbers being given shelter and accordingly the hostel was transferred to premises at 58 Newton Street on 17 July 1928. The new hostel had six of the then 15 women police attached to it. It is worth noting that the hostel, which was a gift to the Watch Committee and Chief Constable, from Mr and Mrs Barrow Cadbury was situated next door to a new Children's Court which they had also generously donated to the City. The Children's Court opened in 1905 was also a first in the country. Up until that time children in Birmingham appeared in the Magistrates Courts with adults. The new building was opened in 1927 and stands to this day.

The evolution of women in police work continued apace to this form of welfare work. Four months after the appointment of Rebecca Lipscombe and Evelyn Myles three more women were recruited as women police. On 1 December 1920 we find that Miss D O G Peto, OBE was appointed Female Enquiry Officer attached to the Criminal Investigation Department. Miss Peto was paid £200 per annum, received £27 per annum for plain clothes and 2s per week boot allowance. Some value must have been attributed to her work as her starting salary was just below that of a 12 year constable.

The work of policewomen at this time is described by the Watch Committee as being of a 'protective and preventive character'. Their duties were to patrol the streets and parks and pay visits to public resorts. It is said that they were able to protect and assist females who were in distress, out of work or in bad company. Most of all the benefit of Birmingham's women police was said to lie

principally among girls, 'who can be removed from evil influences.'
A confirmation of the value of these early women police officers can be obtained from the 1934 Chief Constable's Report. At this time the policewomen department had an establishment of 17 officers. In that year 704 women and girls were taken to the Newton Street hostel, 141 girls were sent to other hostels, 648 visits were made to homes, numerous interviews were made at the hostel following complaints from parents, guardians or others, 107 girls were found employment, 60 girls reported missing from home were traced and restored and finally 200 girls and women were taken to hospital.

On 5 July 1922 the Watch Committee approved the appointment of the women police as permanent members of the City of Birmingham Police, thereby justifying their own initial approval of women police.

CRIME AND DETECTIVES

Other than the wartime conditions the First World War had little direct impact in the social field on citizens and police in Birmingham. It was fought far away in a line of trenches that crossed from Northern France to Switzerland. Crime during the war years maintained a fairly constant rate in the indictable offence categories. The most common offence of simple larceny hovered around the 850 a year mark. The maximum number of murders occurred in 1916 with two offences being committed. Housebreaking and burglary never rose above an average of one offence per week. Halcyon days! No wonder there was always a copper on the beat. One noteworthy item is the gradual reduction in the number of attempted suicides from 134 in 1915 to 71 in 1916 and 59 in 1918. What were the causes of this? A better standard of living from regular munitions work? Increased awareness of the value of life when so many were giving theirs? Or less domestic conflict through spouses being absent in the Forces or working longer hours?

After the end of the War the strength of the Criminal Investigation Department in 1919 stood at 70 officers. From their original headquarters in Crooked Lane the detective branch had moved to the Lock-up attached to the Moor Street Public Office in 1849. By 1881 the establishment consisted of a superintendent and 15 detectives. When the new police headquarters was established in Corporation Street in the Victoria Law Courts in 1894 the department moved there and had reached 25 officers. In the last year of the First War the CID, as they were now known, dealt with 39,100 enquiries and proceeded against 1,341 persons for 1,537 indictable offences.

Point duty at the junction of Bull Street, 1930's

POST-WAR TRAINING

Training was carried out in the Police School at Digbeth Police Station and the school was recognised as the most efficient in the country. With the resumption of recruiting the school was reorganised in 1919. Instruction was given not only to officers of the Birmingham City Police but also to members of many other forces in the country. The school was responsible for the training of police officers from around the world. Men from countries as far away as Siam, Columbia, Afghanistan, China and Egypt came to Birmingham to be instructed in the ways of the British Police Service.

Recruits in Birmingham were attached to the school for three months. As can be seen from the timetable, they received full time instruction in police duties, law, general education, drill, fire and ambulance work, swimming, life saving and patrol work. Graduation from the school as a probationer to perfom beat duty did not mean the end of classwork as probationers were required to attend evening classes in educational subjects. This further instruction was carried out by members of the City Education Authority. These extra classes are not surprising when considering that most recruits had attended only elementary schooling that did not fit them for the changing, more comprehensive form of police work.

It must be remembered when examining the subjects taught that the City Police were responsible for the accident ambulances for all street accidents within the City and those within a reasonable distance of the boundary. In 1901 the Watch Committee had approved the purchase of a horse drawn ambulance. Prior to this any casualties or victims were taken to hospital by handcart. Hospital ambulance service was under the control of the St John's Ambulance Brigade and the Birmingham Hospital Control Association.

The police ambulances were stationed at Duke Street Police Station and eventually eight motor ambulances were in use. These vehicles passed to the Fire and Ambulance Service on 5 July 1948. Ambulance and first aid training was to St John's Ambulance standard. A constable was trained to obtain his first certificate in his first year and progress to his third certificate and medallion at the end of his third year. The medallion was worn on the right sleeve of the tunic between the shoulder and elbow. Police orders of this time show great lists of men who had been successfully examined or re-examined in first aid by police surgeons. The Chief Constable's Report for 1917 compliments several officers for this type of work but in particular the following, 'PC E 138 William Spiers rendered first aid to Edith Griffiths (22) who was suffering from severe haemorrhage (internal) by undoing all tight clothing, giving ice to suck, sprinkling the face with cold water and bandaging the extremities from the

68

Birmingham City Police.

DUTIES OF RECRUITS.

HOURS DAILY.	MONDAY.	TUESDAY.	WEDNESDAY.	THURSDAY.	FRIDAY.	SATURDAY.
9.30 a.m. till 10.30 a.m.	Gymnasium.	Drill.	Gymnasium.	Drill.	Drill	Gymnasium.
11.0 a.m. till 12 noon.	Court.	Court.	Court.	Court.	Court.	Court.
12 noon till 1 p.m.	School.	School.	School.	School.	School.	School.
1 p.m. till 2.30 p.m.	Dinner.	Dinner.	Dinner.	Dinner.	Dinner.	Dinner.
	Drill 2.30 p.m. to 3.15 p.m.	Drill 2.30 p.m. to 3.30 p.m.	Drill 2.30 p.m. to 3.15 p.m.	Fire Drill 2.30 p.m. to 3.30 p.m. Lingard Street Fire Station.	Drill 2.30 p.m. to 3.15 p.m.	
	School 3.30 p.m. to 4.30 p.m.	School 3.45 p.m. to 5 p.m.	School 3.30 p.m. to 4.30 p.m.	School 3.45 p.m. to 4.30 p.m.	School 3.30 p.m. to 4.30 p.m.	
	Patrol 6 p.m. to 10 p.m.	Evening for Home Study.	Evening for Home Study.	Patrol 6 p.m. to 10 p.m.	Evening for Home Study.	Patrol 6 p.m. to 10 p.m.
	Council School Classes during the winter months from 7.30 till 9 p.m. on Monday, Tuesday, and Wednesday, take the place of Home Work and Patrol. Ambulance Classes will be attended after Recruits are dismissed drill.					

Recruits are required to devote their spare time to study.

They are expected to make themselves reasonably efficient within a reasonable time.

December, 1905.

Fig. III — Training Programme for Recruits, 1905

Results are posted at Digbeth Police School in 1930's

ankles to the hips and hands to the shoulders. Dr Heapy states that he considered the constable had saved the woman's life'.

THE 1919 POLICE STRIKE

Some would consider that the year 1919 was probably the blackest in police history but from the dispute of that year came better conditions and the establishment of the Police Federation of England and Wales. This was the year of the Police Strike. Troops were on standby in London and they patrolled the streets in Liverpool with tanks and the warship *HMS Valiant* was brought south to the Mersey from Scapa Flow. Birmingham also played a part in these developments.

There were two main causes of the strike. The first was the demand for the 'right to confer', in other words the recognition of the Police and Prison Officers Union. The second was the fact that police pay during the war years had failed to rise with the cost of living which had doubled. In comparison with that of munitions workers police pay was inadequate. As Critchley states, 'By 1918 many policemen and their families had sunk so low in poverty that they were actually undernourished and the temptation held out by bribes of food and money must at times have been irresistible'.

Rafter and the Watch Committee were aware of the discontent brewing within the Birmingham Force. After an initial strike in London the Home Office circulated forces announcing that there was no longer any objection to police officers holding membership of the National Union of Police and Prison Officers. However, the Government in the form of Lloyd-George stated that he could not, 'in wartime sanction the recognition of a police union'. In October of 1918 the Chief Constable of Birmingham, Charles Rafter announced that the union, 'Would not only be contrary to Police Regulations, but would be highly subversive of good order and discipline, in fact the two things cannot exist together in the same force'. He continued, 'The recent disgraceful strike of police in the Metropolis, of which we are all ashamed, should act as a deterrent to members of this Force, not to ally themselves in any way to an organisation which took part in such a disloyal occurence'. It is not clear whether the Birmingham officers agreed with their Chief Constable but what was clear that in April 1919 the local union branch was claiming a 90% membership in the City. The motto of the union was 'Discipline is not Tyranny' and this gives us a flavour of the conditions the union were pledged to fight.

Rafter and the Watch Committee were obviously worried and anticipating strike action when the new Police Bill was published, as a result of the

National Union of Police and Prison Officers, Birmingham Branch.

OUR CASE.

We are out on strike in Birmingham to secure recognition for the Police and Prison Officers' Union. This recognition, we understood, was secured for us by the Prime Minister last August, but it now appears as if the whole fight the Union was engaged in has to be gone through again.

We are also on strike because the Police Bill at present before the House of Commons takes away from us liberty of action in regard to any organisation to secure proper conditions of service and dealing with matters of complaint. Victimisation has been frequent, and we in Birmingham have been great sufferers in this respect.

Clauses in the Police Bill to which we take greatest exception are 1, 2, and 3. These clauses provide for an internal organisation which is not on democratic lines. They have the effect of dividing the ranks, and so largely rendering ineffective any recommendations being discussed on a general representative basis. There is no guarantee that any recommendations made under the provisions of the Bill will be given effect to.

NOT CONSULTED.

We have not been consulted in any way with regard to the principle or details of the Bill which is being thrust upon us. Clause 2 has the effect of robbing us of the restricted liberty we have had in the past, and the penalties laid down in this clause for belonging to our National Union are that we must cease to be policemen and forfeit all pension rights.

Clause 3 is of vital importance to the public, because it states that any person who, in the opinion of the authorities, is guilty of action calculated to cause disaffection in the service will be liable to varying terms of imprisonment from two months to two years. If a member of the police discusses conditions of service with another member of the force and thereby, in the opinion of the authorities, attempts or causes disaffection he will be liable to imprisonment and heavy penalties under the Act, and forfeiture of pension.

We are not on strike for any increase of pay, but we acknowledge that our union has secured us increases of pay and better conditions. Before the existence of the Union such demands had been consistently ignored.

A "SECRET" CONFERENCE.

There is one matter to which we call the especial attention of the public, and it is that a telegram was received from the Home Office by the Chief Constable, asking the chairman of the Birmingham Police Representative Board to attend a conference at the Home Office. Practically nobody, with the exception of the Chief Constable and the chairman referred to, had any knowledge of the conference or its purpose, and it was impossible under the circumstances for the Birmingham Police Force to be consulted or to give a mandate to their so-called representative.

To the Home Secretary the chairman of the Birmingham Representative Board made a protest against the way in which the conference had been convened and the secrecy of its purpose.

This is not solely a policeman's fight but an effort to safeguard the elementary rights of citizenship and freedom.

Our Union is about to be smashed, ruthlessly, once and for all.

This Union is, up to now, a perfectly legal organisation ; but if once the present Police Bill becomes law, you will witness the unprecedented occurrence of a properly constituted

TRADE UNION BEING WIPED OUT

by Act of Parliament ! If that happens, a serious blow will have been struck at Trades Unionism in this country.

Fellow countrymen, will you stand tamely by and witness this attack of British Prussianism on our hard-won liberties ? Our fight is yours ! We stand or fall together !

Birmingham Printers, Ltd., 42, Hill Street.

Fig. IV — Union handbill for strike support

Desborough Committee recommendations, issued the following order:—

POLICE ORDERS 30 May 1919
POLICE AND PRISON OFFICERS' UNION
THREATENED POLICE STRIKE

The Watch Committee have under consideration the threatened declaration of a strike by the Executive of the Police and Prison Officers' Union and have decided that any officer or man of the Birmingham City Police Force, of whatever rank, who participates therein and fails to report in the ordinary course of duty, or when called on, will be forthwith dismissed from the Force.

They have also decided that such officer or man will under no circumstances be permitted to rejoin Birmingham City Police and dismissal will result in the loss of all service counting towards pension.

The Watch Committee have the approval of the Government for this course.

It will be seen from the Home Secretary's reply to Mr Wallace's question in the House of Commons on Wednesday last, a copy of which appeared in Police Orders yesterday, that the Government have definitely decided not to recognise the existing Police and Prison Officers' Union.

An organisation will be set up by the Authority within the Police Service to enable the men to protect their own interest. Particulars will be published as soon as possible.

It will not be confined to a purely local organisation, but will include provision to enable the men to make their representation on a national basis on questions of pay etc, which effect the Police as a whole.

It is pointed out that the Trades Disputes Act 1906 does not apply in the case of a strike by the Police, as the Police are not 'workmen' within the definition of Section 5(3) of the Act.

Any forcible prevention or interference with a police officer who is parading for duty is an obstruction of the Police within the meaning of the Prevention of Crimes Act 1885 and will be dealt with accordingly.

This notice is issued by the direction of the Watch Committee.

The Chief Constable feels assured that the large majority of the Birmingham City Police Force have no association with the organisation referred to and he has the utmost confidence in the good sense and loyalty of the Police Force as a whole. He feels sure that the members of the Birmingham City Police Force will not take part in any movement such as described but which seems to be in contemplation in connection with the Police Union which claims to have a membership in Birmingham.

By Order
Charles Haughton Rafter
Chief Constable

The Chief Constable and Watch Committee could not have been more explicit.

When the full implications of the Desborough Committee were being debated in Parliament the Union leadership recognised that the battle was on for the survival of the Union which was to be replaced by the Police Federation. On 31 July 1919 when it was obvious that the Police Bill would be passed into law, the Birmingham branch of the Union sent two delegates, who were prison officers, to London to seek direction.

The local branch chairman was Sergeant Edward Taylor, the same officer who had lent his uniform to Lloyd-George who was now the Prime Minister. Sergeant Taylor had 22 years service in the Birmingham Police. He worked at Kenyon Street Police Station and is said to have been a well respected, trusted and conscientious officer. On 1 August Taylor called a meeting of the branch committee at 15a Spiceal Street, Digbeth. But with no news from London, he went to Kenyon Street at lunchtime and telephoned all divisions to tell his members to report for duty. Later that afternoon he chaired a meeting of 40 union members and is said to have told them he was opposed to a strike but reminded those present that they had pledged to strike for union recognition. The two delegates returned on a late afternoon train and told Taylor that London was on strike and wanted Birmingham's support.

At 9.30 pm Sergeant Taylor sent a message to all divisions asking all men to come out on strike. However, the timing of the call was the eventual downfall of the strike. By then news of the weak response to the London strike call had been in the evening papers and the Force had been paid that day and received £10 extra pending the Police Act. There was much discussion that night as to the wisdom of striking and the benefits which that course of action would make. The impetus was lost. At Digbeth Police Station eight men reported for duty, three of whom refused duty and went on strike.

The following day 2 August the Judicial Sub-Committee were informed by the divisional superintendents as to the identity of the men who had gone on strike. From the 'A' Division the report was 42, the 'C' Division 21 and the 'E' Division reported 26 officers. In accordance with the Police Order they were summarily dismissed. At the next meeting of the sub-committee on the 4 August the report was that from the 'B' Division one officer had taken strike action, in the 'C' Division 14 and the 'E' Division reported a further 13. They too were dismissed making a total of 117 police officers on strike. The final recorded total of men dismissed during the Birmingham Police Strike is 119.

The days that followed the initial action were taken up by claims and counter claims, between the Union and the Chief Constable as to the numbers on strike.

The Union claimed 300 and gaining more support, Rafter maintained the correct figure.

On Saturday, 9th August 1919, after no headway had been made, Sergeant Taylor and five members of his committee, perhaps feeling their position as insecure, went to London to find out what was happening. To their dismay, they found out that even there the full membership had not struck. The men returned to Birmingham. Sergeant Taylor's intention was for mercy and reinstatement for his members. He called a meeting of the Union branch at the Barton's Arms public house and sought out a Police Inspector and short hand writer who were present on the Chief Constable's instructions at every such meeting. He told them that he believed the strike had done good, because it had exposed the Bolsheviks in the Union and that they had been told 'nothing but a pack of lies by officials' and by the *Daily Herald*, a socialist newspaper. In a clear attempt to get the message to Mr Rafter, the Sergeant continued, 'We all want to go back and there need be no question of our loyalty in the future. We admit defeat. We are neither mutineers nor criminals and I am convinced that we shall all be better policemen for our experience'.

Mercy was sought but Mr Charles Haughton Rafter showed no quarter. The strikers were discharged and would remain so, as a warning to the rest of the Force. On 15 August 1918 the first of many applications for reinstatement was received. 12 strikers from the 'A' Division applied to the Watch Committee without success. Members of the 'A' Division asked permission from the Chief Constable to submit 'round robins' of support for each applicant for reinstatement. Their suggestion was dismissed. An application for mercy by the Birmingham Trades Council also fell on deaf ears. On 27 October 1919, the full Council refused to hold an enquiry into the Birmingham Strike.

Sergeant Taylor's record of service, shows that he had been commended on 19 occasions and awarded two merit stripes. The last entry is dated 2 August 1919 and reads: 'Reported by Supt. Penrice for inciting men to leave their duty in the Police Force and going out on a Police Strike, and themselves declaring about 10 pm, 1st August 1919 that they were on strike — Dismissed the Force.'

Most works and articles on the strike describe the future of the strikers as grim and full of unemployment and hopelessness. As yet there is no published evidence of this. The most they lost was their pensions. In the case of Sergeant Edward Taylor this was £140 8s 0d. Perhaps they were all soon in work and success.

IMPROVED CONDITIONS

The Police Act 1919 was the enabling act for the Police Regulations of 1920. These changed the conditions of service for the City of Birmingham Police. It saw the foundation of the Police Federation Branch Board in Birmingham. Pay for constables was increased from £3 10s 0d to £4 15s 0d and other ranks were rewarded similarly. Other payments were made, such as 1s per day for officers on point duty, 2s 6d per week for drivers, CID outdoor duty entitled an officer to 8s per week and use of one's own bicycle paid an extra 4s per week. Officers on mortuary duty were paid 10s per week for days and by some strange logic 4s per week for night duty. The regulations empowered a Chief Constable to dispose of the services of a probationer without reference to the Watch Committee. Discipline authority for lesser matters was removed to the Chief Constable. Where complaints by the public were concerned or the punishment was either dismissal, being required to resign, loss of merit stripe, reduction of pay or rank, discipline remained the province of the Watch Committee. Importantly the regulations introduced promotion regulations and made the Chief Constable responsible for making promotions. On 3 September 1920 the Watch Committee recorded their annoyance at the restriction upon their authority.

As members of a borough force the Birmingham City Police, with a population of over 150,000 became entitled to benefit under a Police Bonus Scheme on 25 October 1920. Constables, sergeants and inspectors received a non-pensionable sum of 2s, 2s 3d and 2s 6d increase to cover a cost of living rise.

The 1920 regulations also introduced an obligation on the Watch Committee to provide rent free houses or quarters or in lieu to grant non-pensionable allowances. In Birmingham the Watch Committee set this new rent allowance at the maximum limit payable. This meant that constables received 13s per week. The Council elected to build houses for occupation by police officers on Corporation housing estates in 1925. These houses were to cost £550. By 1939 339 such houses had been provided and one third of these were on the Heybarnes Estate in Small Heath. In 1954 there were 838 police houses provided by the Corporation for the Police. The final development which led to the rapid decrease in the number of police houses was the decision of the Watch Committee in November 1965 to waive the restrictions of service qualification on house purchase by members of the Force allowing the Chief Constable to decide each case.

A development which is worth recording is the appointment of Mr F A Smith from the Accounts Department of the City Treasurer's Department to the Watch Committee. Mr Smith, it could be claimed, was the first civilian employee in the modern 'support' sense. The Chief Constable and his staff recognised that the burgeoning administrative work of the expanding post war police force required professional expertise. This was highlighted by the requirements of the Police Act 1919 and the regulations made thereunder. F A Smith's appointment was made in June 1920 and he was paid £500 per annum and allowed an annual increment equivalent to a superintendent's. The Watch Committee minutes record that, 'It is not proposed that Mr Smith shall become a member of the Police Force, but that he shall be employed in a civil capacity as will his staff'. Here we can discover an early form of creative accounting. By their course of action the Watch Committee ensured that these employees would be paid from the Exchequer grant and not totally by the City Council. The Watch Committee had engaged shorthand typists and junior clerks on a short time basis as support for the Police. In 1922 these posts were made permanent and by 1946 there were 18 such posts. In April of that year there was an increase to 47.

The formation of a Mounted Branch was considered by the Watch Committee on 1 October 1919 for the first time since 16 August 1839 when the night horse patrol was founded. For a trial period horses had been loaned from the Government to assess the suitability of such a branch. It was suggested to the Chief Constable that he should approach the Government to hire these horses. In this he was successful because on 2 June 1920 he was empowered by the Watch Committee to purchase 50 pairs of jack-boots at 55s a pair and the same quantity of riding breeches. In 1922 a mounted section of 22 officers was established using 20 horses hired from the Corporation Stud.

In October of 1920 a problem arose in relation to the housing of single men. On 6 October 1920 it was reported that no accommodation could be found for 61 single men who were receiving the princely sum of 4s per week lodging allowance. The answer to this problem appeared to be found in the suggestion of a Mr Coffey of the YMCA that the Watch Committee could have the use of a YMCA hut in Worcester Street. What the constables thought of living in a hut is not recorded. The offer was for 25 beds with meals provided at a charge, the accommodation being charged at 7s per week. This subject takes up several mentions in the Watch Committee meetings and by the 1 December an agreement had been reached for the use of the hut at £455 per annum. Fortunately for the officers the idea was discontinued on 2 February 1921 when difficulties arose with the owners of the ground used by the hut.

However, all was not lost as accommodation was soon found for 20 single police officers in Newton Street. On 1 December 1920 the Soldiers and Sailors Club which was situated in that street decamped to Harborne. The premises were altered to provide accommodation for 20 officers and a caretaker, together with CID offices and a police club. The club was built for the use of officers attending at the Chief Constable's office and the Victoria Law Courts. There was no liquor licence in force but it was used to provide refreshments.

In this year examinations which had been standardised and authorised as a means to promotion by the Desborough Committee were held under this new system in Birmingham. In the examinations held between 17 and 19 November 1920 there were 286 candidates. 40 out of 48 sergeants qualified to inspector and 183 constables qualified to sergeant. This is an approximate pass rate of 80% in both cases. The examinations were set in two parts. Firstly candidates had to answer questions on criminal law, evidence and procedure, acts, local acts and police orders. Secondly they were tested on English, dictation, arithmetic, geography, general knowledge, principles of local government (civics) and 'reading aloud'. As a guide to promotion prospects in the Birmingham City Police at this time promotions made on 7 December 1921 are as follows and are an average guide.

Henry Cook	47 years	25 years service	8 as inspector to senior inspector
Beaman Harrison	35 years	13 years service	2 as inspector to senior inspector
William Hale	42 years	21 years service	7 as sergeant to inspector
Joseph Plevin	38 years	16 years service	7 as sergeant to inspector

Mr Harrison, who gave sterling service to the City Police, was clearly what is known in police circles as a 'flyer'. He was promoted superintendent less than four years later.

POOR PC CAPEWELL

The sad case of PC Arthur Capewell, aged 22 years, was reported in the *Birmingham Mail* on 4 March 1921. Capewell had appeared before Birmingham Assizes charged and indicted on four offences of arson and one of breaking and entering. On 25 October 1920 the premises of Mr Yardley, a furniture remover, in Wheeler Street had been fired and damage to the cost of £200 caused. On 3 December 1920 a workshop in Great Hampton Row was also fired and damage caused costing £320. On 7 December the premises of Brightside Plating in Brearley Street were completely destroyed by fire. On this occasion the cost of the fire was put at £5,000. All these fires were on PC Capewell's beat and he had raised the alarm.

On 8 December he found another fire in a workshop in Wheeler Street. At the scene he was seen by another officer with a padlock in his hand and said, 'There is someone doing all this: Keep it to yourself'. Poor Arthur was only stating the obvious but he forgot he was working with professionals who were quite capable of putting two and two together. He was kept under observation and later that same evening was seen breaking into 296 Summer Lane. He was arrested and taken to Bridge Street West Police Station. He handed a detective a piece of iron and said, 'That's done it. It's all over for me now.' Capewell admitted causing the fires saying that he had wanted to give the impression he had been working hard and admitted feeling funny. His one request was that his mother was not told of his misdeeds.

A common enough type of story. But what separates Arthur Capewell from the run of the mill attention seekers was his defence. He had joined Kitchener's Army in 1914 by lying about his age when only 15 years old. He had been buried alive by a shell explosion in the trenches on the Somme and later gassed at Ypres. He then developed epilepsy and was given a 100% disability pension which was unknown to the police. At his trial he admitted all the offences except the most serious at Brearley Street adducing a defence of automatism. The jury found him guilty but insane. He was sentenced to be detained at His Majesty's Pleasure.

THE HOCKLEY BROOK DISASTER

The year 1920 was the occasion of the Hockley Brook disaster in Birmingham. This brook which rises in Warley Woods and flows into the Tame at Bromford ran through the Hockley area. Hockley at this time was a hotch-potch of back to back houses, courts and workshops crammed into one area. On 15 August 1920 following a heavy downpour of rain the brook suffered a flash flood. The water level rose inexorably. Whilst patrolling the area Police Constable C 187 Bell saw eight children leaning against a wall. As he later told a Coroner's Inquest from where he stood on a bridge he saw that the wall was being washed away. He shouted at the children, 'Get away from that wall, I say,' and made his way towards them. As he drew close the wall collapsed into the current. He grabbed out and caught one child at risk to his own safety. However, two 14 year old boys were swept away and drowned. On 6 September PC Bell was awarded five guineas by the Watch Committee and given three merit stripes. Superintendent Penrice was also rewarded for his action in helping those rendered homeless in the flood which by the time it had abated had covered an area of one square mile.

MODERN TIMES

The Police were now definitely into the twentieth century. On 6 October 1920 electric lights were fitted in the Lock-Up at a cost of £270. The gas lamp holders which they replaced were still in place in the tunnel connecting the Lock-Up to the Courts until the late 1970's. In July of 1920 the Watch Committee in a fit of spending voted £347 18s 8d for the purchase of a new Lock-Up prison van. The horse drawn vehicle was deemed unsuitable and unequal to the work and was replaced by a Ford one ton truck with the added luxury of pneumatic tyres!! By 1921 the Watch Committee were again spending money on transport. They report that the horse used to convey stores around the Force and children to the Remand Home in Moseley Road was worn out. The poor beast was replaced by another one ton Ford motor lorry purchased for £372 from George Heath & Co. In September of that year the last horse drawn vehicle, the mortuary van, was replaced. On this occasion, to save money, the vehicle body was mounted onto another one ton Ford.

On 2 March 1921 the Chief Constable on behalf of the Watch Committee offered the Home Office £100 for four motorcycles that were on loan to the Force. Eventually they were bought for £200. These were the first motorcycles belonging to the City of Birmingham Police. However, they were not used for traffic patrols but seem to have been used for general transport and despatch riding. These motorcycles were gradually replaced by BSA Combinations. The first motorcycles that were purchased specifically for traffic patrols were six BSA 650cc 'Golden Flash' machines in 1951. This was followed by three further bikes in 1953. In 1952 the first motorcycle course was held and the 12 constables who attended were successful. It had been necessary earlier that year to send a sergeant to the Metropolitan Police for training as a motorcycle instructor.

It is worth recording that in 1921 the Chief Constable was obliged to increase the number of officers employed in the Central Mortuary by three because of the eight hour shift system and additional leave entitlement. In his submission to the Watch Committee he states, 'The duties are very unpleasant. The officers have to strip and prepare bodies, often in an offensive condition. They also have to receive bodies and keep the place clean and tidy'. The mortuary could hold 28 bodies and was equipped with refrigerating equipment. If that wasn't enough these men were also employed on reserve duty at Newton Street Divisional Station. The poor officer on night duty still received less than those on days.

Increased payment was made in 1921 to constables on fatigue duty. This consisted of whitewashing etc. when they were employed morning and night at the time of annual cleaning. For this duty they received an extra 2s 6d per day. Officers 'getting in coals' were paid 1s per load. Those who attended to cells and lamps were to receive an extra 3s. Whilst completing fatigue duties constables were allowed to wear their own old clothes but receive no compensation.

The establishment of the Force at the start of the decade in 1920 consisted of: one chief constable, one assistant chief constable, one secretary superintendent, seven superintendents, 61 inspectors, 154 sergeants, 1,172 constables. There were vacancies for 34 officers. The establishment therefore was for 1,431 police officers. For reasons of economy it was decided in 1922 that the actual establishment should be kept at 10% below authorised strength. In 1928 the establishment of the Birmingham City Police reached 1,587 officers.

Recruits to the Force came from all walks of life. The occupations of those joining on 6 September 1920 were five soldiers, three farm labourers, three musicians, four clerks, six labourers, four butler/valets and three butlers. One further recruit was PC E 203 Ambrose Myatt who had been an asylum attendant. Perhaps Mr Myatt saw a similarity in the two jobs.

In March 1920 Councillor Hackett, a member of the Watch Committee, raised the question as to the 'non-employment of local men in the Force'. The Judicial Sub-Committee resolved to investigate this matter but the results are inconclusive, speaking only of equal opportunity of recruitment for all. What is known is that in 1935 the breakdown of the Force was, Englishmen 1,348, Scots 101, Welsh 73 and Irish 63. This gives the lie to hordes of six foot 'Paddies' maintaining the King's Peace in Summer Lane on a Friday night.

In August of 1920 merit stripe pay was commuted. The system continued as an award for meritorious conduct until the end of the Force. One exotically named award that was made in this year was the 'Palms in Gold of the Order of the Crown' by HM Albert, King of the Belgians to Inspector William Tudor for his work among Belgian refugees in Birmingham during the First War.

Developments in uniform and equipment in the 1920's were straightforward. On 9 August 1920, £10 was paid for application of transfers onto 1,000 special constables' staves. In 1921 a contract was placed with the London Rubber Company for capes. A Wooton re-chargeable lamp was first issued in 1929 and remained in use until 1945. It seems surprising in the present day when nickel cadmium cells appear to be a modern innovation that a rechargeable lamp was in use so long ago. A white traffic control tunic was taken into use for officers on point duty. This was a normal style tunic with white plastic buttons. A white helmet was used for the same duty. These items were taken out of use in 1938.

A parallel with modern times occurred in 1927. On 3 May 1927 a resolution was passed by the Watch Committee asking for information from a minute proposed by Councillors Simmons and Watkins of the Labour Party. The primary question was, 'What control can the Council through the Watch Committee, exercise over the Police Force?' A summary of the other two questions was, what powers had been lost by the Watch Committee? and how should they go about regaining those lost powers? They were answered by the fact that even though the Watch Committee was a Committee of the Council it derived its powers from separate legislation and therefore the full Council could not exercise any control. It was stated that any attempt to exercise control may result in there being no certificate of efficiency being granted and thereby a loss of the Exchequer grant to the Police. It was also pointed out that the Watch Committee could not exercise control over the Police, as the Police derived their powers from the Common Law and Statutes. In answer to the other two questions the Watch Committee were told that the Police Act 1919 had certainly reduced the powers of the Committee and if they wished to change this they should seek legislation. The previous year, 1926 had seen the general strike in the United Kingdom, and the roots of the Labour questions can probably be found in the unrest of that time.

Crime in the 1920's shows no pattern of any change throughout the whole decade. Over that period of time there were 23 murders, 24 attempted murders and 18 offences of manslaughter. In the whole ten years there were only nine recorded offences of rape in the City. Simple larceny was the most common offence averaging 1,000 offences a year. Noticeably attempted suicide continued to be one of the more common offences with an increase in numbers towards the end of the twenties. The most common methods for this offence were by gassing or throat or wrist cutting.

THE THIRTIES

The 1930's saw little development or change in the organisation of the Force. If one remembers that this was the time of the depression, hunger marches and the immobility of two National Governments then this is not surprising.

A 1933 report on the work of the policewomen's department, signed by Sergeant Eileen Slevin, to the Chief Constable makes interesting reading. The policewomen's department were preoccupied with the work of the girls' hostel. The hostel had moved from Dale End to better accommodation at 58 Newton Street, which was part of the Children's Court, in June 1928. The policewomen occupied a great deal of their time in obtaining employment for numerous girls, who had either arrived in the City or had left home. The majority of the posts found were in domestic service or the catering industry. Miss Slevin states that in 1933 her officers had dealt with 75 girls aged 18 or under who were pregnant and were unable to give any information as to the identity of the father. The policewomen attributed this moral collapse to 'the habit of going out with different motorists'. This is clearly seen as a problem as the report also states that 'the number of girls brought into the City on motor lorries etc is decreasing'. Policewomen in the main patrolled areas of public resort such as railway waiting rooms, public toilets, parks and cafes. In her 1934 report Miss Slevin points out that the department had dealt with 70 females suffering from venereal disease and had arranged treatment for these unfortunate females. She also points out that her officers were by then in the habit of patrolling in plain clothes between 12 and 4 pm in the principal drapery stores, obviously on the look out for wide eyed country girls and thieves.

In October 1934 the Watch Committee saw fit to increase the cycling allowance to 3s 6d per week. This was not born from any largesse on their part but from the simple expedient that the more officers using bicycles meant larger beats and thereby fewer officers! But we must not be unkind to the Committee. Their generosity is a matter of record. In November 1924 an estimate of £22 by Walter Green and Son for the provision of an internal lavatory in the chief inspector's house at Woodbridge Road Police Station was approved.

By 1935 the BSA Combination motorcycles were said to be worn out. Approval was granted to replace them with 12 7HP Austin Ruby saloons. The changeover was to take two years and cost £1,242. The one way system around New Street and Corporation Street had been introduced by this time together with the 'gyratory' system of traffic islands. The major reason for the change to motor cars, though, was the necessity to provide corroborative evidence in cases of exceeding the speed limit set in 1936.

The most important change in the uniform worn by City constables in the thirties was the discontinuance of duty armlets. Over the years there had been two styles used, a horizontal stripe and vertical stripe. The armlets were last used on 31 March 1936 and were only withdrawn after consultation with the Licensing Justices. Obviously the armlet, which signified that the officer was on duty, could easily be taken off and hidden by any thirsty constable when passing a 'friendly' pub.

Uniforms throughout the country were standardised in 1934 following Home Office recommendations. In Birmingham this meant the loss of the leather belt with the City crest buckle for ordinary day wear. However, there

September 1939: Sand bagging at Steelhouse Lane

were no recommendations as to a pattern of helmets, they were left very much to local preference. It was not until 1936 that the Birmingham City day duty helmet was changed. The helmet lost its spike and distinctive helmet plate. It was replaced by a black rose on top and a black helmet plate of the standard star burst pattern with the City coat of arms in silver placed centrally making it similar to the night duty helmet.

STEELHOUSE LANE POLICE STATION

The most important building development in this period was the building and opening of Steelhouse Lane Police Station. By 1923 the Central Police Station in Newton Street had been condemned as insanitary and unsuitable by the HMI. The accommodation had consisted of four basement rooms without cells. This necessitated walking prisoners along Steelhouse Lane to the Lock-Up. Other problems also existed due to departments being located in separate buildings. In October of that year the Corporation purchased the leasehold on numbers 52 to 60 Steelhouse Lane. A tender for building a new Central Police Station for £73,000 was accepted by the Watch Committee in May 1930. The foundation stone was laid on 30 May 1932 by Alderman W A Grist, the Watch Committee chairman. Alderman Grist is still remembered by the West Midlands Police as he endowed a prize, awarded to this day for the successful officers in the competitions for the mounted section and promotion examinations. Steelhouse Lane Police Station was formally opened in December 1933. A three storey building, much loved by those who work and who have worked there, it originally had accommodation on the ground floor for the superintendent, inspectors, sergeants, the women police and other departments. The first floor accommodated the Force clothing store, doctor's room and common rooms for single men. The second floor was made up of two classrooms, linen stores and 20 bedrooms. The third floor had 26 bedrooms, four sick rooms and a further linen store. The charge office on the ground floor had direct access to the Lock-Up cells. Over the years the building's interior has been much changed and due in no small part to the burgeoning police bureaucracy the single men's accommodation is now office space.

Steelhouse Lane is synonymous with Police and policing in Birmingham. The very name is suggestive of the Lock-Up itself but in fact is derived from the steel masters and their businesses that were situated there. The site of the present car park alongside the station housed a former steel mill until 1966.

It was in the late 1930's also that a proposal was made to replace Kenyon Street Police Station, which had been condemned in 1923, with a new building to act as 'C' Division headquarters. Premises were examined in Warstone Lane

D

Marching to their beats, Steelhouse Lane 1935

and in Newhall Street. The final choice was made to build in Newhall Street. The land was purchased and the building was to stand at the junction of Newhall Street, Brook Street and St Paul's Churchyard. The site is presently an NCP car park. An architect was appointed and the building was finally costed at £63,869. This met with Home Office approval and the expenditure was authorised. However, with the outbreak of hostilities in 1939 the plans were shelved never to be resurrected.

Some new buildings were erected in this period at Bridge Street West, and Kingstanding. Kingstanding had come within the City boundary in 1928, at the same time as Canterbury Road Police Station and Perry Barr had been incorporated into Birmingham. Plans were also made for the building of a new police garage in Duke Street. For this purpose the lease of the land in Lawrence Street where the garage then in use stood, together with numbers 80-89 Duke Street were bought. On 2 June 1938 land at the junction of Bordesley Green East and Station Road, Stechford was purchased for the building of the proposed new police station. This of course did not materialise until 1976. A property known as *The Elms* stood on this site and had been used as a police station since 1925, when the station had moved from Victoria Road. Further land adjoining *The Elms* was proposed to be used as a home for canal boat children! Much discussion was also made at meetings of the Watch Committee in the 1930's as to the future of Coventry Road Police Station. Plans for road widening were even then in hand and the Committee were loath to invest in any improvements for the building. Needless to say the building remained in use until the new Stechford Police Station had been built. It remained vacant for some time until it was demolished. With the expansion of the City and police work in general there was a growing need for more working space. In January of 1939 the Lord Chancellor's Office gave permission for the police courts at Victoria Road Police Station to be appropriated for use as police office accommodation. The tradition of make and mend with police buildings is therefore steeped in historical precedent.

PAY AND CONDITIONS IN THE 1930's

Pay and conditions in the Birmingham City Police during this period were of course governed by the politics of the day. The 'Geddes axe' is the term applied to a policy pursued by the National Government in the early 1930's whereby pay of public servants was reduced by 10% to cut public expenditure. It was as a result of this that the last Naval Mutiny occurred at Invergordon. However, as politicians are masters of the pragmatic they only enforced a 5% cut on the wages of the Police. After the first year the Government prolonged the life of the cuts by a further year. The Watch Committee recorded their discomfort at this and only imposed the continued cut after expressing their views to the Home Office. In Birmingham this meant a loss of 4s 3d per week to constables and a pro-rata loss throughout the ranks. This was not an inconsequential sum out of only approximately £4 per week. To add insult to injury the Police Regulations were changed whereby on 30 September 1931 constables who joined the Force after that date started at 8s per week less than previously. However, there was some small cheer for those unfortunate enough not to live in police accommodation as rent allowance was increased in 1933 to £1 per week for inspectors, 17s 6d for sergeants and 15s for constables. The end of 1934 saw the resignation of Mrs Rebecca Lipscombe, one of the two first women police. By this time she had returned to duty as a Lock-Up matron. Mrs Lipscombe received the princely pension of 7s per week after serving the City for nearly 20 years. Sergeant Miss Evelyn Miles fared much better, when she retired just before the outbreak of hostilities. She was granted a pension of £104 per annum. In an age without social workers and supplementary benefits, Miss Miles and her colleagues did sterling service for the poor and corrupted in Birmingham. There must be many alive today who owe a lot to the staff of the girls' hostel. As previously stated the City of Birmingham Police and their Watch Committee were fully aware of the advantages of women police. This can be seen in the promotion on 7 December 1938 of Woman Sergeant Bushnell of the Criminal Investigation Department to inspector. It would probably be fair to consider Miss Bushnell as the first woman detective inspector of the Force.

The equipment used by the City Police was updated in this period to keep pace with modern trends. On 26 October 1932 approval was given to install telex machines on each territorial division together with a machine on 'R' Division, the Chief Constable's office. On 3 May 1933 negotiations were held with the Post Office and Fire Brigade concerning the installation of police pillar posts where members of the public could contact the emergency services. The telephone was housed in a metal box, above a pillar on top of which was a light which could be illuminated to attract the attention of patrolling officers. Initially 11 posts were erected on the 'C' Division in the Kenyon Street area. The first such post was officially inaugurated by the chairman of the Watch Committee, Alderman Lovesey, in Warstone Lane, Hockley beside the clock tower. The posts spread to the rest of the City. They were finally withdrawn in 1967 with the advent of unit beat policing, but there is an exception to every rule and post A1 situated in the Bull Ring was allowed to linger for a few years longer. The Force vehicle fleet continued to be changed and in 1938 thanks to revenue received from the Road Fund Grant the Baby Austins were changed for 12 10HP Austin saloons and 14 10HP Austin fixed head saloons at a cost of £1,544. The joys of open topped motoring were still enjoyed by some officers in the summer months. The Chief Constable had use of a Daimler saloon and the CID enjoyed the status of an Alvis saloon.

4
End of an Era

On 25 August 1935 Sir Charles Haughton Rafter died whilst on holiday in Ireland. By then he was 75 years old and had completed 52 years police service in Birmingham and the Royal Irish Constabulary. As a final valedictory memorial the Watch Committee passed the following minute as a tribute to the Chief Constable,

> 'Sir Charles Rafter's long police service of nearly 53 years in all was distinguished by great sagacity and efficiency and he proved himself to be a wise administrator and to possess in very full measure tact, patience and a deep understanding of human nature. He also possessed supreme qualities of organisation. Consequently the Police Force under his control attained a very high standard of efficiency. These qualities combined with a genial personality and dignified presence enabled him to preserve the peace and good order in the City with marked success. In 1909 he was awarded the Kings Police Medal. In 1920 he was made Commander of the Most Excellent Order of the British Empire and in 1927 was made Knight Commander of that same order. On the occasion of his completing 25 years with the Force in 1924 he was presented with a life size painting in oils together with an illuminated address by the Force.'

It would probably be fair to assume that one or two disgruntled policemen were glad to see his demise. But we can be sure that he was held in high esteem by his men as a collection was made amongst the Force for his widow, Lady Rafter, in the tradition that all widows were so aided. Lady Rafter received a gratuity from the City of no less than £7,583 6s 8d to be placed in trust for herself and the children. She was also allowed to remain in residence at Elmley Lodge, Harborne, the Chief Constable's residence for a period of time, even though the house was to be demolished for road widening purposes.

On 1 September 1935 Mr Cecil C H Moriarty C.B.E. LL.D was appointed Chief Constable. He had spent a long time as heir apparent having being the Assistant Chief Constable since 1918. Like his predecessor, Mr Moriarty had been a District Inspector in the Royal Irish Constabulary. He had joined the RIC as a cadet officer on 4 March 1902 and served until 6 July 1918. His reference to the Watch Committee states, 'His service has been diligent and faithful', and is signed by J Byrne Inspector General. Mr Moriarty was an

Mr C C H Moriarty, Chief Constable, September 1935 – September 1941

international rugby player and in his youth was capped for Ireland on several occasions. He will be remembered most as 'That famous old Irish author, C C H Moriarty' by all policemen, as in 1929 he published the first edition of Moriarty's Police Law. This handbook of law and police duty has helped many officers down the years either to greater efficiency or promotion and is still published in an updated form.

Mr Moriarty inherited the top police post in Birmingham at a time of decreasing crime. Remembering that this was the age of the depression, hunger marches and means testing it is hard to believe that major reported crime fell in the thirties. In fact the figures raise a question against the new-left criminologists who suggest that the causes of crime lie in social deprivation. Offences against property in the form of simple larcencies fell by nearly 50% in the first half of the decade and house breakings by 70% over the same period. Murders and woundings fell by the same figures and in 1933 no offences of rape were reported. Perhaps the key to this lies in the loss of a whole generation of males in the horrors of the First War, but the numbers of City population had increased in the 1928 boundary changes. We can only assume that the behaviour of the Brummies improved.

THE BOMBERS RETURN

The major incidents of crime in the 1930's occurred during an intense period of IRA activity towards the end of the decade. On 22 March 1939 a car parked at the junction of Moseley Road and Balsall Heath Road exploded, completely destroying the vehicle. No clues were left as to why the device had exploded or who had left it there but the later assumption was that those carrying it had accidentally triggered the bomb and fled. The *Birmingham Mail* points out that all the senior officers of the Force turned out to the scene with the exception of Detective Superintendent Baguley who had taken to his bed that morning with a bad cold. However, he was probably fit again by 31 March when a further bomb exploded in a house at 12 Trafalgar Road, Moseley. The occupants of the house debunked and the City Police announced they were seeking two Irishmen. Matters did not end though for on the evening of 5 April there were three explosions in the City Centre. The first the Force knew about the incidents was the arrival of a Public Works Department Crew at Steelhouse Lane Police Station with a bomb they had found in a waste litter bin in Martineau Street. The bomb consisted of gelignite and the detonator device was a child's balloon containing acid. The device was defused. One can only imagine the success the IRA would have achieved if the bomb had exploded in the police station. Shortly after this a similar bomb exploded in Snow Hill by the site of the present police headquarters at Lloyd House. At the same time Police Constable Blunt was on patrol in Congreve Street when he saw a smoking parcel in a litter bin. He took it out and, breaking the golden rule, threw it along the street, it exploded and in doing so buckled the tram standards and smashed all the windows in the Norwich Union building. Unfortunately for PC Blunt a sergeant coming to his aid was badly shaken by the blast. History does not record the sergeant's revenge on the foolhardy constable. A third explosion occurred outside the George and Dragon public house at the junction of Weaman Street and Steelhouse Lane but the only damage was to the windows of *Loo Blooms the Tailors* premises.

Police and public were put onto their guard for at 8.25 pm on 6 April 1939 Lawrence Dunlea of 35 Moilliet Street, Winson Green was arrested in Newhall Street by police and passers-by. He was found to be in possession of explosives, a gun and ammunition. Appearing in court the next day he was asked by the Stipendiary if he had anything to say. He replied 'I am afraid not. As a soldier of the Irish Republic I refuse to ask any questions or make any statement.' He was later sentenced to penal servitude for life.

This was not the end of the activities of the IRA in Birmingham for this period as they continued their dark deeds into the next decade. On 14 February 1940, at the time of hostilities with Germany further bombs were placed in the City. One such bomb was found by PC A 139 Ivan Fishwick on a window ledge of Murdoch and Company, piano dealers in Corporation Street. He rushed into the milk bar next door obtained a pan of water and dropped the bomb into it. This was not such a daft idea as the triggering devices used acid. Moreover, in the history of the City of Birmingham Police this was Ivan Fishwick's night. Continuing to search his beat he found another bomb outside Greys Store in Bull Street and disarmed that. Not to be outdone PC A 143 Sheppard also found a bomb between the telephone kiosks in Stephenson Street. In the finest traditions of resourcefulness of the City policeman he took the bomb into nearby public toilets and immersed it!

Unfortunately this was not the end of the campaign. The following day, 15 February 1940 two Irishmen were executed at Winson Green Prison for murder by explosions in Coventry. As a last farewell the IRA exploded a bomb at Dolcis shoe shop in Corporation Street at Cherry Street. Again, luckily, there was no loss of life.

*PS C24 Christie and PC C601 Grills together with PC C114 Leslie Thomas: all recipients of **BEM**'s for air raid bravery*

The Second World War

It has often been said that the workpeople of Birmingham were the first to know that war with Germany was inevitable. The First War had been fought as Birmingham v Krupps and so would the Second. The change from commodity production to war weapons began in the City's factories and workshops from 1937 onwards. At the same time every police station in Birmingham was being fitted out with decontamination rooms to be used in case of chemical and gas warfare. As the war clouds thickened the centenary of the Birmingham City Police was celebrated in 1939. The Chief Constable Mr Moriarty produced a vignette to celebrate the occasion. 4,500 copies were produced at a cost of £65. As an end to this epoch in human affairs a description of the City of Birmingham Police as given by him is quoted as an appendix.

As international affairs deteriorated in a downwards spiral after the Munich Agreement preparations were put in hand to place the Force on a wartime footing. City police officers were trained in the use of firearms, combating the effects of the use of poison gas and general war duties such as the training of air raid wardens. The number of firearms held by the Birmingham City Police can be assumed from the fact on 3 July 1940 the Chief Constable placed an order for 451 revolver lanyards.

At Police Headquarters in Newton Street a war room was prepared by fortifying the basement. Once built, standing orders decreed that the Chief Constable or one of the Assistant Chief Constables should always be present in the war room during an air raid. It was quickly apparent that the use of telephones as a command and control device would be easily disrupted by air raids. The Chief Constable sought help from two local radio enthusiasts who acting in a private capacity, fitted their wireless equipment in Newton Street as an experiment. Mr Moriarty was impressed and by July 1940 two main transmitters together with 19 receivers at police stations and 12 fitted in cars were in use. The system, one of the earliest police radio networks in the country, was therefore limited as only the headquarters sets could transmit. This was soon overcome by fitting transmitters at divisional stations. Great foresight was seen in the installation of a duplex system which allows two way conversation at the same time between stations, similar as over a telephone. A further inovation of Birmingham Police was the introduction of a mobile police station which by use of wireless could be kept in contact with the war room and used at the scenes of emergency.

Remembering the sudden rush to the Colours at the outbreak of the First War, the Secretary of State wrote to the Birmingham Watch Committee and told them that police officers should be discouraged from enlisting because, 'experienced men will serve the state more usefully by continuing to perform police duty.' However, the Watch Committee resolved on 8 November 1939 to pay any officer who was enlisted in HM Forces the difference in pay that would result as pay in the Forces was lower than in the Police. But they also expressed the caveat that any officer who insisted on enlistment would not be paid the difference. In fact the Police were made a Reserved Occupation exempting members of the City Force from conscription. This ended in 1942 and the Chief Constable's Report for that year shows that 281 constables had been 'Called up'. In fact he states that a total of 375 were in the Services which presumably means that 94 had volunteered for the Armed Services up to that time.

As in other forces, police recruiting to the Birmingham City Force was suspended for the duration of the War. In consequence of hostilities police duty changed and the volume of that duty increased dramatically. In order to cope with this, and the shortfall on establishment caused by the suspension of recruiting, police auxiliaries were enlisted. The first of these auxiliaries was the Special Constabulary Reserve. The specials had been in existence in the City since 1919 and were particularly well regarded for the custom of using their own motor vehicles to patrol the City, for which they were reimbursed. The Special Constabulary had been depleted initially due to its members enlisting but volunteers and the introduction of the National Service Scheme to the Special Constabulary soon restored the balance. The maximum strength of the City of Birmingham Special Constabulary Reserve during the War was 2,150 men together with 54 men who were paid for their duty.

The second body of auxiliaries were the First Police Reserve and the Police War Reserve. The FPR's consisted of retired police officers who volunteered to return to duty when called upon for which they received a retaining fee. The PWR were volunteers aged over thirty recruited for war service only. During the period of the War 798 men saw service as PWR's and 211 as FPR. Needless to say the rigours of policing during a war soon took its toll on the older FPR's. One such man was PC A 402 John Barrier who joined Birmingham City Police on 8 June 1898 and retired in December 1924. As his country tumbled inexorably towards the Second World War he volunteered and was accepted for FPR duty on 25 August 1938. PC Barrier lived in Alcester Street and in late December 1940 he took cover with his wife and daughter in their air raid shelter. The shelter took a direct hit from a high explosive bomb. The only remains found were part of a respirator case and piece of police whistle chain. Mr Barrier was 63 years of age.

The other major source of police auxiliaries were the Women's Auxiliary

Police Corps (WAPC). On 29 October 1941 the Women's Auxiliary was established in Birmingham. The initial recruitment was set at 50 women to be paid at £2 7s 0d per week. They were engaged on full-time duties as drivers, shorthand typists, clerks and telephonists. The Women's Auxiliary wore similar uniform to the Women's Auxiliary Fire Service and very fashionable it was too. The maximum strength achieved during the War years was 142 and the Corps was eventually disbanded, on 31 March 1946, but several of the women were retained for secretarial duties.

On the same date that saw the introduction of the WAPC, the Police Auxiliary Messenger Service was inaugurated. This service, was made up of boys aged 16-18 years who acted as messengers to supplement normal communications. The Watch Committee initially planned on 30 such boy messengers but were worried that the attraction of high earnings in munitions work would prove too competitive for the police service. By the end of the hostility the maximum strength attained was no fewer than 515.

The final factor which influenced the size of the war time establishment was the Police and Firemen (War Service) Act 1939 which suspended the right of officers to resign on pension without a medical certificate. The members of the auxiliary services were prevented from resigning by the Defence Regulations.

The authorised establishment of the Force at the outbreak of war stood at 1,888 and by the time recruiting was resumed less than 1,200 remained. More than 500 members of the Birmingham City Police served in His Majesty's Forces. The largest number 235 served in the Army, 168 in the Royal Air Force, 86 in the Royal Navy and 36 in the Royal Marines. Commissions were held by 144 of that number ranging from colonel in the Army to sub lieutenant in the Navy. Six members were awarded Distinguished Flying Crosses, one received the Air Force Cross, one was honoured with the Croix de Guerre, and in that nice rank-conscious tradition where officers have crosses and the 'other ranks' medals, one member of the Birmingham Police received a Distinguished Flying Medal and one the Military Medal.

In his annual report for 1945 the Chief Constable announced, 'I deeply regret to record that 44 men were killed on active service or their death was presumed and five died whilst serving in the Armed Forces. Eight members of the Force were captured and made prisoners of war'. One such POW was PC E 105 Thomas Albert Rose who died whilst a prisoner of the Japanese. His wife Rose Rose was given a pension by the Watch Committee of £62 16s 8d per annum and his two sons were paid £10 per annum until their 18th Birthday. PC Rose exchanged the cold grey flagstones of some pavement on the 'E' Division for the deprivations of a tropical prison.

ADJUSTING TO WARTIME DUTIES

The major change in police duty over the war period was brought about by the necessity to organise Civil Defence. The Chief Constable was also the Chief Air Raid Warden and for some time Chief Fire Guard. During the war there were 20,000 wardens and nearly 200,000 fire guards. The Police were the prime authority at air raid incidents and all officers were trained to act as incident officers. Liaison officers were also appointed to the Military. It is worth recalling that the Police were involved in the establishment and organisation of the Local Defence Volunteers which became the Birmingham Home Guard. The Police were also responsible for the air raid warning system and the correct maintenance and use of the 150 sirens fitted across the City. This system to signal 'Air Raid Imminent' and 'Raiders Past' could be activated from one central control point or locally in the case of failure.

The Police also had to cope with new war time legislation. They had to enforce a welter of defence regulations, statutory rules, lighting restrictions, control of noise, photograph and maps regulations, petrol restrictions and food rationing. Throughout the war over 127,140 enquiries were received from the Military authorities. These enquiries concerned absenteeism, welfare, family circumstances and compassionate leave, and were undertaken for the most part by women police officers.

Mutual aid to other forces was given and received during the War. After particularly heavy raids on 19 and 22 November 1940, 85 officers from Staffordshire and 25 from Wolverhampton performed duty in Birmingham for four days. This was done because at the time 100 Birmingham officers performed duty in Coventry from 15 to 24 November after the Coventry Blitz, when that City teetered on the edge of collapse and the imposition of martial law. But every cloud has a silver lining and 35 Birmingham City officers assisted Portsmouth City Police for several weeks before 'D' Day and the invasion of France.

During the War three members of the Force were awarded the George Medal for Gallantry. The first two were awarded to PCs E 157 Thomas Henwood and E 335 Ronald Jackson, for rescue work on 9 April 1940 in Abbotsford Road and Garrison Lane respectively. 14 officers were awarded B.E.M. and a further 14 were awarded Commendations for similar gallantry.

Pay and conditions of the City Force saw no general improvement during the war years, in fact the opposite was true. In June 1940 the Watch Committee sought advice from the Home Office as to the case of P S Richard Hawkins. Sergeant Hawkins was a first police reservist, in receipt of a pension of £300 per annum, who was to be promoted inspector. The promotion would have given

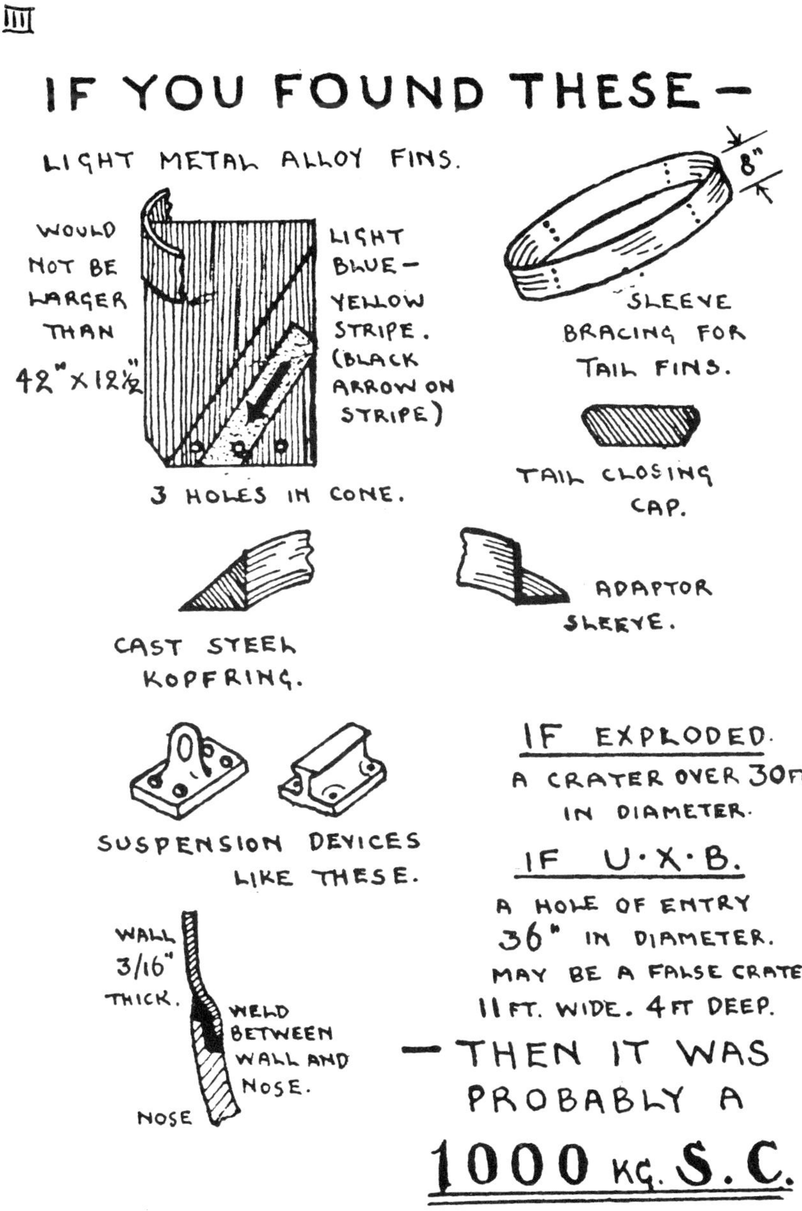

IF YOU FOUND THESE—

LIGHT METAL ALLOY FINS.

WOULD NOT BE LARGER THAN 42"×12½"

LIGHT BLUE-YELLOW STRIPE. (BLACK ARROW ON STRIPE)

3 HOLES IN CONE.

8"

SLEEVE BRACING FOR TAIL FINS.

TAIL CLOSING CAP.

CAST STEEL KOPFRING.

ADAPTOR SLEEVE.

SUSPENSION DEVICES LIKE THESE.

WALL 3/16" THICK. WELD BETWEEN WALL AND NOSE.

NOSE

IF EXPLODED.
A CRATER OVER 30 FT. IN DIAMETER.

IF U·X·B.
A HOLE OF ENTRY 36" IN DIAMETER. MAY BE A FALSE CRATER 11 FT. WIDE. 4 FT DEEP.

— THEN IT WAS PROBABLY A

1000 KG. S.C.

Fig. V — Wartime duty: How to identify 1000kg bomb

him £300 per annum salary thereby giving him £600 per annum total income. The Watch Committee balked at the thought of his receiving the same income as a chief superintendent. The Home Office did not and advised that he was quite entitled to the monies. In August of 1940 the City Police received new pay allowances. A supplementary allowance of 5s per week non-pensionable was paid to constables and 4s women police, to compensate for the rise in the cost of living and to make comparability with civilian pay. A War Duty allowance was also paid of 3s per week for constables and 4s for sergeants, with 3s for both ranks of women police. This second allowance was to compensate for the fact that police were by then working 12 hour shifts, with no overtime, no time off in lieu and no right to a weekly rest day. By the end of the war the allowances were also paid to inspectors and had reached 14s for constables.

This retention on duty for long periods, especially at the time of enemy action, raised problems of supplying refreshment for large numbers of officers and in December of 1940 four mobile canteens were purchased at £58 each for use on outer divisions. They were fully kitted out with urns etc. and the inventory also shows a good stock of half pint earthenware mugs. It was possible to attach the canteens to any police vehicle. The Chief Constable worried that they would have to be manned by a PC proposed that the work should be offered to police officers' wives at 10s per turn out. In June 1945 the canteens were sold for £160 each, a nice profit on the original investment.

At the same time the Chief Constable saw fit to replace the fleet of patrol cars. On approaching the Home Office he was told by the Secretary of State that only 25 cars would be available to the Police and that was for the whole of the country!! Fortunately for Birmingham City Police somebody knew somebody who could replace the City patrol cars which had done 58,000 miles with 14 second hand models that had done between one and 8,000 miles.

AIR RAIDS ON THE CITY

After the first heavy air raids on the City in late 1940 the Police Surveyor, Mr Moon was granted travelling expenses due to his increased work. In his application it is stated that 'Many police houses have been damaged, some demolished and several police stations have been much damaged.' This is the first indication of the results of the bombing, actual details of course were never published at the time to save the danger of the enemy knowing the results of their work.

Altogether during the War the Force had 16 members killed and 111 injured during the air raids. The first officer to lose his life was PC E 329 Harold

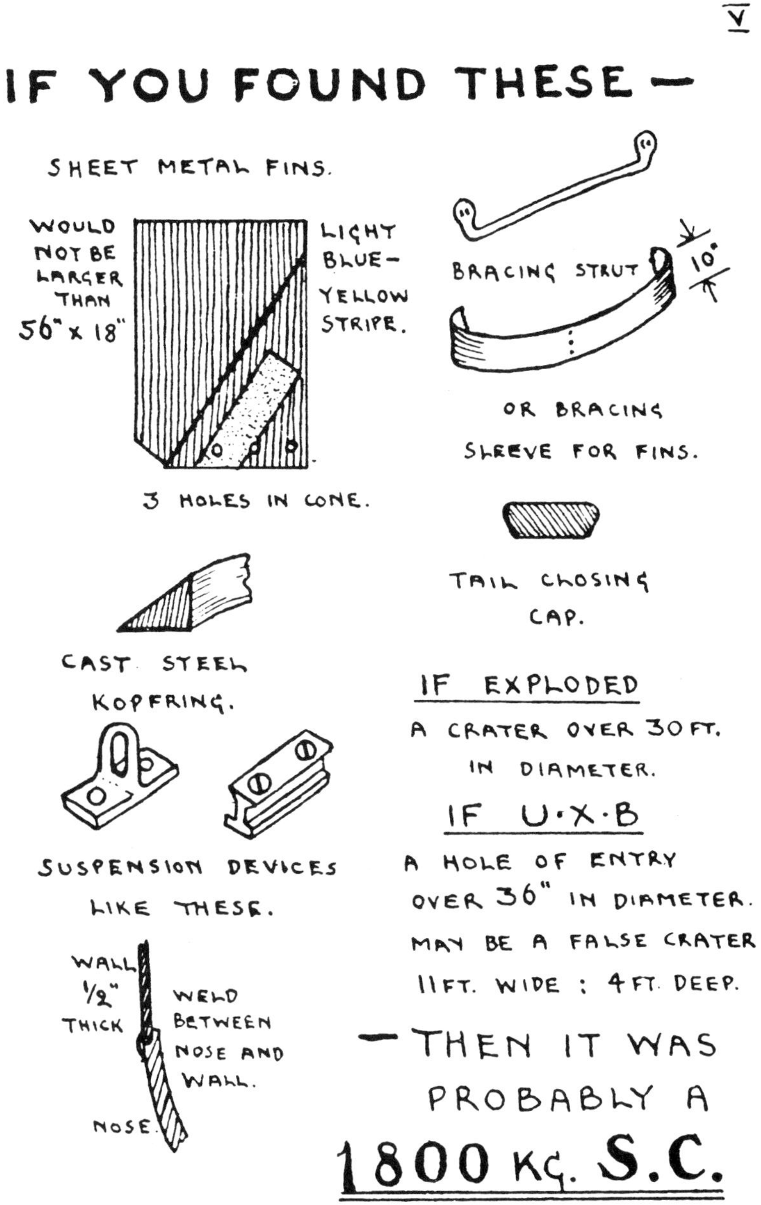

V

IF YOU FOUND THESE —

SHEET METAL FINS.

WOULD NOT BE LARGER THAN 56" x 18"

LIGHT BLUE — YELLOW STRIPE.

3 HOLES IN CONE.

BRACING STRUT 10°

OR BRACING SLEEVE FOR FINS.

CAST STEEL KOPFRING.

TAIL CLOSING CAP.

SUSPENSION DEVICES LIKE THESE.

WALL 1/2" THICK   WELD BETWEEN NOSE AND WALL. NOSE

IF EXPLODED
A CRATER OVER 30 FT. IN DIAMETER.

IF U·X·B
A HOLE OF ENTRY OVER 36" IN DIAMETER. MAY BE A FALSE CRATER 11 FT. WIDE ; 4 FT. DEEP.

— THEN IT WAS PROBABLY A
<u>1800 KG. **S.C.**</u>

Fig. VI — Further instruction for 1800kg bomb

Benbow, who was killed on 27 September 1940 when a bomb demolished his home in Alfred Street, Kings Heath. The worst raid occurred on 10 April 1941 when three officers, Detective Inspector Mark William Selleck, PC A 97 Bertie Gready and PC E 217 Jack Frederick Goodchild, were killed. PC Gready was on duty at Digbeth Police Station when a bomb fell and exploded at 1.05 am. Detective Inspector Selleck was on duty at Police Headquarters in Newton Street when the building received a direct hit from a 1,000 lb high explosive bomb at 1.11 am. On the same night another high explosive bomb fell on the mortuary and a delayed action bomb dropped on the Juvenile Court. The worst damage was caused to the Chief Constable's office at the junction of Newton Street and Steelhouse Lane. The following day trams and buses passing along Steelhouse Lane caused the whole building to vibrate. Mr Moon, the surveyor reported that the building should be taken down to the level of the first floor window sill and be capped off with corrugated iron to make an office for the use of the Chief Constable at an ultimate cost of £3,000. The damage was so bad that the steel frame had to be cut in small pieces by oxy-acetelyne torch in order to prevent further collapse. The mortuary was demolished. In all bomb damage was caused to Police Headquarters, Victoria Law Courts, the Mortuary and superintendents' flats, the Coroner's Court, the Forensic Science Laboratory, Juvenile Court and the Girls' Hostel. To this day the change in brick work on the Newton Street building is visible where the rebuilding repair work took place. The bombs caused little more than inconvenience to the Birmingham City Police. The direct hit was shrugged off.

As to exemplify this we can examine the conduct of Inspector Frank 'Panto' Goddard of Steelhouse Lane Police Station. At the time of the raids in 1941 he was informed that a bomb had dropped in the Bull Ring markets area and had failed to explode. Together with a lieutenant of the Bomb Disposal Squad, he made a search and found the bomb in a house cum shop in Sherlock Street. The lieutenant tried to defuse the redundant ordnance but was unsuccessful. It was therefore necessary to take it to the bomb pit at the Austin Works at Longbridge. The bomb weighed 35 kilos and both men decided it was too sensitive to place in the boot of the lieutenant's car, so Inspector Goddard sat with the bomb on his lap for that long journey through Selly Oak and Northfield. When they arrived at Longbridge and the bomb was dropped in the pit; well you've guessed it, it exploded before it reached the bottom. Courageous work? It was in its own way, but no more courageous than the normal method of searching for unexploded bombs. Officers would go out armed with a 20 foot steel pole and a sledge hammer to probe holes in the ground. None were found in this manner, either by good fortune or good sense!

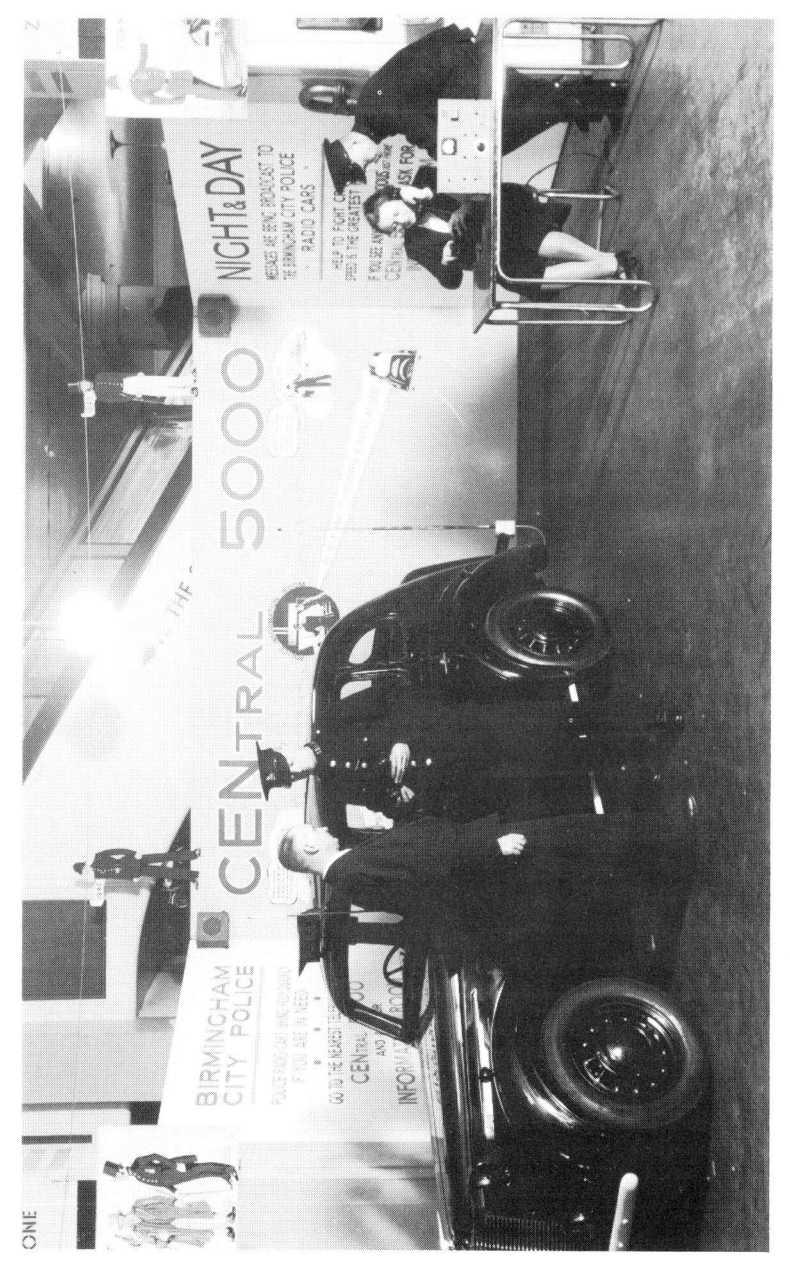

An exhibition at Lewis's Ltd to publicise the new radio area cars in 1943

Mr Moriarty Retires

On 23 July 1941 the Chief Constable, Mr Moriarty applied to the Watch Committee for permission to retire on pension on 4 September 1941. He points out in his application that by then he will have served 39½ years in the Police, 16 years and four months being in the Royal Irish Constabulary and having been in the Birmingham City Police since 7 July 1918. Mr Moriarty tells the Watch Committee that he was born on 28 January 1877 and was by then 65 years old. It was his intention to serve until the end of the war but found that, 'The war has lasted two years and may continue for some more'. He was granted leave to retire because of his age and awarded a pension of £1383 6s 8d. It is easy to sympathise with his position and at 65 years of age the war time duties of a Chief Constable must have taken its toll on his health.

Due to the prevailing defence regulations no interviews were held for the post of Chief Constable and 1st ACC Mr William Clarence Johnson, who had joined the Force on 16 January 1936 was appointed Chief Constable with the Secretary of State's approval. Mr Arthur Young took over the position of 1st ACC and out of seven applicants Mr Edward J Dodd, a Metropolitan Police sub-divisional inspector was appointed 2nd Assistant Chief Constable.

At this time the Chief Constable was provided with a house at 29 Elvetham Road but this was not thought to be satisfactory. The Watch Committee sought another house at 79 Westfield Road, Edgbaston as the Chief Constable's residence. They had it examined by the Council's Estates Department who reported, 'It is a bijou residence situated in a charming part of Edgbaston', but warned the Committee to beware of, 'The flat roof which may leak because of expansion and contraction and the poor cement rendering.' They were further warned that the house was, 'very attractive but likely to damn itself in the future'. At least they didn't describe it as 'deceptively spacious.' The Watch Committee purchased the house.

Developments on the Home Front

At the end of 1941 Chief Superintendent Beaman Harrison also resigned on ill health pension. As proof of the esteem he was held in the Watch Committee presented him with an illuminated address, a rare compliment. But it wasn't all resignations. A Mr Edward George Brown of the Birmingham 'Eddystone Wireless Company' was appointed directly as an inspector in the First Police Reserve. The reason for this unprecedented appointment was his experience in wireless engineering with the City Police. He received a salary of £200 per annum plus a further £200 per annum expert's pay. The City Police obviously

Mr William Clarence Johnson, Chief Constable, September 1941 – October 1945

One of the first area cars fitted with radio in 1940's

gained from this appointment because on 28 August 1942 the Birmingham Police Ultra High Frequency Wireless Communication Service was inaugurated. The City was divided into areas for area car patrols which were linked by radio to the Information Room at Police Headquarters. The Chief Constable and Watch Committee were very enthusiastic for the new system and pointed to the first success of the area cars when a man was arrested trying to dispose of stolen property within an hour of the system commencing. The Chief Constable urged the public to use the Central 5000, telephone number to contact the Information Room for police assistance and displays of the new system were held in stores such as Lewis's. By 1946 however, the first rumblings against the system were heard and are still being advanced to this date. On 30 October 1946, Alderman Crump brought to the Watch Committee's attention a statement by ex-Superintendent Wensley of the Metropolitan Police suggesting that the modern method of mobile radio patrols was not an effective substitute for bringing police into personal contact with the public. However, there can be no denying that their use in wartime Birmingham was a boon to effective policing.

There was no new police building in Birmingham during the war. After the opening of the new Bridge Street West Police Station and Kingstanding Police Station in 1939/1940 such work was suspended for the duration. The move from Kenyon Street still presented problems for the Force. On 2 June 1943 the proposal was made to move the 'C' Division Headquarters from Kenyon Street to Thornhill Road Police Station. The idea of a new building in Newhall Street was abandoned as the business premises in that area were moving away from the City centre to the suburbs. The Watch Committee announced, 'The Kenyon Street premises are obsolete and utterly congested and are not suitable even for peace time requirements'. The Divisional Headquarters were moved to Handsworth but the death knell of Kenyon Street was a long time coming. In May 1942 the 'E' Division Headquarters were also moved from Moseley Street Police Station to Acocks Green. Again the reason was that the Moseley Street building was 50 years old and had suffered bomb damage which had destroyed the cell block rendering the police station unsuitable for wartime duties.

CHANGES IN PERSONNEL

As the War progressed further changes were made in the Senior Officers of the Birmingham Police. The tide of the war was turning by early 1943. Montgomery broke out of El Alamein in victory to pursue the Afrika Corps back across Northern Africa and the Germans were beaten at the Battle of

Stalingrad. The unbeatable were reduced to human proportions. Plans were laid for the policing of Europe after liberation and the Chief Constable, Mr Johnson was nominated to be a 'Police Commander' under the future Allied Commission. He was sent on a 14 week course for this purpose. The Watch Committee were none too pleased about this and announced that in the absence of the Chief Constable the 1st Assistant Chief Constable was to assume the duty of Deputy Chief Constable. In July of 1943 Mr Johnson was appointed, for a time, Lieutenant Colonel Commandant in charge of a course for junior police officers who were to be sent overseas. This was suitably followed by the appointment in July of the 1st ACC Mr. A E Young as a Lieutenant Colonel on special military duties and he saw service in Italy with the Allied Control Commission. E J Dodd Esq. was then moved to 1st ACC duties on 20 November 1944.

The continued enlistment of younger officers led to the Watch Committee resolving in July 1944 that all war time promotions were of a temporary nature only, thereby safeguarding the interests of all Birmingham Police officers serving in HM Forces. The Watch Committee minutes for this period show for the first time confirmation of appointment of seven policewomen probationers on 5 January 1944. Amongst these ladies is PW 39 Jean S Law who had joined the Force on 13 October 1941. She was 27 years of age and prior to joining the Force had been an optician. Miss Law rose to high rank as Assistant to the HMI from 1962 to 1976. During her service she was honoured with the OBE and awarded the Queens Police Medal. The previous occupations of the other six women, whose average age was 24 years, was two shorthand typists, one florist, one assistant sales manageress, one stock room assistant and one lady of no previous occupation. At this time 12 policewomen and two WAPC lived in the girls' hostel in Newton Street to be readily available for duties in the police war room. From 1 February 1940 one policewoman had been attached to the B-E Divisions due to the expansion in the use of policewomen in general police duties.

As the War drew to a close in 1944 Mr Young, who had come to Birmingham from the Leamington Spa Borough Police on 5 September 1941, was appointed Chief Constable of Hertfordshire on 22 September. On 30 September 1945, Mr William Clarence Johnson the Chief Constable resigned to take up appointment as Her Majesty's Inspector of Constabulary. At this time he had 25 years service. He had joined and rose to detective superintendent within 10 years in Portsmouth and with 12 years service was appointed Chief Constable in Plymouth. He was made OBE in 1939 and raised to CBE in 1945.

Mr E J Dodd was appointed Chief Constable of the City of Birmingham

Mr E J Dodd, Chief Constable, October 1945 – September 1963

Police on 1st October 1945, nine years after being a sub-divisional inspector in the Metropolitan Police.

It is worth recording the responsibilities of the senior officers of the Force as they stood in 1945, they were:—

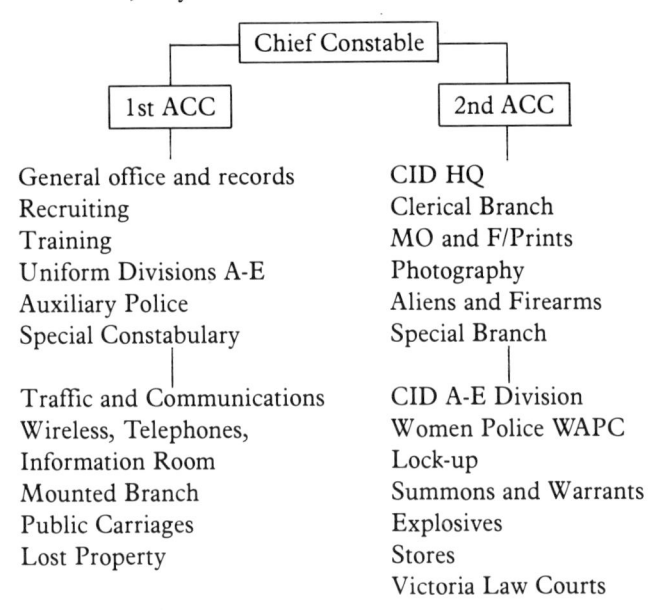

```
                    ┌─── Chief Constable ───┐
              ┌─────┴─────┐           ┌─────┴─────┐
              │  1st ACC  │           │  2nd ACC  │
              └─────┬─────┘           └─────┬─────┘
```

General office and records	CID HQ
Recruiting	Clerical Branch
Training	MO and F/Prints
Uniform Divisions A-E	Photography
Auxiliary Police	Aliens and Firearms
Special Constabulary	Special Branch
Traffic and Communications	CID A-E Division
Wireless, Telephones,	Women Police WAPC
Information Room	Lock-up
Mounted Branch	Summons and Warrants
Public Carriages	Explosives
Lost Property	Stores
	Victoria Law Courts

A not inconsequential work load when one remembers that the bureaucratic system required every report and minute to be passed ever upwards through the hierarchy.

WARTIME CONDITIONS AND CRIME

The Chief Constable's Report for 1945 details the picture of crime in the City in the War years. Due to austerity and the shortage of paper the reports for the War years are brief and succinctly worded. It is amusing in this day and age to read that, 'The decrease of 124 indictable offences is greatly appreciated.'

Overall there was an increase in reported crime over the six years of war time, this is not surprising due to the increase in City population and the war time impersonality of a changing populace. House breakings rose from 304 in 1939 to 673 in 1945, other breakings, of shops and warehouses, also rose from 518 to 977 offences. Offences against the person stood at 263 in 1939 and reached 359 by 1945. Indecent assault on females rose from 59 offences to 127. Early in

1940 the Chief Constable recorded that in his opinion the rise in crime was not attributable to the 'black-out' conditions imposed in September 1939. By 1941 the Chief Constable was claiming that, 'Damaged premises, black-out conditions and houses temporarily void by reason of evacuation or nightly absence from the City have afforded valuable opportunities to thieves.' A special offence of 'Looting and kindred offences' was created by defence regulations and, no doubt to speed disposal, was made non-indictable. In 1940 there were 239 such recorded offences ranging from stealing small unattended articles to deliberately planned theft.

Even though the War led to less vehicular traffic in the City, congestion and accidents increased. The times of greatest strain were immediately post air-raid and the Military Police and Military Traffic Company were used to assist in the regulation and diversion of traffic. It is reported that the black-out caused special problems when traffic lights, of which there were 55 installations in 1940, were switched off at night. The lights themselves were modified by an opaque lens in the form of a vertical cross and the fitting of small repeater lights of the form used on the Continent.

The Watch Committee minutes for 1944 contain an interesting report by the Chief Constable dated 29 December 1944 and titled 'War time conditions in the centre of the City.' The report is two pages of A4 paper and spends most of its time as a preamble without ever revealing the true nature of its message. It starts, 'The presence of large numbers of members of the British and Allied Forces in the City, combined with the war time restrictions on lighting... Undoubtedly produce a very difficult problem in the central area of a City of this size.'

After a time it reaches a definition of the 'very difficult problem' when the report states 'Unfortunately a great many young girls have been attracted into this area for the purpose of associating with members of the Forces, in particular the American soldiers, with result that a very undesirable standard of conduct became increasingly apparent.' The report continues with a list of police duties undertaken in the City Centre such as the numbers of National Registration Identity Cards checked. The answer to the perplexing reason for the submission of the report is found in the last item on the list, the number of 'Persons moved from doorways.' Therein lies the reason for the report; the serious matter of persons indulging in sexual intimacy in doorways. In 1944 14,440 persons were moved on and in 1945 no fewer than 26,674 were also moved on. In all probability the increase was due not to abandonment of morals in 1945 but the fact that the policy was enforced to move these people on and the need to record more figures for the benefit of the outraged Aldermen.

Whilst on the same subject, the historian, Lord Blake records that in London on VE night, Hyde Park was a mass of people engaged in sexual acts. No such record exists in Birmingham, probably due to the abundance of unpoliced doorways, but what is recorded is the following minutes by the Watch Committee for 6 June 1945, 'Your sub-committee have pleasure in recommending to the Watch Committee to record by minute their appreciation of the satisfactory manner in which the members of the Birmingham City Police remained at their posts and carried out their duties on the occasion of the recent VE Day and the VE plus one day celebrations in City'.

All well and good we may think, but not for Mr G T Mole a builder of Ormond Street, Newton who subsequently sued the Watch Committee for riot damages. He claimed that a group of riotous young men broke into his yard and stole a large quantity of materials which were consumed on bonfires to celebrate VE Day. His claim failed but in the spirit of rejoicing at the end of hostilities he was given an ex-gratia payment by the Committee.

Problems persisted in the City Centre with young girls and American servicemen. The major complaints were of theft when the girls asked the soldiers to be allowed to hold and admire an item of value. Once in their possession the girls would take the article and run off never to be seen again. The Americans also complained of being duped by larceny by trick when they would loan money to a girl for accommodation for the night. They never saw the money, the accommodation or the girl again. Disgraceful!

5
The Very Thin Blue Line

The War had ended. The eulogies and plaudits to the Police began. In 1942 the Prime Minister, Mr Churchill had singled out the Police in a broadcast for special praise, saying 'The Police have been in it everywhere all the time. And, as a working woman wrote to me in a letter, "What gentlemen they are".' The City Council of Birmingham stated in 1945, 'The most valuable of the innumerable contributions made by the City Police Force was the maintenance at all times of public order and a high morale. By personal courage especially under air attack and by cool and efficient control of 'incidents' the members of the Force rose in public esteem to a point never previously equalled or ever likely to be surpassed'. The thin blue line of pensioners, like the 63 year old PC Barrier, special constables and Auxiliaries had held, and saw the City of Birmingham through its darkest hours.

The War had indeed ended but the battle to rebuild the City of Birmingham Police had begun. On 31 December 1945 the Police (Employment and Offences) Orders were revoked. The implications of this were that the numbers of auxiliaries fell immediately from over 1,000 to 78 as members were freed to take up their old trades or new employment. The First Police Reserve fell to 27 members and the Police War Reserve were left with 51 officers. These reductions occurred notwithstanding the offer of favourable short term engagements. The number of special constables also fell to around 1,000 and continued to fall until 1949, when women were allowed for the first time to become members of the City of Birmingham Special Constabulary. Only 40 Women's Auxiliary Police Corps members remained on 31 December 1945 and the Corps was disbanded on 31 March 1946. The Watch Committee offered work in a clerical capacity to those remaining in order to preserve the pool of experience.

Recruiting to the City Police Force in 1945 shows a shortfall of 62 officers with more leaving than joining. The Chief Constable stated, 'It is regrettable that experienced officers — many with not inconsiderable pensionable service — should be influenced by present economic conditions to exchange the security and prospects of the Police Force for what in the great number of cases appears to be employment offering immediate and possibly temporary advantage only'. The main reasons given by these officers for resigning were,

Bomb damage repairs to the Chief Constable's office, Newton Street

inadequate pay and lack of ability to readjust to Police work on returning from the Armed Services. Out of an authorised establishment of 1,888 officers, the actual strength was 1,425, that is 455 officers short. With the loss of auxiliaries, the Chief Constable must have thought his force was haemorrhaging away. To make matters worse the Police Auxiliary Messenger Service was also disbanded at the end of 1945. The loss of these young men must have been missed, because they were used for extraneous duties around Police Stations.

Police pay was without doubt the major cause for the continual resignations. After the Desborough award in 1919, Police pay in the City was high in relation to average income and the cost of living. At one time it was estimated to be 55% above the average for a manual worker. New pay scales were introduced in April 1945 and 1946 to offset the loss of the War Duty Allowance and Supplementary Allowance. These rises re-established the Police pay to 17% above normal. However, in an industrial city such as Birmingham, there was a deficit of workers and wages were high, which only served to attract disgruntled Police. The pay barrier was again soon eroded. In 1949 the Home Office appointed the Oaksey Committee who recommended a pay increase of 15% in line with the Labour Governments Wages and Prices Policy. This came as a blow to both the Chief Constable and the Birmingham Police Federation, who were confidently expecting a rise between 33½% and 54%. Recruiting still struggled.

THE SEARCH FOR EFFICIENCY

To make matters worse the Chief Constable recognised that by 1946 the Force would have to be re-organised. The size of the City had grown contemporaneously with its population and by now needed to be policed by six divisions. This meant an increase of the authorised establishment to 2,062 plus a further two policewomen. The changes could not be introduced without the benefit of a full establishment and changes in Police buildings which were not achieved until 1 July 1952.

The Proposed changes were:

Division	Sub-Divisions	Division Headquarters	Sub-Divisions	Stations
A	Central	Steelhouse Lane		Bridge Street West
	Digbeth		Digbeth	Duke Street
B	Selly Oak	Selly Oak		Longbridge
	Stirchley		Stirchley	Kings Norton

C	Handsworth Hockley Ladywood	Thornhill Road	Kenyon St Ladywood	Holyhead Road Dudley Road Lozells Road Bristol Street Speedwell Road Harborne
D	Aston Kingstanding Erdington	Victoria Road	Kingstanding Erdington	Bloomsbury Street Canterbury Road
E	Acocks Green Bordesley Green Washwood Heath	Acocks Green	Bordesley Grn. Washwood Hth.	Hay Mills Coventry Road Stechford
F	Kings Heath Sparkhill Balsall Heath	Kings Heath	Sparkhill Moseley St	Woodbridge Road Billesley Robin Hood Edward Road

A further change that was incorporated in January 1946 was the alteration of the long established system of working beats in a fixed pattern to a system of discretionary patrol. This placed the onus of the policing of a beat on to the officer himself. It allowed greater initiative and enterprise and was welcomed by the Officers as giving greater interest and responsibility. On 25 February 1946 the '999' system of emergency telephone calls was introduced and was quickly adopted by the public adding to the increased work load. By 1949 the Chief Constable was reporting that, 'An observant member of the public who does not hesitate to inform the Police without delay of anything that may arouse his suspicions, is the greatest potential danger a law-breaker has to risk' and encouraged further use of the 999 system.

Recruiting and Recruits

The added work of the Force was compounded by the lack of recruitment and resignation throughout the rest of the decade. Recruiting to the Police was on a regional basis. Birmingham was the Headquarters of No 4 District Recruiting

Board. Who could blame a recruit for accepting an appointment in a force where he could be guaranteed accommodation in Police housing, which the Birmingham Force could not guarantee? The Chief Constable, Mr Dodd became exasperated and announced,

'The Police Force now offers an attractive career, security and excellent prospects to suitable candidates of both sexes possessed of the necessary educational and physical qualities. Young men anxious to establish themselves in regular employment of an open-air character affording a wide variety of interest, requiring intelligence, initiative, and self-reliability, with unlimited prospects of promotion to higher ranks would be well advised not to overlook the opportunity of a career in the Police.'

But overlook it they did. The expected increase in recruitment after the publication of the Oaksey Report did no materialise in the long run. It must be pointed out though, that the Watch Committee and the Chief Constable did not allow standards of recruitment to drop. In 1946, 389 candidates attended for final examination and 229 were appointed. In 1949 the figures were 215 attended and 158 appointed. The nationalities of post-war recruits up to 1950 are given as 594 English, 75 Scots, 58 Welsh, 20 Irish and 2 Canadians.

The Force was compelled to distribute illustrated leaflets extolling the virtues of a career in the City of Birmingham Police. The Police (Consolidation) (Amendment) Regulations of 1 July 1949, the enabling Act for Oaksey, not only increased the pay of Birmingham police officers, but also increased their refreshment breaks to three quarters of an hour and increased the payment of overtime to time and a half for leave day working. Detective Duty Alowance was also introduced, together with Detective Expenses and increased subsistence payments.

This dearth of recruits led to the philosophy of 'Catch 'em while they're young' and 1945 saw the establishment of the Police Cadet Clerks Scheme, the forerunner of the modern Police Cadets. The qualifications for entry were a good education and physique. Youths were enrolled at 16 years of age and gained knowledge of Police organisation and procedure by working in administrative offices. At that time young men were still conscripted at 18 to the Services, making their eventual appointment after National Service at the age of 20 years. By 1952 the training of the cadets had changed, whereby they did attachments to various departments or divisions for four months, were trained in first aid, physical training and drill.

After the war recruits to the City Police were no longer sent to the Digbeth School for their initial training. Instead they went to the No 4 District Police Training Centre at Ryton on Dunsmore, Coventry for a 13 week course. This

E

"A" DIVISION AREAS.
NUMBERED 1 to 32.

STEELHOUSE LANE.
  AREAS. 6,7,8,9,10,11,12,13,14,15,16,17,29,30.
DIGBETH
  AREAS 18,19,20,21,22,23,24,25,26,27,28.
BRIDGE ST.WEST.
  1,2,3,4,5,31,32.

SECTION SERGEANT'S VISITS.

SEQUENCE OF TIMING OF POINTS ON VARIOUS AREAS FOR THE THREE CODES. ADJUSTMENT HAS BEEN NECESSARY FOR LAST POINT OF TOUR ON CERTAIN AREAS.

STEELHOUSE LANE.
  'A' CODE
  6,7,29,30,8,9,10,11,12,13,14,15,16,17.
  'B' CODE
  15,16,17,13,12,11,10,14,8,9,29,30,6,7.
  'C' CODE
  29,9,8,10,11,14,13,12,17,16,15,6,7,30.

DIGBETH.
  'A' CODE
  24,27,28,26,25,20,19,18,21,22,23.
  'B' CODE
  23,22,21,18,19,20,25,26,28,27,24.
  'C' CODE
  20,19,18,21,22,25,26,28,27,24,23.

BRIDGE ST.WEST.
  'A' CODE
  1,5,4,3,31,32,2.
  'B' CODE
  2,32,31,3,4,5,1.
  'C' CODE.
  5,4,31,32,3,2,1.

Figs. VII & VIII (opposite) — Beat Card for Section Sergeants to time visits to Constables

DOUBLE BEATS

7/9	11/13	14/15	16/17
18/19	20/21	22/23	24/25
26/28	29/30	1/2	4/5
31/32			

TRAFFIC CONGESTION IN CITY CENTRE

Beat Cards contain a general instruction for all P.Cs. to report to Steelhouse Lane cases of serious traffic congestion in the City centre <u>at once</u>. This instruction is to enable Inspectors and Section Sergeants to take the appropriate action.

NO. 8 AREA
(STRAIGHT BEAT)

Beat consists of both sides of Corporation St., from Lancaster Place to New Street.

CONFERENCE POINTS

1. Corporation Street & Coleridge Passage.
   Tel. CEN.6497.
2. Old Square   Tel. CEN.2156 & CEN.2258.
3. Corporation St., & Lower Priory.
4. Corporation St., & Bull St.   P.P.
5. Corporation St. & Martineau St.

SYSTEM "A"

POINTS	1	2	3	4
1st. W.	6:35	8:45	10:45	12:45
2nd. W.	2:35	4:45	6:45	8:45
Nights.	10:35	12:45	2:45	4:45

SYSTEM "B"

POINTS	2	4	3	1
1st. W.	7:15	9:15	11:15	1:15
2nd. W.	3:15	5:15	7:15	9:15
Nights.	11:15	1:15	3:15	5:15

SYSTEM "C"

POINTS	2	4	3	5
1st. W.	6:30	8:30	10:30	12:40
2nd. W.	2:30	4:30	6:30	8:40
Nights.	10:30	12:30	2:30	4:40

SPECIAL ATTENTION
Observe Police Pillar Bull St. & Corporation St.
Traffic lights at Bull Street & Corporation St. at Peak periods.
REPORT SERIOUS CASES TRAFFIC CONGESTION AT ONCE.

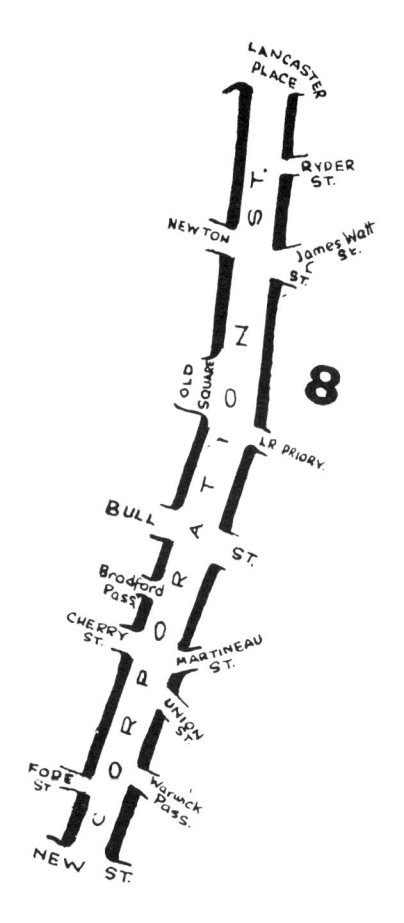

Figs. IX (opposite) & X — Constables Beat Card showing conference points and the times at which points should be made on visits and conferences

Victory Celebrations: Special Constabulary March Past, 1945

was followed by a two week course at the Digbeth Police School in local legislation and procedure, soon to be known as Local Procedures Courses. Probationers at this time were still obliged to attend evening classes in educational subjects, three nights per week between 7 pm and 9 pm. Rehabilitation courses for men returning from HM Forces of four weeks duration were held at Digbeth. The Police school at Digbeth had, in the modern expression, been a 'Centre of Excellence' for detective training courses for officers throughout the country and from overseas. This instruction was continued by Birmingham officers at Ryton. In 1948 after the establishment of the Police Staff College at Ryton, recruits were sent first for training at Cannock and then to Mill Meece, near Eccleshall in Staffordshire, where the centre remained until the mid-1960's.

BACK ON THE ROAD

The end of the War and the easing of petrol restrictions, saw an increase in the number of vehicles using the City roads and in consequence, more accidents and congestion. In May 1946 a sergeant on each division was appointed Road Safety Officer. They were responsible for all aspects of road safety, in particular visiting schools for talks and later for examination of the children's pedal cycles. At the end of 1946 new Police vehicles again became available. A mobile kitchen was purchased for the feeding of officers at incidents and special duties such as football matches and race meetings at Bromford. In 1947 the vehicle fleet stood at 84 and the Chief Constable's limousine, a Humber together with two Wolseley 18 HP, the CID van and other vehicles, were changed. In 1948, 32 of the Force's vehicular fleet were said to be fitted with wireless and seven more were planned. In 1949 the Watch Comittee purchased 15 Austin A70 Hampshire Saloons amongst other vehicles. The Sports and Social Club in that year purchased a 29 seater Bedford coach with permission of the Watch Committee.

Traffic patrols were resumed in Birmingham in 1946 and at first, because of the lack of vehicles, courtesy patrols were established. Officers would give warnings on the spot for minor infringements of Road Traffic Offences or the Highway Code but, the Chief Constable is quick to point out, 'proceedings are always taken for excessive speeding.' In 1949 a brake testing machine was purchased, due to the high number of disputed accidents. The same year saw the implementation of the Motor Spirit (Regulation) Act 1948 and traffic patrols had the duty of testing vehicles for commercial petrol, somewhat like the present day search for 'pink' diesel. Out of 8,000 tests only 42 cases were

PC A30 uses a Police Pillar in Dale End, 1949

found. This year also saw increased use of loud-hailer equipment, fitted to patrol cars, at junctions and crossings to draw attention to the proper use of pedestrian crossings and traffic lights.

While recruitment of men proved extremely difficult in this period no problem was found in the recruitment of women. At the end of 1946 the establishment of policewomen stood at 22, being made up of two inspectors, five sergeants and 15 constables. By the start of 1949 the numbers had risen to 27, but one inspector post was lost. At the end of that year the Authorised Establishment rose to 35 with posts for one chief inspector, two inspectors, four sergeants and 28 policewomen constables. The work of the Policewomen's Department expanded and throughout 1949 constables were attached to the woman detective sergeant for training. In this year the first woman constable attended a CID Course at Wakefield Detective Training Centre. The Policewomen's Department continued their work with the Girls Hostel which had been temporarily rehoused whilst the premises in Newton Street were used for policewomen's accommodation during the war.

By 1945 new premises were sought for a hostel and, after much haggling with the owners' premises at 31 Aston Street were obtained. On 1 February 1946 the Salvation Army took over the administration of this work which changed its name to the Girls Night Shelter. The premises in Newton Street were vacated on 31 March 1946 and made offices for the Probation Service which they are to this day. In 1961 the girls shelter moved to 37 Portland Road, Edgbaston. After 73 years the Watch Committee were no longer responsible for the shelter.

The Crinimal Investigation Department at this time suffered from a shortfall in Establishment similar to the Force total. Their work had been made more professional by the establishment of the West Midlands Forensic Science Laboratory in Newton Street in 1938. During the War years in 1943 the change was made from the investigation of all crime by the CID to being the responsibility of every officer. It was said that uniform officers were disgruntled, that once having arrested an offender the work was taken from them and they were then kept in the dark leading to a sense of frustration and injustice. By 1950, 46.34% of all persons prosecuted were dealt with by the Uniformed Branch. A reading of the literature available for the period makes it cleat that relations between the two branches of the Force were strained. 'Aides' to the CID, being officers who were attached to the department for six months for evaluation as to their suitability to transfer, had been introduced before the war, but the system had been suspended for the duration. In 1946 they were reintroduced and by 1948 uniform sergeants and constables were being attached for training. In his Annual Report for 1947, the Chief Constable mentions that the CID and

Uniform Branches 'Co-operated well'. In 1948 he mentions 'a high degree of co-operation between the various branches... reflected in the high percentage of arrests for all indictable offences, nearly 50% made by officers of the Uniformed Branch.' In 1949 the Chief Constable saw fit to state, 'The very cordial and co-operative relations that exist throughout the City between members of the Uniformed Branch and CID reflect creditably upon the individuals in both branches of the Force,' and, 'The high percentages of arrests for crime made by uniformed officers (46% of the whole) is in no small part due to the encouragement and assistance given by the detective staff.' One could expect that if over a five year period there was no strain in the working relationship between Uniform and CID, then by the end of the decade there would be no need for the Chief Constable to keep returning to the point. It is an axiom of Police work that uniform officers make most arrests but Mr Dodd thought it worthwhile to prove that Uniform and CID were equal on work rate.

However, everybody, Police and public alike love the Mounted Branch. In the late 1940's the section, known colloquially as the 'Donkey Wallopers', had an establishment of one inspector, one sergeant, 24 constables and 20 horses which were practically all 'greys.' The Branch carried out patrols throughout the City every day and concentrated on the outlying districts. The horses were maintained by the Corporation's Stud of Horses, belonging to the City Veterinary Department, but were provided for by Watch Committee. In May 1946 the Committee resolved to increase the weekly upkeep from 30/- per horse to 35/- for the provision of feeding, bedding and shoeing. Contemporary readers are advised that Police Orders of the day together with Chief Constables' Reports also have long accounts of winners of tent pegging, lancing and best horse and 'jockey' as we see regularly. On the practical side though the Mounted Branch were widely valued and in 1949 were called upon to assist Wolverhampton Borough, Worcester City and Shropshire Police. For this purpose a two horse trailer box was purchased at the time.

Post War Austerity

The issue of uniform clothing in the period, 1945-1950, posed particular problems. This was the period of austerity and rationing. As the Auxiliaries, special constables and Reserves resigned in droves at the end of the war the stores at Steelhouse Lane Police Station in 1946 alone handled 50,000 items of uniform either received or issued. After the war, periodic issue of new uniform was resumed but this was soon changed back to a one for one exchange basis and items of serviceable uniform were cleaned and re-issued by the stores. The problems of obtaining new stocks became so grave that by 1949 a contract was placed for uniform to be cleaned and repaired by a private firm. In October 1946 the Police Council announced that open neck tunics, collars and ties could be worn by all ranks. The Watch Committee announced that when stocks became available the use of the new style tunics would be restricted to summer months only in order to get full value and use from existing tunics. The new uniform was first worn in Birmingham on 10 May 1946 for the visit of HRH Princess Elizabeth and was voted a great success by all. At the same time the Join Branch Board of the Police Federation balloted their members as to whether helmets should be replaced by flat caps. The result was a resounding 'yes' for the retention of the helmet.

In February 1946, a motor driving school was established at Duke Street. Courses of instruction lasted four weeks and students were graded, 'First' 'Second' or 'Failed'. In the first year out of 94 students, 54 obtained First grades, 36 Second grades and four failed. In the second year, courses were also held for inspectors and sergeants to teach them how to drive and the elementary knowledge of the mechanics of motor vehicles. Courses leading to the award of a Ministry of Transport Driving Licence were also held for CID, policewomen and summons and warrants officers.

October 1946 saw the introduction of the Accident Report Book. This greatly facilitated the beat officers work as the book provided ease of compilation of statistical records.

Throughout these years the Victoria State Police and the New South Wales Police sent food parcels from Australia to members of Birmingham Police. The parcels are said to have contained sustantial quantities of the types of food which were in short supply. The kindness of this gesture was appreciated by the City Police and those parcels that were sent to the Force itself were given to police widows.

Crime in this period had doubled across the board from the 1939 levels and this increase together with the shortfall in force strength must have been exasperating. However, the detection rate of 45% was a sign of headway being made against the tide. With petrol being 'taken off' ration in 1947 there was a clear indication of the return of vehicles to the road in the drastic falls of theft of pedal cycles and a contemporaneous growth in theft of motor vehicles and, because of the greater number of cars, theft from motor vehicles. The increase in the last category of offences led to the practice of police leaving a printed card inside vehicles which were unattended and unlocked, warning of the dangers from thieves. This was the great age of bigamy, the stuff that the Sunday newspapers thrived on. There were no fewer that 44 prosecutions in 1948 and

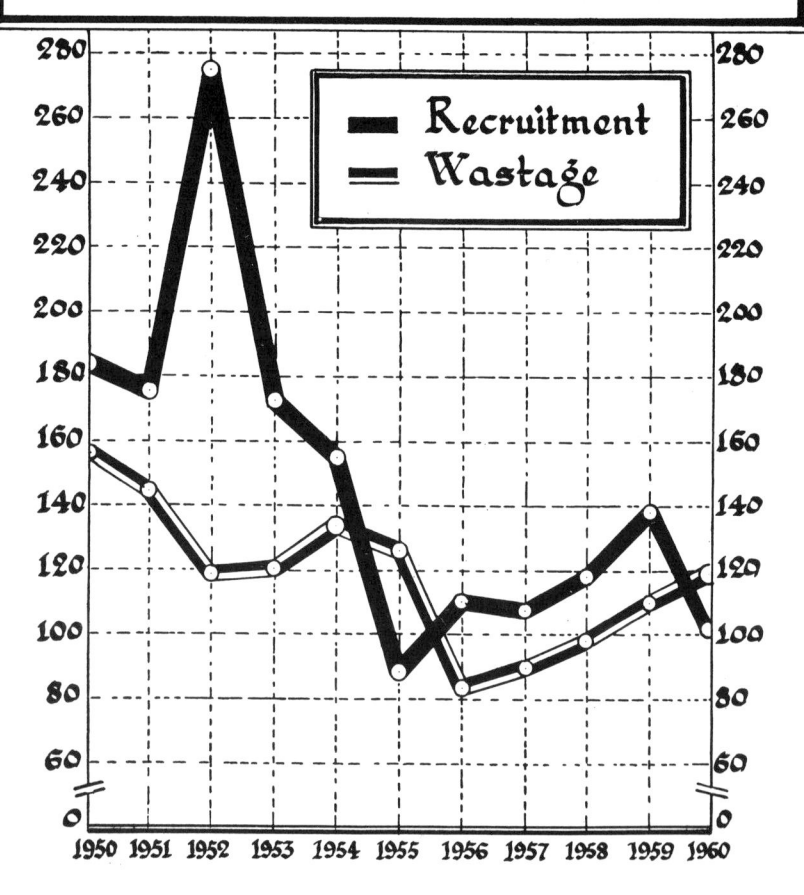

Fig. XI — Graph showing how recruitment went into reverse in the 1950's and 60's

an average of 30 for the other years. Divorce was difficult and the change in morality and family links during the War, probably made bigamy the easy way out.

Building for the City Police was also strictly controlled at the end of the War but the City was expanding outwards. Large council housing estates were being built at Shard End and Sheldon in the east and Quinton in the west. Accordingly, sites were examined and purchased in Packington Lane, Hengham Road at Garretts Green Lane and Quinton Road West for new police stations.

THE RECRUITING PROBLEM

The one recurring theme, the 'leitmotiv' of police and policing, in Birmingham between 1950 and 1959 was that of recruiting. The pay and improvement of conditions which resulted from the Oaksey Committee, had no positive effect on recruiting. In his 1950 Report, the Chief Constable points out that in a City such as Birmingham with 'more remunerative occupations, with regular and less working hours, the security and prospects of a police career are not likely to appeal'. A further blow was caused in the first year of the decade, by the extension of National Service from 18 months to two years, thereby depriving the Force of its cadets for longer periods. The Chief Constable was forced to swallow his pride and he solicited the Chief Constables of more popular Forces for the files of candidates who had failed by height or some local requirement. Even this did not increase the number of recruits.

The Authorised Establishment of the City of Birmingham Police on 31 December 1950 was 2,058 men and 35 women. The actual strength was 1,522 men and 33 women. This made a shortfall of 538 officers, a quarter of the Force. At the end of the decade in 1959 there were only 160 more constables and 32 more women on the strength.

The disappointing failure to attract quality recruits was continuous. A new pay rise on 3 August 1951 caused a very temporary blip on the graph. The Watch Committee were told that every form of recruiting had been tried from distribution of leaflets to advertising in newspapers and Service magazines. Standards were unofficially dropped. Between 1952 and 1954 an average of one third of all recruits were below the height requirement and one third were over 26 years of age. In fact in 1953, three quarters of all recruits were over 26 years of age. Force Orders of 7 August 1879 state 'A six foot PC to be transferred from E to A Division.' The tradition was maintained that only men over six foot tall were posted to Steelhouse Lane Police Station. As the officers in the City centre would be the most visible, where better to put the taller men to prevent the public perceiving that standards had dropped. At a meeting of the Judicial Sub Committee on 21 October 1953 the Chairman informed the Committee that since their last meeting in September, 14 probationary constables had resigned. He had been approached by his counterpart in Manchester, where they were suffering the same damaging wastage, and agreed that with other members of Municipal Authorities they would make representation to the Home Office. This must have had some success, because in 1954 another pay rise was granted to the Police. To coincide with the pay rise, there was a 'massive' recruiting campaign in Birmingham. It made no difference.

The year of 1955 was particularly bad in the history of the Force, more officers left than joined. The slow drip had turned into a rush. Yet another pay rise was made in December 1955, but again that made no difference. It was only the recruitment of police cadets and policewomen that kept the figurative head of the Force above water. The Chief Constable took heart in 1956, when the first recession hit Birmingham's car industry. But these were the days when you could quite literally leave a job on Friday afternoon and start a new one on Monday morning. Mr Dodd's enthusiasm was short lived. The candidates for the Force who had offered themselves for appointment were either too old, below physical or educational requirements or not prepared to accept irregular hours. By 1957 things were no better. At a meeting of the Watch Committee on 18 September 1957, the Chief Constable was advised to 'Consider the question of the extent to which civilians might be employed on administrative work in order to release police officers for other duties.' That sounds very familiar. However, the Chief Constable did as he was bid and not only in clerical posts. The mortuary attendants were replaced by civilians and the six police officers responsible for policing of the markets were replaced by Council employees. It had been the duty of the Police to regulate the question of who would obtain which stall and to achieve this, tokens were placed in a helmet and the traders had to take their pick.

In his report for 1959 the Chief Constable reluctantly had to admit that in the 15 years of recruiting since the end of the war, no less that 35% of men who had joined Birmingham Police had left. At last he recognised that this costly problem was more retention than recruiting. The Royal Commission eventually set up under Sir Henry Willink, to report on this and other problems, correctly called the loss 'a crippling handicap.'

Throughout the period there is no record until 1957 and 1959, as to the causes of resignation. In 1957 it is stated that out of those voluntarily resigning, six transferred to other Forces, five started their own business, 11 were

Recruits in training at Digbeth Police School c.1940's

BIRMINGHAM CITY POLICE

Station House Rules

In order to ensure cleanliness and good conduct essential for health and comfort when a number of officers are residing together, the following regulations have been made and will be observed by all persons living in the Station House.

1.—Residents will be personally responsible for the cleanliness and tidiness of their rooms and must be properly dressed when using communal rooms.

2.—Residents will report to the Station Officer any woman cleaner or cook who is not carrying out her work efficiently or is otherwise unsatisfactory.

3.—Men on night duty, except those engaged at Court or on some other special duty, should normally leave their rooms not later than 3-30 p.m. To allow adequate time for cleaning and ventilation, other officers should not return to their rooms before 4-30 p.m.

4.—Smoking will not be permitted in dormitories, but is permissible in bedrooms and communal rooms. Care must be taken, however, to avoid risk of fire.

5.—Gambling or playing for any consideration is strictly prohibited. Borrowing and lending money among residents is undesirable. Any officer in financial difficulty should consult his Chief Inspector.

6.—Articles of clothing and footwear should be cleaned only in the rooms set apart for the purpose.

7.—No offensive or improper article is to be kept in quarters.

8.—Visitors will not be allowed in sleeping rooms.

9.—Residents must take adequate rest and those on First Day Watch the following day must be in the Station House by 12 midnight unless they have permission to be absent. Any officer who enters the Station House between 12 midnight and 6 a.m. whether on or off duty, must report his arrival to the Station Officer.

10.—Residents on the sick list must not be absent from their quarters so late as to be likely to retard recovery.

11.—Residents are particularly warned against making use of any article of clothing, property, or appointments belonging to another man. Lockers should be kept locked with the keys provided and no officer must interfere with the locker allotted to another.

12.—Members of the Force are forbidden to leave money or other valuables lying about the Station insecure or in pockets of garments. Any loss of money or other property is to be reported at once.

July, 1957.

13.—Wireless or television receiver sets may be installed by residents subject to compliance with the following conditions

(a) receiving sets only may be installed ;
(b) a communal set may be installed in the lounge ;
(c) headphone sets only may be used in dormitories ;
(d) loudspeaker sets may be used in *bedrooms* provided the noise does not interfere with other residents ;
(e) the consent of the Police Surveyor has been obtained where it is proposed to operate the set off the mains or to use an aerial ;
(f) the cost of making good any damage is met by the resident ;
(g) all private installations must be withdrawn at one month's notice in the event of interference with any official installation ;
(h) a current licence is produced to the Chief Inspector annually.

14.—Other musical instruments may be kept provided no disturbance is caused to other residents.

15.—Where a messing system exists, no resident may derive any profit by supplying articles to the Mess nor have any interest in supplies.

16.—The members of the Mess will appoint a Mess Committee, under the chairmanship of the Chief Inspector, to be responsible for catering. Mess accounts must be paid within three days of their presentation. Complaints will be made to the Chief Inspector through a member of the Committee.

17.—Presents to the Messes will not be accepted without prior consent of the Chief Constable, as in the case of other gratuities.

18.—All men must be in Mess except when on leave, on night duty, or on any other special duty which prevents them from returning to the Station for refreshment. Notice of intention to be out of Mess when on leave or otherwise must be given to the Mess Caterer not later than mid-day on the day prior to that on which the man concerned wishes to be out of Mess.

19.—No resident may adjust or interfere unnecessarily with any heating, electrical, mechanical, ventilating or other technical service provided.

20.—Lights are to be extinguished when rooms are vacated or lights not required.

21.—Residents must exercise the greatest care in all that relates to the property of the police authority and will be held responsible for any damage or loss caused by negligence.

22.—The senior officer present is responsible that any disorder or infringement of the "Station House Rules" is brought to the attention of the Station Officer.

By Order of the Chief Constable.

Fig. XII — New Station House rules for a relaxed atmosphere in Quarters

emigrating to Canada or Australia and the remainder considered they were unsuited to the life. The majority resigning, cited their wives' dislike of shift work as the main reason for quitting. In 1959 out of 52 resignations, 16 men claimed they were leaving because of inadequate pay, nine because of shift work, six because they could not settle, five because of lack of prospects, three to join other Forces, three for domestic grounds and only one officer claimed to dislike the discipline of Police life. A further nine men declined to give clear reasons for resigning.

There is a hint of arrogance in the Chief Constable, Mr Dodd's statement in 1957 that, 'A proportion also left the service under the impression that they could obtain more lucrative jobs in other walks of life.' Perhaps therein lies the key to the answer. He saw his problems of recruitment and retention in the form of a cash nexus. Some policemen have always voted with their feet and what he had to offer wasn't good enough. The City of Birmingham Police were pitching their level of recruitment to a generation of men who had either seen service in the War or endured the rigours of discipline and separation of National Service. The post war consumer boon was on and work and wages were plentiful in Birmingham. A Police career promised a rent free house or, in lieu, a rent allowance. Men came to join the Police in Birmingham and discovered no Police houses available and because of war damage and the boom, no houses to rent. The Police service separated men from their families.

Those men who were then forced to live in single men's accommodation in Police Stations were subject to 40 different rules as to what they could or could not do. That was more than a Benedictine Monastery. In 1956 the rules were dropped to 22 in number. The main changes were that no longer had a resident to be in quarters by midnight, he could now, except if on First Watch, stay out as long as he wanted, providing he reported to the Station Officer on return. TV sets could also be fitted in rooms or cubicles, but licences would be regularly inspected. Men on sick leave had been obliged to be in quarters by 7 pm in the winter and 9 pm in the summer. The change allowed no specific time, but warned men as to retarding their own recovery. Smoking in bedrooms was made permissible. The rule of lights out at midnight was abolished. Men on night duty were excused from taking meals in the mess, (their dinners had been prepared and then allowed to go cold). Because of the large number of married men living in quarters, they were referred in the rules as 'residents' and not 'single men.'

Even though only one man gave his reason for resigning as dislike of discipline, life for the policeman in Birmingham was hard. A small personal experience can be found in *Forward*, The Birmingham City Police Magazine, in 1971. An article by an officer obtaining some degree of anonymity by use of his warrant number wrote;

'A Quarter of a Century'
by W N 11779

Somehow a quarter of a century seems longer than 25 years, but the term has a historical flavour, which is perhaps why it is the best one to use when committing to paper thoughts and memories common to many of us who joined the Police Service in 1946.

Practically without exception we were all ex-servicemen and women with both the advantages and disadvantages that went with it. We were readily disciplined, but too many of us possessed a narrowness of outlook which came not only from the Services but also from the conditions under which we were educated and brought up before the war. This suited the Police Service admirably at that time, for the supervising officers were cast in the same mould and we were harried and disciplined for such trivia, things as failing to walk to the end of each little cul-de-sac on our beat. For this, we were paid the princely sum of 90/- per week.

The 'wastage' was high and yet, under those conditions, one may ask why did some of us stay? One reason was that the job was secure, we were reared in the traditions that security of employment was the be all and end all; secondly, that we lacked the initiative to seek other employment when we became disillusioned, and lastly that we found in Police work a rewarding (not, of course, financially) occupation.

There have been many changes since those early years, and now the memories come flooding back, happy and miserable ones, some tragic and some comic, for if there is one thing that can be said about a policeman's job it is that he has probably a greater experience of life than any other occupation can provide. The birth of a child, death in all its forms, the visiting of luxurious dwellings and witnessing the squalor of the slums; being the deliverer of happy, but more often sad news and then having to deal with the reactions of arresting criminals and being involved in drunken brawls and, above all, the cold austerity of the Courts.

My first experience was on my first day in uniform as I boarded a tramcar in Bristol Street and my helmet broke the lamp on the platform. I stood there with my shoulders covered in broken glass whilst the conductor said, 'Officer, I have to have your number for my report.' This, together with all the passengers turning in their seats, would have made a marvellous cartoon for *Punch*.

You may ask, 'Would you do it all again?' and I would answer, 'Not on your life,' and yet on reflection I think I would, for although I might not be as rich in worldly goods as I might have been, I do know that I am wiser and a more understanding creature for the experience.'

The Search for an Answer

During the 1950's there were 12 different Police Regulations issued in an attempt to improve the policeman's lot. However, such piecemeal changes made no impact on conditions of service. A Supplementary Allowance was paid to officers separated from their families. Officers were allowed to count service in HM Forces as an entry point for pay. A further pay increment was introduced for constables after 25 years service. Rent allowance was increased. Annual leave entitlement was increased by two days a year. Most importantly hours of work were reduced from 48 to 44 per week. This resulted in the necessity of awarding an additional rest day to the Force each fortnight. The Watch Committee decided that it could not be done and officers were paid that day as overtime from 1955 onwards. The Chief Constable and the Joint Branch Board of the Federation, became concerned that the overtime was becoming accepted as part of pay. Even so the Chief Constable lamented, 'But for this supplement to pay, the Police wage in industrial areas such as Birmingham, would compare even more unfavourably with outside rates of pay.' In fact a constable's maximum pay had fallen to 5% below the average industrial earnings and the minimum pay of probationers and recruits to 30% below by 1959.

Neither the Chief Constable or the Watch Committee made any statement about the morale of the Force. Perhaps, they felt that in all the circumstances it could only be low. To compound the problems of the City Police, levels of reported crime in Birmingham doubled unexpectedly in all cases from 1954 to 1966. The detection rate slipped to 38% in 1959 and this must be an indicator of the increasing difficulties facing the City Police. Crime became a vicious circle. The more offences that were committed the more persons were arrested and blocked the Criminal Justice System, causing longer waits for disposal. The Magistrates at Victoria Law Courts felt obliged to bail more prisoners who in turn committed more offences. Moreover, social morality was changing, not only in Birmingham but across the country and especially amongst the young. This was the age of the 'Teddy Boy', increased prosperity, educational opportunity, greater social mobility and Bill Haley 'Rocking around the Clock'. The old order was changing and a sadly depleted Police Force was expected to deal with it.

In order to cope with the outbreak of serious crime a City Crime Squad, known initially as the Special Crime Squad, the forerunner of today's Serious Crimes Squad, was formed in February of 1952. 'Seasoned and experienced' detective officers were drawn from the City's divisions, relieved of routine duties and equipped with wireless cars. They were successful from the start and broke up a number of organised gangs of metal thieves, which were operating in the City and neighbouring areas. The City Crime Squad were also available to assist divisions in the investigation of other serious crimes.

A Watch Committee minute for 9 November 1952, sums up the annoyance of authority when the Chief Constable is asked to investigate the sale of toy truncheons which are, 'easily converted into rubber coshes,' and the common sale of 'knuckle dusters'. At the end of the decade, we find Mr Dodd bemoaning, 'the spirit of avarice that exists among well paid and well provided for people in Birmingham,' and, 'The use of physical violence both in committing crime and in acts of general hooliganism which is symptomatic of the deterioration in regard for the law,' also, 'Clearly much begets a desire for more and there is little or no relation between need and theft'.

His answer to the problem in Birmingham? More Police. Like so many before and after him, Mr Dodd, failed to recognise that such increases in public misbehaviour are not only affected by the number of patrolling policemen, but by problems that are the responsibility of governments. The symptom was to be attacked but not the cause. Harold MacMillan, the Prime Minister won the 1959 General Election with the slogan 'You've never had it so good', but there are several ways in which that was not true for the City of Birmingham Police.

LAW AND ORDER IN THE 1950's

Two incidents from either end of the 1950's that show the problems of Birmingham City Police in maintaining the rule of law and order are the shooting of PC Sommerville and the murder of Stephanie Baird, and are worth discussing in more detail.

Police Constable D173 Thomas Bryce Sommerville was on patrol in Lichfield Road, Aston at about 4.30 am on Friday, 4 May 1951 when he came upon a Kenneth Millington aged 23, an escapee from Highcroft Mental Hospital. The officer examined Millington's identity card and having had his suspicions aroused, asked what he was carrying in his bag. Millington obliged by showing PC Sommerville a .38 revolver and shooting him once in the left side of the stomach. Millington ran off. A Mr Sid Joyce, the proprietor of the Aston Cross Cafe, was later to tell the *Evening Mail* that he was awoken by the persistent blowing of a police whistle. He looked out and saw a police officer staggering along the road, clutching his stomach and continually blowing his whistle. A Mr George Mansell a worker at Ansells Brewery also heard the whistle and traced it to its source at Wainwright Street and Aston Road, where he found PC Sommerville lying against a horse trough. Two officers from the same shift at the completion of their tour of duty at 6 am, put on plain clothes and carried on patrolling. They were PC D172 Cameron Murray and PC D180 Robert Leo Lamont. Their actions and professionalism are to this day worthy of note. The officers spotted Millington in disguise in Rocky Lane, Aston. As they challenged him, he tried to get his gun out of his haversack. They overpowered him. He was also found to be in possession of a stiletto knife.

PC Sommerville was later awarded the Kings Commendation for Brave Conduct, PCs Lamont and Murray received the British Empire Medal. Mr Sommerville retired as Licensing Inspector from Steelhouse Lane Police Station in the 1980's.

The murder of Miss Sydney Stephanie Baird must have confirmed the public's conception that their worst fears were being realised. An horrific murder that a beleaguered Police Force, at first, appeared unable to solve, seemed to be a sign of the times.

At the time of her death, Baird was aged 27 years. In July 1959 she had attempted suicide and had received treatment at the Midland Nerve Hospital. It was known that she was strongly adverse to confrontation with members of the opposite sex. Baird lived at Edencroft House a YWCA Hostel that stood in Wheeleys Road, Edgbaston. Her room was in an annexe to the building known as Queensway. At 7.30 pm on 23 December 1959 a woman working in the laundry at the hostel was attacked with a brick, by a man she had disturbed. The Police were summoned and a search was made which proved fruitless. A Police officer went to Baird's room. On entering he found her decapitated body. The clothing had been cut away and the body was mutilated and excessively scarred. Her head lay on the bed. A pool of blood was on the floor but little had been splashed about. A broken and bloodstained bone-handled table knife was in the room. A casement window had been left open and a well defined footprint had been left outside the window. Importantly an envelope was found on a tall-boy in the room. Written in biro on it was, 'This was the thing I tought (sic) would never come'. A post mortem revealed that Stephanie Baird had been manually strangled and then decapitated. There was no evidence of sexual assault.

An Incident Room was established in the cramped conditions of Speedwell Road Police Station. Enquiries were commenced but were soon bogged down by the Christmas holiday. The mass coverage in the media caused two men to come forward and admit the crime. When they were interviewed it was soon obvious that they knew nothing of the murder and were attention seekers. The popular press soon started the cry of 'Bring in the Yard' but this was something the Birmingham Police were not accustomed to doing. Door to door enquiries were made and 30,000 people were interviewed as to their movements on the night of the murder. Approximately 2,500 statements were obtained, 5,000 telephone messages were received and more than 4,000 letters were despatched.

As a result of the routine house to house enquiries, it was revealed that a Patrick Joseph Byrne had left 97 Islington Row, close to the YWCA, on 24 December. He was alibied by his cousin for his movements on the night of the murder. A follow up enquiry was sent to Warrington, Lancashire for Byrne to be interviewed. By appointment he attended Warrington Police Station on 9 February 1960 and was interviewed by a Detective Sergeant Welborn. After the preliminary questions Byrne blurted out, 'I want to tell you about the YWCA. I have something to do with that'. He was cautioned but said, 'I cannot sleep its been on my mind, I was coming down to see the Police. These last seven weeks have been no good to me'. The Detective Sergeant probably could not believe his luck.

Byrne made an initial statement admitting going to the hostel to peep through the windows. Emboldened he had entered the annexe and stood on a chair to peep at Baird over a glass partition. She had caught him and they had struggled, whereupon he had strangled her. Byrne was arrested and taken to Birmingham. He was interviewed again and admitted murdering Baird and decapitating her, freely admitting that his motives were sexual. He had stripped to his socks and shoes before mutilating the corpse. Byrne provided a sample of handwriting which matched that on the envelope. The final clue was the shoe print from the soil outside the window. Police enquiries had been hampered by the size of that print, being measured as size 11 when the true size as they found out was 9½. Byrne stated that he had left the shoes at his lodgings in Islington Row. Enquiries revealed that they had been left for the dustman to cart away. By a stroke of fortune the dustman had placed the shoes in the cab of his vehicle and the Police were able to collect them. They matched the print as the 9½ had expanded due to wear.

Patrick Joseph Byrne appeared before the Learned Judge at Birmingham Assizes on 23 March 1960. He was found guilty of murder and sentenced to life imprisonment. This was later reduced on appeal to manslaughter, but even though he was clearly of diminished responsibility, the sentence remained the same.

The inquiry was probably the most exhaustive in the history of the City of Birmingham Police. By meticulous application of the 'system' and thorough door to door enquiries, checking on the movement of everyone in the area, a potential suspect was discovered. Suspicions were roused and Byrne was as good as caught. Diligence was the keyword of this gruesome enquiry. The result is a credit upon the memory of Birmingham Police.

BIRMINGHAM'S POLICE DOGS

One of the innovations of the 1950's was the introduction of police dogs and on 27 December 1951, PC J. Ford and his dog 'Flash' first patrolled the City.

On 9 July 1952 the Watch Committee were pleased to pass a resolution noting the success of Police Constables Richardson and Welsley and their dogs 'Tex' and 'Rex' at the Metropolitan Police Training School. It is obvious that they did not win any prizes for originality of canine naming. The number of dogs gradually increased over the years and there were good examples of tracking and detection. The dogs were Alsatians and were either gifts to the City Police or were bought cheaply. In 1956 a radio equipped van was used for dog patrol in the City area at night. By 1957 there were 27 dogs and the van patrol was established as a 24 hour service, the other officers and dogs being used as foot patrols. In the same year, one of the section's sergeants spent four weeks at the Police Dog Training Establishment at Mulheim in Germany and on his return a Force Dog Training School was established. Facilities for the training of dogs were used at Sutton Park, the Lickey Hills, Yorks Wood Scout Camp at Kingshurst and at the ICI factory at Witton. Plans were laid for the importation of dogs for breeding stock from the Continent. In 1959 a permanent home for the Dog Training Centre was found at Home Farm, Harborne Golf Club.

POLICE MOTORCYCLES

In 1950 the City Police vehicle fleet stood at 71 cars, 31 vans and one lorry. Out of these vehicles, 46 were fitted with radio. The greater number of cars were Austin A70 Hampshires and a policy was introduced where the smaller 10 HP cars were replaced by small vans for despatch delivery and such duties. Congestion in the City centre became an intractable problem by 1951 and accordingly the Watch Committee decided to reintroduce motor cycle patrols after 25 years. Six BSA 650cc 'Golden Flash' machines were purchased, followed by a further three in 1953. The fleet stood at 12 in 1955. The Chief Constable and the Committee were obviously pleased with the extra mobility provided by two wheeled transport, for on 30 May 1956 an order was placed for the purchase of 20 Vespa motor scooters.

Liverpool City Police had experimented successfully with scooters and this is what swayed the Chief Constable. However, within a year there had been too many accidents involving the Vespas, due to their low centre of gravity. The Watch Committee resolved on 5 June 1957 to replace the Vespas by Velocette lightweight motor cycles, manufactured by Veloce Ltd of Hall Green, Birmingham for £155 each. This was the start of a long love affair between the Birmingham City Police and the Velocette. It was an ideal vehicle for Police patrol and a maximum of 61 were held in 1967. The machines were particularly silent in operation. So much so that they sounded more like an electric motor than an internal combustion machine. Offenders and miscreants would never hear the approach of the vehicle, until it was too late. They are fondly remembered by all officers who had the pleasure of patrolling on them.

Another vehicle purchased at this time which proved valuable for police work were the Austin A90 Westminsters. Eight of these vehicles were first purchased on 24 November 1954. The specification was black in colour with a laminated windscreen and the luxury of synchronised speedometers.

OLD AND NEW POLICE STATIONS

The work of building and reorganisation of the City Force in the 1950's was initially concerned with the rectification of war damage to the building stock. In 1950 it was reported that the work of rebuilding at Victoria Law Courts and the Chief Constable's office was nearing completion. Work that had finished was at Steelhouse Lane, Bloomsbury Street and Duke Street Police Stations, together with the Central Lock-Up. Further work saw the conversion of Selly Oak Police Station into a Divisional Headquarters to replace Ladywood Police Station as 'B' Division Headquarters. At the same time, Kings Heath Police Station was also converted to make a headquarters for the 'F' Division for the proposed reorganisation of the Force into six divisions.

By the middle of 1951 the Watch Committee were seeking a replacement site for the police station in Bristol Street which had closed in 1946. It was agreed that a site at Spring Vale and Bristol Road should be acquired. At the same time that the Committee were informed that the building of the new police stations in Shard End and at Sheldon was to be postponed due to a post war national steel shortage. Building work at Shard End had been due to start on 1 March 1952 but was postponed until October. The work at Sheldon was virtually postponed sine die. In the event work started at the Sheldon site first.

Plans and developments were continued into 1953. However, in the early hours of Thursday, 26 March 1953 a fire broke out in the CID offices on the second floor of Newton Street Headquarters. The roof of the building was severely damaged. The cause of the fire was attributed to faulty telephone wires and the cost of damage was estimated at £1,730 8s 4d. One can almost hear the Chief Constable saying, 'Don't worry we've got the builders in anyway!' The first post-war police station to be built in the City was the police station at Quinton Road West, which was officially opened on 14 November 1953. As a point of historical interest, this was the first police station to be built without accommodation for single men. Notwithstanding this, a pressing need for accommodation for single policewomen existed. This was evident from the loss of the girls hostel in Newton Street which had been used as wartime quarters. A search for suitable premises resulted in the Watch Committee purchasing a large house at 106 Anderton Park, Moseley, known as Burgess House. This had previously been a nurses' hostel and was converted in the first instance to provide accommodation for nine policewomen and a resident housekeeper. By September 1954, the adjoining property at 108 Anderton Park Road had been bought, to provide further accommodation. It must also be remembered that 97 Anderton Park Road had been used as an annexe to Burgess House for some eight to nine policewomen. Burgess House remained in the possession of both Birmingham and the West Midlands Police for many years. In the latter time it was used as accommodation for girl cadets. During its time it was known by many names, the most respectable being, 'The Convent.'

The year of 1953 saw the beginning of the end for two of the oldest police stations in the City. On 6 May 1953 the Chief Constable informed the Watch Committee, that Home Office approval had been granted for the reconstruction of Moseley Street Police Station. This police station had been badly damaged during the air raids upon the City. However, once Government approval had been gained for the capital expenditure, the police authorities changed their tack and announced that the site of Moseley Street was, 'insufficient for modern needs', and the search was on for a new site. In 1954 the Watch Committee resorted to the Compulsory Purchase Order scheme to buy land in Bradford Street, close by, to build the new police station. It was anticipated that work would commence in 1955. The Committee reckoned without the continuing shortage of building steel and the work progressed very slowly. Bradford Street Police Station, (or to cognoscenti Moseley Street Police Station, due to the front door of the station opening onto that road), was opened on 1 April 1959, providing accommodation for 36 single officers and police flats for married officers, together with a modern spacious police building. Moseley Street Police Station, that long link with the past, was demolished.

The end of the road for the oldest police station in the City, came on 31 December 1953 when Duke Street Police Station 'shut up shop' for police business for the last time. It had served Birmingham Police and public for 101 years. In a report to the Watch Committee, dated 14 November 1953, the Chief Constable announced that the old station had come to the end of its serviceability. He stated that the building, first opened in 1852, was then beyond repair. The building was heavily shored up to prevent collapse and the top floor was unusable. The roof over the cells and ablutions, leaked continually and the whole was only fit for demolition. This included the police garage, which he described as inadequate. The Chief Constable announced that there was little need for a police station in the area. The figures for arrests had gone into decline in 1951, 201 persons were taken in custody then and by 1953 only 148. He pointed out that offenders arrested in Dale End, Gosta Green and Newtown, could equally be taken to Steelhouse Lane or Bridge Street West Police Stations. It was agreed that Duke Street and its area used to be an unruly population with large gangs that used to roam Summer Lane and Newtown Row. However, the wartime bombing had dispersed the elements who made up the gangs. The area had 'died' and therefore the police station could go with it. The Chief Constable proposed a new garage, stores and stables for 1956.

On 7 November 1955 the Traffic Department evacuated their accommodation at Duke Street and moved into temporary accommodation in the disused bus garage in Barford Street by the markets. It was not until three years later that they returned on 1 January 1959 to Duke Street. The new building provided a garage workshops, driving school accommodation, radio maintenance accommodation, a new police store and developed quarters for the mounted branch. By 15 July 1959, six months later, the roof of the new building moved, due to a heat wave. The police surveyor announced it would cause no problem. It was as though he had a premonition that within 20 years or so, it would no longer be a police building.

It was in the mid 1950's that the proposition for a new police station in the area of Walsall Road was first mooted. On 2 May 1953 the Watch Committee were informed that the population in this area was growing and had passed the 38,000 mark. Industries and factories had moved out of the City Centre area to what might now be called, 'Green field sites'. Importantly it was noticed that the nearest police station for the area was three miles away and the Walsall Road itself was now one of the main thoroughfare arteries of the City. So began a long period of discussion and procrastination over the building of Walsall Road Police Station.

Sheldon Police Station was opened on 19 July 1954 and its sister 'E' Division

Station, Shard End, was opened on Friday, 11 February 1955. The latter police station was opened by the Rt Hon Gwilym Lloyd George, maintaining a perhaps inappropriate link between the City Police and his father, from the Town Hall Disturbance in 1901 and the Police Station.

One of the last acquisitions in the 1950's was the compulsory purchase of The Manor at 1783 Pershore Road, Cotteridge to provide a new police station to replace Victoria Road Police Station at Stirchley. The Manor came with two acres of land and was seen as ideal for a police station and as a building site for police flats. In December of 1955 a Public Inquiry was held into the purchase of The Manor, by a Compulsory Purchase Order. The result was approval for the police, but in his Report for 1957 the Chief Constable, Mr Dodd, expresses regret that the police had to resort to the compulsory purchase as the other interested party was the Kings Norton Ex-Servicemen's Memorial Institute. Perhaps, with hindsight, he was right. The Manor was an exceptionally well appointed building, pleasing to the eye with a wealth of character and history. It is still held in high regard by all policemen who served there. Unfortunately the building was demolished, like so many others for road widening purposes, that have not as yet come to fruition, when the West Midlands Police took possession of Bournville Lane CEGB premises. The police flats that were built in Breedon Road remain, but are now used as singlemen's quarters. The police station in Victoria Road, Stirchley is also used for the same purposes.

Modernisation

Other developments that took place in the 1950's can perhaps be termed modernisation. One point of interest was the demise of the Birmingham Tramway System, which on 4 July 1953 saw the last tramcar leave the City at 10.30 am. This occasion was treated as a civic ceremony and Birmingham police were well represented on what people saw as a happy occasion. Alderman James Crump of the Watch Committee, drove the tram a short distance towards Erdington. This was a fitting tribute as he had driven the very first electric tram in Birmingham at the turn of the century.

School Crossing patrols were appointed in the City on 16 December 1953. The 'Lollipop' men and women, became a familiar sight in Birmingham, thereby relieving the police of this important task. However, it was not all good news, as on 18 November of the same year the free issue of coffee and sugar to men on night duty was discontinued by the Watch Committee at the insistence of the District Auditor.

The re-organisation of the Force took place on 1 July 1952, when the area was divided into six divisions. A fortunate result of this was a co-terminous boundary system with the City Fire Brigade. The breakdown of the Force establishment at this time is shows as:

	A	B	C	D	E	F
Superintendent & Chief Inspector	2	2	2	2	2	2
Inspector	9	8	12	12	12	12
Sergeant	26	25	36	36	36	36
PC	232	159	251	230	202	238
CID	13	7	18	15	14	17
Mounted	5	2	6	6	4	3
Policewomen		2	4	4	4	4

It is interesting to note that on 18 September 1957 the Chief Constable was urged by the Watch Committee to, 'Consider the question of the extent to which civilians might be employed on administration work, in order to release police officers for other duties.' In an age when the establishment shows a PC groundsman at the Richmond Hill Sports Ground, this is not at all surprising. On 8 June 1952 the policing of the City, between 2 pm and 10 pm on this Sunday, had been handed over to the Special Constabulary. With the exception of station staff and specialised departments the Specials were responsible for patrolling the City divisions. This annual occasion continued for many years and without doubt was a success. However, with the loss of those Specials who had been 'full time' during the war years, it is doubtful if this could happen now.

There were no major changes in the appearance of the City police uniform in the 1950's. In 1950, gaberdine raincoats were issued to the Force for use during the summer months for the first time. These coats had the effect of the demise of the police cape. In 1954 the Watch Committee baulked at the idea of the issue of leather gloves to the Force. An experimental issue of woollen gloves with leather palms and inside of the fingers, was tried and abandoned in favour of all leather.

Mention has already been made of the heat wave in 1959 and on 16 September of that year the Watch Committee were informed that constables had requested permission to patrol in shirt-sleeve order by removing their tunics. The largest voice against this move, came surprisingly from the Federation, who opposed it on the grounds that the officers were issued with a lightweight summer uniform anyway. But let us remember that the policewomen were allowed to remove their tunics whilst on patrol. The gentlemen in blue had to sweat it out until the 1960's.

6
'All Change'

If the recurring theme throughout the 50's was recruiting for the Birmingham City Police, then in the 60's it was the literal explosion of recorded crime throughout the City.

The simple fact of the matter was that by 1960 the crime rate had doubled from the 1955 figures. The increase in crime alone for 1960 and 1961, which was 6,963 offences, was the total for 1939. The happy period of the mid 1950's when Birmingham was less crime prone than Liverpool, Manchester, Hull and Coventry, was over for good. At the same time, the detection rate started to tumble. The battle against crime was on, but its roots were deep and complex.

With portentous foreboding the Chief Constable wrote in 1960, 'A serious crime problem exists in this City to which the forces of law and order have so far failed to provide an effective answer.' In searching for an answer to the problem, he points to the vast increase of the numbers of offences committed by persons on bail. The solution was held to be a Crown Court, instead of the Assize and Sessions Courts, as held in Liverpool and Manchester. Mr Dodd claimed that the law was held in utter contempt. By the following year he was blaming the increase on the materialistic age. The changes in society were recognised. The fall in the number of larcenies from automatic machines and meters was seized upon and used to show that slum clearance could prevent crime. The reason? In the older houses, electric and gas meters were housed in the cellars and basements and entry was soon gained through the coal grating. The new motorway and trunk roads were blamed for bringing travelling criminals, especially London thieves, to the City. The violence involved in the commission of offences was disturbing to the Chief Constable and the Watch Committee.

THE CRIME WAVE

The following examples show this change in readiness to use firearms and explosive.

> 'On the morning of 9 July, two men entered the Municipal Bank in Great Lister Street, one of whom produced a sawn-off shot-gun and threatened bank officials and customers, whilst the second man jumped over the counter and stole some money. Two members of the public who were in

the bank at the time, Mr T A Cheshire and Mrs D F Thorne, made a gallant attempt to detain them, but the bandits escaped.

In recognition of their brave conduct Her Majesty awarded the British Empire Medal (Civil Division) to Mr Cheshire and gave orders for Mrs Thorne to be Commended in the *London Gazette.*'

'During the afternoon of 9 November 1960, as a junior clerk was about to lock the doors of the Municipal Bank at Billesley, two men, who were both armed and wearing masks, pushed their way in. The manager of the bank, Mr J L E Edwards, finding himself faced with two armed men, immediately grappled with them. After a fierce struggle, during which the bank manager was struck on the back of the head and two shots were fired, the intruders retreated and ran out of the bank. Mr Edwards who followed them out, saw them leave in a motor car. This vehicle was subsequently seen by a motorist, Mr L G Baker and with his help the two men were traced. In recognition of his bravery, Her Majesty the Queen awarded Mr Edwards the George Medal, whilst Mr Baker was presented with an inscribed silver cigarette case by the Police Authority.'

'During the afternoon of 20 October 1961, three young men entered the post office in Whitmore Road, Small Heath. One of them pointed a gun at the postmaster, Mr P Reece, saying 'This is an armed hold-up.' In spite of this the postmaster rang the alarm bell, whereupon the young man fired the gun. Fortunately the postmaster was not injured and the three young men ran out of the post office after seizing a handful of notes from the counter. A butcher, Mr Geoffrey Deekes, who was in his shop nearby, saw the youths running, heard the alarm bell and noticed that one of the men held a bundle of notes. He immediately chased them and eventually detained one of them and took him back to the post office, in spite of a hostile crowd which had assembled not realising the nature of the crime the youth had committed. In recognition of the brave conduct of these two men the Postmaster General decided to make monetary awards.'

'When two men, who were in possession of explosives, attempted to break into Camp Hill Post Office, they were seen by Mrs Jessie Banner, who was waiting for a bus in Camp Hill. Mrs Banner ran to Bradford Street Police Station, which is about a quarter-of-a-mile away, told the Police and the men were subsequently arrested. Mrs Banner was congratulated on her presence of mind by the Learned Judge at the trial and was subsequently presented with a wristlet watch by the Police Authority in recognition of her help.'

By 1962 the crime rate was double that of 1952 and four times that of 1939, the crime detection rate continued to fall and stood at 35%. Blaming greed the Chief Constable asserted that, 'The luxuries of yesterday are now the necessities of today, causing people to steal to obtain without working or considering the feelings of others. This resembles the slogan in Brixton in 1981 that, 'Looting takes the waiting out of wanting.' Trying to find a scientific explanation of the sociological cause for the rise, it was pointed out that 45% of all those proceeded against had been born during the war or immediately post war. They had suffered at a time of general moral decline from shortage of food and essential commodities. The family units were broken up by fathers going on active service, mothers working and children being evacuated. In September of 1962 in an attempt to go on the offensive against crime, the local television company, ATV, offered the Midlands Police Forces a five minute slot at 8.55 pm on Fridays. Hence, *Police 5*. The Police were able to tell the public at large of the crimes in their area. So began the long contact between Birmingham Police and Mr Shaw Taylor the presenter. The results from the programme were very encouraging and *Police 5* has been of such benefit that in 1987 the programme celebrated its Silver Jubilee.

In 1963 the Force was able to record that crime in the City was still increasing but for the first time the rate of increase was slowing. By 1965 the rate of increase had gone into decline, so that in the following year the increase was the lowest since 1955. A peak was reached in the near vertical graph of increase and in 1967 the first reduction in numbers had been reached. Unfortunately this only provided a breathing space as from then onwards the number of crimes in Birmingham continued their upward, ever upward growth. The detection rate of those offences had taken on an inverse ratio and has started to fall away from 36% in 1963 to a regular average of 34%.

The crime wave of the 1960's placed a severe strain on the already depleted City of Birmingham Police. A high crime rate was to be expected in a prosperous City such as Birmingham. Expressed simply there was more property lying around waiting to be stolen. In a 'car town' the vast increase in thefts from and of, motor vehicles was inevitable. People had more money to spend on entertainment and holidays and were therefore absent from their homes for longer. In 1963 the Chief Constable pointed out that one half of all crimes were larcenies of pedal cycles, unattended motor vehicles, in houses of property valued at less than £5 and other simple larcenies. To his obvious annoyance they were all preventable with a little more care by the owners. Other demands were placed on Police such as the escape in 1964 by Charles Frederick Wilson, one of the 'Great Train Robbers' from Winson Green Prison. The abduction and murder of Margaret Reynolds from her home in Aston by Raymond Morris in 1967, led to 20 officers being seconded to Walsall Police and the interviewing of 5,000 local owners of Austin motor cars. A

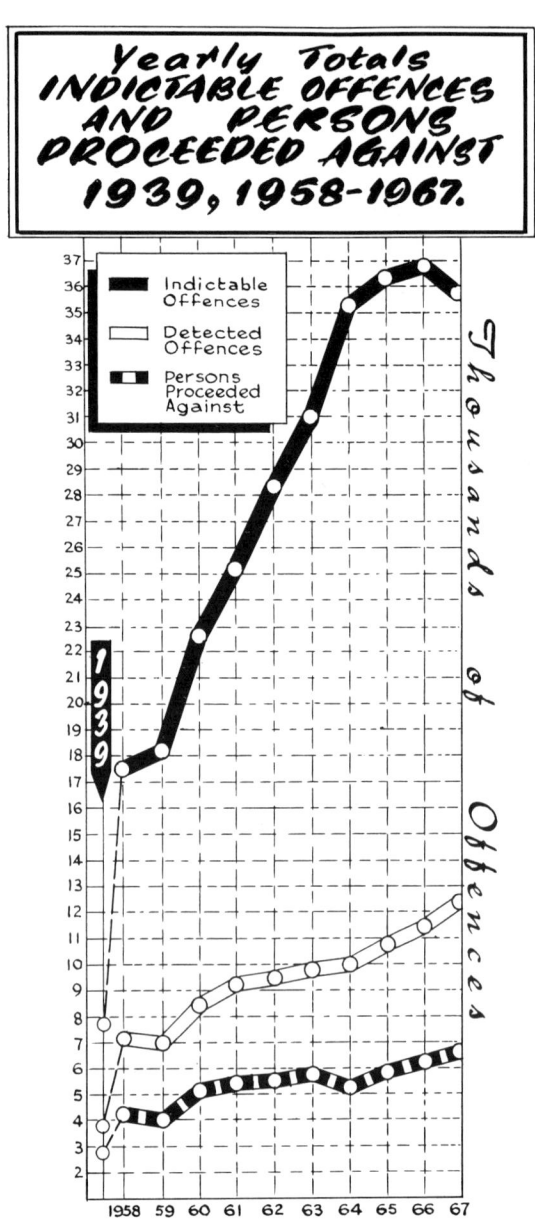

Fig. XIII — Graph of the near vertical record of crime in Birmingham in the 60's

further 40 officers were engaged in the murder enquiry of Sylvia Whitehouse in the same year. This enquiry also crossed force boundaries as she had accepted a lift from a stranger on the Coventry Road, Small Heath and was later found dead in Elmdon just over the boundary in Warwickshire. Difficulties were also compounded by the large number of senior CID officers tied up with the investigation of complaints against the Police.

Tackling the Crime Problem

The Birmingham Police and especially its leadership did not take the crime wave lying down, but went on to the attack. In the late 1960's, Mr Michael V Argyle MC QC was the Learned Recorder of the City of Birmingham. It is tradition, and probably only apocryphal, that he announced that any person appearing before the Assize Court for burglary in Birmingham would be sent to prison. The tradition is that the number of burglaries fell. The reality is that these offences continued to grow until late in 1967 when the introduction of panda cars and personal radios made an impact on such crime. Help for the City Force had to come from within and this was emphasised time and again by the Home Office refusing requests of the Watch Committee to pay an under-manning allowance to Birmingham Police.

A Night Crime Patrol was organised experimentally in October 1961 and became known as 'Cappers Commandos.' The patrols were led by an inspector assisted by three sergeants with 27 police constables. The brief of the patrols was to pay particular attention under the direction of the detective chief superintendent to areas of high crime. In effect radio shops, tobacconists, jewellers and wines and spirits premises were watched. The results were said to be effective. However in the case of the night crime patrol, their activities were suspended in the summer months due to the manpower requirements of annual leave and the consequent fall in crime during the days of longer daylight. But the pressing problem of crime in Birmingham continued and as a further experiment a Special Crime and Accident Prevention Squad was formed. Notwithstanding that the reason for the suspension of night crime patrols was manpower problems, the new squad was made up of an inspector, two sergeants, 24 police constables and two policewomen. Members of the squad alternated fortnightly between crime patrol and accident prevention.

In modern parlance the squad would be known as a Theft from Vehicle Squad and this was their major remit. The Accident Prevention Squad work consisted on the enforcement of Road Traffic legislation, Police presence at black spots and advice to motorists. This had a dramatic effect on the number of

F

accidents in an area chosen for patrol, but the effect was lost when the patrol moved on.

At the turn of the decade in 1960 the strength of the Criminal Investigation Department stood at 180 officers. In 1964 it had risen to 230. However, senior officers were quick to point out, that at that time, reported crime had increased three times since 1953 and the establishment of the CID had only increased by 55%. The Home Office recommended case load of 150 cases per detective, was used initially in the 1960's by the Force to beat the drum of undermanning. When the case load reached over 100% of that figure and the detection rate continued to slump, without any acknowledgement of the special problems in Birmingham, the futility of the argument was acknowledged and allowed to wither away. The answer was again found in the formation of squads.

A Regional Crime Squad was established in 1956, with detective officers from Staffordshire, Warwickshire and Worcestershire, working with Birmingham officers under the supervision of the officer in charge of the Birmingham Crime Squad. Both squads had a noticeable effect on the detection of the more serious offences. In April 1965, the No 4 Regional Crime Squad was formed and given offices in Newton Street, which were converted flats above the Coroner's Court.

March 1966 saw the formation of a small specialist Drug Squad. Police efforts were expanded on the misuse of cannabis and according to the Chief Constable, 'addiction to heroin and cocaine'. The squad was based at Bridge Street West Police Station and its objectives were stated to be primarily to identify drug addicts and their associates, to discover the sources of supply and to reduce or contain the spread of addiction. This was abbreviated to prosecuting 'persons who have been peddling drugs.' The Drug Squad were successful in Birmingham, but in an age when the editor of *The Times* claimed that the prosecution of Mr Mick Jagger for possession of controlled drugs was, 'Breaking a butterfly on the wheel,' they had little overall effect in stemming the tide of drug misuse.

In 1964 to cope with the problem of increased numbers of motor vehicles taken without consent, a Central Index of Stolen Motor Vehicles was introduced. The problem of vehicle thefts from the motor works and showrooms caused the formation of a Specialist Stolen Car Squad in 1966.

Every effort was made to use the available manpower to best advantage. On 3 April 1967 an antecedents section was formed to relieve numerous detective officers from spending long hours in Court waiting to give details of a prisoner's background.

On 3 November 1969 a Criminal Intelligence Section was set up and in that same month a revised method of crime reporting was introduced. The laborious Divisional Crime Register was abolished and in its place, revised part prepared forms were introduced. These revised forms saved time and effort and avoided passing papers in a bureaucratic paper chase between departments. Even though it is claimed that the new system broke the paper chain, it is worth noting that 'crimes' were still sent up the hierarchy to HQ where persons were arrested, if they were of special interest, for murder/manslaughter, breaking offences, robberies and offences against the person. In November of that year a system whereby minor crime was investigated by uniformed officers was introduced. The wheel had been re-invented. The reasons put forward for this were to raise the interest of uniformed officers, increase their responsibility and 'afford some relief to the detective branch.'

Police orders for 10 November 1967, suggest that the ideal forms of crime for such investigation were theft of pedal cycles and stealing from unattended motor cars. However, it is worth pointing out that the uniformed officers were not allowed to retain any papers concerning the investigation. These were to remain in the CID office. With the benefit of hindsight, it seems a strange way to increase the responsibility of uniformed officers. Was the status quo threatened?

An important change was made on 12 June 1967 which affected control and management of the Criminal Investigation Department. Up until this date, even though detective officers were posted to divisions, they were still members of 'R' Division, the Headquarters Division, for the purposes of administration and control. Without doubt this led to elitism and difficulties over supervision. From the date of the decentralisation, detectives on division came under the control of divisional chief superintendents and were allocated a divisional number in order that, 'Their identity with their division be emphasised.' At the same time, six officers were trained in scenes of crime investigation work for posting to divisions for the same purposes.

It must be mentioned at this point, that popular local feeling attributed the escalation of crime to 'Coloured immigrants and immigration'. The Chief Constable, Mr Dodd, announced in 1958 that, 'The general standard of conduct of the very large coloured population in the City, is highly commendable and causes the Police very little concern.' In fact Mr Dodd, did point the finger at those responsible when he wrote, '. . . . a high proportion of those arrested for crime, particularly the more serious offences, are persons who have come to Birmingham from outside to find work.' Ever the diplomat, the Chief Constable did not point his finger north.

Austin Mini Cooper 'S' on Traffic Patrol in 1968

Traffic Congestion and City Centre Reconstruction

To compound the difficulties of the Birmingham Police, in their fight to stem the rising number of crimes, the early 1960's saw the vast redevelopment of the City centre. What Hitler and the Luftwaffe had failed to do, it is said the Lord Mayor and Aldermen of the City Council did, by the destruction of the old town. Included in this was the re-organisation of the road system. It was estimated in 1960 that Birmingham had over 1,000 miles of roads and being the home of the motor car and cycle industry, it had the number of vehicles to match. The first section of a new inner ring road, the Smallbrook Ringway, was opened on the 11 March 1960 by the Transport Minister, Mr Ernest Marples. The building of these financially and socially expensive roads, provided Birmingham with freer flowing traffic into the City Centre than any other comparable UK city.

In an effort to defeat obstruction and congestion at the junction of Camp Hill and Coventry Road, a temporary car bridge was erected in the space of thirty hours by J J Gallagher & Co. This temporary bridge, remained in use until the weekend of 25 March 1989, when it was dismantled in fewer hours. A simple, cheap idea that proved invaluable. The main construction, carried on with the building of the Birchfield underpass, the Six Ways, Aston underpass, the Hockley fly-over and the Holloway underpass. At the same time Masshouse Circus, Colmore Circus and Priory Circus were all built, much to the amusement of the locals, who are reported in the *Birmingham Evening Mail* of the time, asking when the clowns who had devised these circuses were coming to use them! The work of the traffic patrols and uniform Police, to control vehicles and frayed tempers in the City centre, was instrumental in speeding the work along. The reconstruction of the railway bridge in Navigation Street and Pinfold Street, as part of the redevelopment of New Street Station, virtually closed one half of the City centre to the other. At the same time, the opening of the new Central Omnibus Terminus in the Bull Ring Centre, which soon became a grim, smoke filled cavern, had a marked effect on traffic due to the diversion of bus routes.

All these constructions were hampered by roads blocked by parked vehicles and especially 'double banked' cars. A new multi-storey car park had been opened in the Bull Ring Centre in 1960 and followed by another at St Martins a short while later, but motorists still insisted on parking as close as possible to the City centre. They ignored these car parks and those on the edge of the City centre itself.

Easing the Congestion

The Police response to the overall problem was initially to form a Central Area Traffic Squad in 1960, to ensure the free flow of traffic. In 1961 a Land Rover fitted with moving equipment, was taken into use under the Removal of Vehicles Regulations. Any vehicles causing an obstruction, were removed to a temporary pound in Masshouse Lane. The first year of operation saw 822 vehicles towed away. The following year 1962, saw the figure jump to 3,884. The increase was due to the fact that in 1962, the Parking Places and Controlled Parking Zones (Birmingham) (No 1) Order 1962 came into effect, creating 856 metered parking areas. The Home Secretary applied the use of Fixed Penalty Notices to the City and the Watch Committee gave authority for the employment of traffic wardens.

On Tuesday, 4th June 1962 the Parking Places etc. Regulations, came into force and 37 traffic wardens patrolled the City centre streets. By the end of the year, there were 49 and plans were made to recruit female wardens. Initially the wardens were housed at Digbeth Police Station and later moved as accommodation became available to Newton Street. The Corps was supervised by an inspector and two police sergeants of the Traffic and Communications Branch and before taking up their duties, they received a one week course of instruction at the Police School. By the end of 1965 the strength of the Traffic Warden Corps was 40 male and 31 female wardens. Turnover was high, as during that year 31 wardens had resigned. Nevertheless, the benefits of the Corps were soon realised by the City Police, who were now freed from being continually involved with parked vehicles.

The Traffic and Communications Department, of course, had the main responsibility for the control and free flow of vehicular traffic, in and out of the City. In 1960 the vehicle fleet stood at 207, being made up of 81 motor cars, 19 vans, 18 dual purpose vehicles, one lorry, one personnel carrier, 36 motor cycles, 50 lightweight motor cycles and one motor cycle combination. With the expansion of the City boundary outwards and the building of large housing estates on the periphery, the vehicle fleet also expanded until by 1966 it stood at 266. Included amongst these was an Austin Mini Cooper 'S' for Traffic Patrol work. This is another vehicle upon which strong men grow misty eyed when asked for their recollections, most of which cannot be printed for legal reasons.

At the same time that the Land Rover was bought in 1961 for the removal of obstructing cars, a further five were bought for patrol purposes on the outer divisions. In the vast new impersonal housing estates, it was believed that contact could be re-established with the public, by parking up the vehicle and waiting to be approached. In all likelihood, the only other voices the crews heard, was that of the Information Room on the radio. Other innovations of the time were the use of disc recording machines in the Information Room for recording incidents. The first 'Peta', Portable Electronic Traffic Analyser, was bought in 1962, followed shortly by another two such machines. In simple terms the 'Peta' were 'radar traps' for speeding offences.

The peak manpower strength of traffic patrols in this period was reached in 1966, with four inspectors, six sergeants, 41 constables, including 21 on attachment to the branch for motor car duty and 43 constables on motor cycle patrols. With the introduction of unit beat policing in 1967, the strength of the patrols was decreased and the vehicle crews reduced to one officer.

Obviously the traffic congestion and increase in the number of cars on the City roads in the 1960's, led to a great increase in accidents. Sadly the majority of these accidents were to pedestrians, and in the course of such things, to children and the aged. Road safety became a major concern for the City Police. Throughout this period there were twelve road safety officers, co-ordinated by an inspector at Headquarters, on the six divisions. This allowed for a sergeant and a constable on each division, to visit schools and old people's clubs and other groups to talk about road safety. Who can fail to remember those visits by the Police to school? The chance to drive a pedal car around the school hall with mock pedestrian crossings and lamps, was something to look forward to. Who can also remember the letter arriving at home to advise your parents, that your bicycle had been tested at school and the brakes were found to be inefficient?

Hands up all the swots who received a 'Safe Cycling' lapel badge for passing the cycle proficiency test? Who can recite the names of the characters in the 'Tufty Club'? The officers engaged on road safety duties did valuable work for the safety of Birmingham children on the roads. However, the instruction was not all one way. The 'Be a Better Driver' campaign, allowed for members of the motoring public, to attend the Police driving school at Duke Street. They received four lectures of two hours duration each and demand was so great, that the courses were fully booked for months in advance and continued until the end of the Force.

Obviously with the increase in the number of Police vehicles and Police drivers, the number of accidents involving them also increased. Unfortunately in 1964, two traffic patrol motor cyclists were killed. In that year, there were 69 Police accidents of which 39 involved Police motor cycles. By comparison, after the introduction in 1968 of unit beat policing, there were 225 Police accidents, involving 132 panda cars and 13 motor cycles. This state of affairs continues. If the figures for 1971 are considered though, when the total fleet mileage was seven million miles, each vehicle had on average an accident every

27,559 miles. Some would argue that rather than pointing to bad driving, this emphasises the relative safety of Birmingham's Police drivers.

In an effort to cope with the amount of time spent by patrol officers investigating accidents by post hoc enquiries, an experiment was held on one division with an Accident Enquiry Squad in March 1964. The experimental squad, consisted of a sergeant and four constables, who investigated accidents where allegations of dangerous or careless driving were made. The results were better than hoped for with greater patrol time for beat officers and a reduction in the time taken to complete an enquiry. In October, Accident Enquiry Squads were formed on all divisions. The search for effectiveness in the use of Police time, was necessitated by the demands of the high crime rate, increased traffic problems and the continuing failure of recruitment.

THE CONTINUING SEARCH FOR RECRUITS

The worst recruiting figures were recorded in 1960, when 119 officers resigned and only 110 joined. The authorised establishment at the start of the decade was 2,067 men and 107 women, the actual strength was recorded as 1,812 men and 69 women, making a total shortfall 292 Police officers. The darkest day for strength of the City Police was in 1965, when the establishment was short of 619 Police officers, just under a quarter of the number officially recognised to Birmingham Police. Great hopes were placed by the Chief Constable and the Watch Committee on the increase in pay scales, awarded by the Interim Report of the Royal Commission in 1961. There was an improvement in recruiting to the City of Birmingham Police, but the most beneficial result was a decrease in wastage through premature resignations.

The Force continued its usual efforts to recruit through advertising in local and national newspapers and the journals of all branches of HM forces. An advertisement placed in a match programme for Birmingham City Football Club in 1961 reads:

THE POLICE SERVICE IN THE MIDLANDS

Offers you a career with security for the future and opportunities for promotion.

Constables pay: £150 to £695 pa 44 hours week — generous leave and allowances — pension after 25 years.

Applicants are required to be over 5'8" in height and under 30 years of age.

APPLY TO: The Hon Secretary, No 4 District Recruiting Board, Police Headquarters, Birmingham 4

By 1962 the mobile Police Station was sited throughout the City and used for recruiting. An 'At Home' event was staged at Police Headquarters, to introduce interested persons to Police duty. On the first occasion, over 100 people attended, the majority being parents of potential recruits. Advertisements were also placed in local newspapers of areas where unemployment was high. All these efforts had little effect. The year 1963 records the lowest proportion of married men amongst recruits since the end of the war, the average age of recruits fell to 21 years and for the first time, recruiting amongst women also fell. To make matters worse wastage also began to rise. By 1964 applications to join the City Police fell by an outstanding 28% and the actual gain of officers over the year, amounted to only 24. Regular surveys were made amongst men resigning. In this year, 13 stated they were leaving for better prospects, 12 for domestic reasons, 11 because of dislike of shift work and four for other reasons. By 1966, 31 officers were resigning for better prospects.

On a currently topical matter, Councillor Collier asked the Watch Committee on 15 July 1964, whether it was the policy of the Watch Committee and the Chief Constable, to recruit coloured persons into the Force, if they were of the required standard. The Chief Constable stated that no coloured person had yet been enrolled. He did point out however, that the first would have to be of an exceptionally high standard, to overcome the inumerable difficulties and prejudice which he could expect from the public. The first such recruit was PC Ralph Ramadha, who joined the City Police in 1967. The *Birmingham Mail* on 2 January 1967 reports that, 'Birmingham's first West Indian Policeman went out on patrol today. One of the first duties of 28 year old Police Constable Ralph Ramadha was to give advice. PC Ramadha, married with a two year old daughter, is only the second coloured policemen to be appointed in Britain. Born in Trinidad, of Indian descent, he came to Britain in 1961.' Mr Ramadha was eventually appointed Sergeant, and resigned to return to the West Indies in 1977.

As a new departure, and modern venture, recruiting was carried out between 2 January 1965 and 27 March 1965, by use of commercial television and follow up advertisements in newspapers. A 60 second spot was purchased for each Saturday afternoon and on three Sunday afternoons throughout the period. In 1966 two 60 second spots were broadcast each Saturday afternoon, between 2.30 pm and 3.30 pm for a three month period. At last professional advertising and the modern medium were used. What better time could there be to catch the attention of fit young men, than when sports programmes were being watched? The results were better than the Chief Constable had hoped for. He reported in 1965 that the figures for applications were the best since 1952 even against a background of low unemployment and increased industrial wages. Even better, in 1966 there was a 23.8% increase over the 1965 figures for applications. From 20 to 24 April 1965, a recruiting campaign for Birmingham Police was undertaken in Northern Ireland. The Chief Constable reported to the Watch Committee that although the response had been excellent, he held little hope for the result of any recruitment. He was proved right. Out of 12 recruits, four resigned at short notice and returned home. Recruiting was definitely on the up, but ominously wastage was increasing. The Force could catch them, but could not hold them.

At last in 1967 the corner appeared to have been turned. What was correctly attributed to the declining economic situation, was a further 44% increase in applications. No less than 269 new recruits were enrolled, half as many again as the previous year. Restrictions on the eyesight standard of recruits were lifted and applicants who wore spectacles were interviewed. The introduction of a 42 hour week for officers, must also have had an effect on the interest shown. The future looked good.

The axe fell in 1968. In a broadcast to the Nation on 19 November 1967, the Prime Minister, Harold Wilson, announced his plans to tackle the economic problems, by devaluing the currency. He said, 'That doesn't mean, of course, that the pound here in Britain — in your pocket or purse or in your bank — has been devalued,' but it did and what it also meant in terms of public expenditure, was fewer policemen on the streets of Birmingham. Restrictions were placed on recruitment. Civilianisation was brought to a standstill and until 30 January 1970, only 170 officers were recruited over the two year period. Unlike the wartime restrictions though, resignations continued which saw 47 officers resigning in 1969 for better prospects, a trend that continued until the Edmund Davies pay award in 1979-1980.

Birmingham's Police Cadets

In real terms, recruiting showed little improvement over the state of affairs in 1950. At the time the major source of recruits, the backbone of the Birmingham City Police, came from its Police Cadet Corps. In a nine page booklet, produced for recruiting purposes in the 1960's, six pages are given to the recruitment of cadets. Like the Jesuits the City Police knew they had to recruit them young. The establishment of the Cadet Corps in 1960, stood at 101 boys and for the first time 10 girls. The starting pay was £260 at 16 years and increased to £325 at 18 years. A candidate with 'O' Level GCE passes in English, mathematics or a science or foreign language and any other pass, received an extra £30 per annum.

The training of Birmingham Police Cadets is said to have been directed towards physical and educational development. An initial four week training course taught the cadets elementary Police procedure, foot drill and an insight into Police practice and procedure. For the purposes of training, the cadet corps was divided into squads, named after former Chief Constables; Glossop, Bond, Farndale and Rafter. Cadets were also enrolled at Matthew Boulton Technical College for the purposes of further education. In 1964 Birmingham Police Cadets gained 23 'A' Level and 14 'O' Level passes at GCE Level. Once the cadet had finished his or her initial training, they were posted to a department or division for four monthly periods. This became the part of their training where most ex-cadets claim they learnt only to make numerous cups of tea. But credit where credit is due, it must be recorded that it was very good tea. However, this system of training was developed in the mid-sixties, so that police cadets continued full time educational studies at Matthew Boulton College until before their induction to the force, when they would be attached to division and departments for training. Cadets were also encouraged to join the Duke of Edinburgh Award Scheme and a regular award of Gold and Silver medals was made to Birmingham Cadets.

With the exemption of police cadets from National Service in 1958, other forms of character forming training were sought. The Water Committee of the City Council were most generous to the Force and gave a site at the foot of the watershed at Elan Valley for an Outward Bound School. Three disused army wooden buildings were obtained and erected by cadets under supervision. During each year, boy cadets attended the cadet camp at Elan Valley for outward bound training. The purpose of the camp was declared as being that, 'The camp is no holiday for the boys. Strict discipline is enforced and a high degree of personal and camp hygiene is demanded. While the rigorous nature of the work and treks in all kinds of weather, is directed at achieving a high standard of physical fitness, self confidence and the ability to meet and overcome difficulties, is also taught.' The girl cadets of this period did not attend the Elan Valley camp, but over the years attended the Ashburton Outward Bound School in Devon, Bisham Abbey in Buckinghamshire, the Birmingham City Education Department's Ogwen Cottage in North Wales and finally established themselves at Rhowniar Outward Bound School in Merionethshire.

The girl cadets were treated differently from the boys in other ways too. They could not at first join the regular force, until they were 20 years of age. This was changed by Police Regulations in 1966, that allowed girl cadets to transfer at

19 years. The opposite case had existed for the boys, who until 1961 had been able to transfer at 18 years 9 months, this was raised to 19 years. Throughout the history of Birmingham Police Cadets, the girls were always better qualified educationally than the boy cadets.

The cadet corps was also always involved in extra-curricular activities other than sport. In 1962, 13 cadets and three constables undertook an expedition to Iceland, to assist in a geographical survey. In the same year, 38 cadets undertook social work amongst refugees in Austria and Germany. Numerous cadets worked in Kibbutz farms in Israel, under the 'Bridge in Britain' Scheme. The story of the training sergeant who accepted a reverse charges call from a cadet, who wanted his mother to know he was going to be late still circulates. When asked where he was, the cadet replied, 'Ben Gurion Airport', the sergeant dropped the phone as though there were 50,000 volts flowing through it.

In 1961, police cadets formed 30% of the intake of recruits to the City Police and any falling off in enlistment was seen as a danger for the Force. In that year the establishment of girls was increased to 15. They were seen as a good investment, obviously because of their better qualifications, but also because the wastage was lower than expected. Four years after the girls had first been allowed to join in 1959, 51 girls had enrolled as cadets and 25 were still serving as policewomen. The Corps establishment was set at 150 in 1965 and by the end of the year, there were only 127 members of the cadets. This was the beginning of the start of recruiting slippage for the cadets. The Chief Constable warns of the problem in his Annual Report, pointing especially to the dearth of grammar school recruits. In 1967 he states that main source of recruiting for the cadet corps was secondary modern schools: (Oh, the shame of it!) In 1968 the cadet corps was made up of only 79 boys and 21 girls. The problems of recruiting was now across the board for the Birmingham Police. In the previously mentioned recruiting pamphlet, the Chief Constable exhorts, young men to apply to him, 'IF YOU ARE SEEKING A CAREER WHICH DEMANDS TENACITY OF PURPOSE, STRONG CHARACTER, MORAL COURAGE AND SECURITY'. The trouble was, in the swinging sixties, it was not the fashion to do so.

Introduction of Personal Radios

The Chief Constable had to make do with the best he had got and that called for revolutionary ideas and equipment. With fewer men to patrol the streets and police greater problems the first answer was found in the use of radios. The

Police Constables' uniform and equipment, 1970

Birmingham Evening Mail for 5 October 1964, announced 'The first step in revolutionising the work of policemen patrolling their beats, is being taken tonight, when several experimental two way radios are being issued to them.' This was an experiment carried out on the 'E' Division, with a base station at Coventry Road Police Station. The radios themselves were a pack set, carried by shoulder strap. The microphone also acted as the earpiece and the set could be used as a loud hailer. The cost of the radios was £100 each. They were referred to by the Mail as the 'policeman's long distance whistle.' Due to their bulk, these radios were not taken into general use and the Force had to wait for the introduction of unit beat policing for coverage by Pye two handset pocket radios.

The changeover in communication systems is perhaps emphasised by the attack upon Police Constable Law. This occurred at 10.35 pm Wednesday, 12 January 1966 when Police Constable B 260 Gordon Law was stabbed in the back when he discovered youths stealing lead from the roof at a school in St Lukes Road, Balsall Heath. The constable was immediately paralysed and fell to the ground. Before he lost consciousness he blew his whistle. A man living in a house some 70 yards away heard the whistle blast and sensed something was amiss. He sent his nine year old son to investigate. The boy knew the locality well and very soon found PC Law. He at once told his father and then ran to Belgrave Road Police Station and informed the officer on duty of what he had discovered. When other police officers got to the scene, they acted correctly and left the knife in PC Law's back and had him conveyed to the Accident Hospital where his life was saved. A Daniel William Roberts, aged 19 years, was later arrested and charged with attempting to murder the officer. He was sentenced to ten years imprisonment.

This was probably the last time that a Police whistle was used to summon assistance in Birmingham, because during that year, personal radios were taken into use. Police whistles were withdrawn in Birmingham in 1976.

Unit Beat Policing: Pandas

The concept of unit beat policing was developed nationally to combat the shortage of police officers by increasing reliance on Police mobility. The whole key to the introduction of this form of policing was the new Pye Pocketphone UHF radios. The system was developed by Police forces, and the City of Birmingham Police in conjunction with the Home Office Research and Planning Branch. In the 1967 publication, *Police Manpower, Equipment and Efficiency*, the aims of unit beat policing are said to be the provision of a more efficient system of policing, closer contact between Police and public, better flow of information to the centre, a more worthwhile and interesting job for the ordinary policeman than traditional beat working and a significant saving in the demand for more Police manpower.

Before the system was applied in Birmingham, it was tried experimentally on the Belgrave Road Sub-Division from the 10 October 1966 and subsequently on the Erdington Sub-Division. The sub-divisions were divided into areas for patrol purposes. To each of these areas police constables were posted to work the area permanently, known as either the permanent beat officer or the resident beat officer. This officer's duty was to familiarise himself with the area and gain the confidence and respect of the residents. The officer was allowed to vary the hours of his duties as circumstances required and could wear uniform or plain clothes. A mobile car patrol which became known as the Panda car, was superimposed on several of the foot beat areas. The mobiles were responsible for 24 hour Police coverage. Each of the Panda areas had a detective officer allocated to it. All three were issued with personal radios and were in contact via the radio, not only with the control, but also the sub-divisional collator, through whom they were obliged to pass any information they obtained or witnessed during their tour of duty. The experiment was claimed as a success and during the same period, 13 further sub-divisions were equipped with radio. The final four sub-divisions were allocated radios and on Monday, 3 July 1967, unit beat policing was implemented throughout the City.

The plans for the introduction of the scheme were published in Police Orders of 16 June 1967. The order claims, 'The policing of the whole of a large City such as Birmingham, will be the first of its kind and the comprehensive planning together with the lessons of its application will undoubtedly be of great value elsewhere.' On the City centre 'A' Division the scheme was adapted to create more foot patrol areas. At the same time an experiment was initiated on the division with the use of closed circuit television. Monitors were placed at Steelhouse Lane Police Station and the cameras fitted at selected points. A cautionary note was made at the time, that to be cost effective one constable would have to monitor three screens. There is no mention of any disquiet being registered as to this form of surveillance of the public.

The vehicles chosen for the first Panda cars were Austin A40's, a mass produced family saloon car from Longbridge. The cars were painted in distinctive blue and white colour, marked 'Police' and fitted with a blue beacon and two tone horns to aid movement through the congested streets. The horns were later removed. The *Birmingham Mail* reports that this was done as an economy measure, the horns being given to the Fire Brigade. The Police

Federation protested about this move and its seems that the probable reason for the removal, was that the horns were believed to contribute to the high number of accidents involving Panda cars at speed. At the same time, black A40's were provided for sub-divisional chief inspectors, together with a differently coloured A40 for the CID on each sub-division. The breakdown of the allocation of vehicles can be shown from the 'D' Division where the ratio was;

Aston Sub-division — 7 cars
Erdington Sub-division — 5 cars
Canterbury Road Sub-division — 6 cars
Supervisory vehicles — 3 cars
Spare vehicles — 3 cars

When the scheme was fully implemented it called for an increase in the fleet of 129 vehicles.

Radios were also issued on the same basis, where for example 'D' Division received 81 sets. The introduction of the sets on such a large scale, allowed for the withdrawal of the Police pillars. A further communications innovation at the time was the issue of a telephone credit card. This allowed an officer to make a phone call by telephoning the operator quoting the card number and then being connected to an ex-directory telephone in the collator's office. The purpose was to save on 'reverse charges' calls or the expenditure of the officer's own money. Recording equipment was also fitted to the collator's telephone in order that information could be passed to him or reports dictated for typing.

Praise and Criticism of Pandas

The unit beat patrol system was a complete sea change for policing in Birmingham. Great successes were claimed for the 'Pandas'. An article in *TV World* on 25 April 1968 starts, 'Crime is a gamble. And ever since Cain murdered Abel the odds have been in favour of the criminal...but in Birmingham, the odds in favour of the criminal are shortening, slowly but significantly.' Dramatic stuff! The article claims a 14.5% drop in breaking/burglary offences and a reduction of response time for 999 calls to around 90 seconds. It continues to eulogise on the benefits of unit beat policing and especially the integration of the three man ideal, beat PC, Panda PC and CID man. A Detective Constable Colin Walker of Belgrave Road CID, is quoted as saying, 'When I joined the Force more than 11 years ago, I had the impression that the CID man, although at the same rank, was a little in front. Now the jealousy between the uniformed man and the CID man has disappeared. We work together on a friendly basis and as a team.' It added, 'Panda Driver John

Booton signified agreement with his team mate. So did Resident Beat Officer Bernard Musson.'

It was an ideal form of Police patrol. However, in Birmingham as elsewhere, it was fatally flawed and doomed to metamorphose into a corrupted form. The major flaw was the lack of manpower to set up the complete system and maintain it in the face of increasing demand from the public. The Panda car became a response and message carrying machine with little time for anything else. The Police Order requiring Panda cars to park up and the driver to patrol the area on foot at quiet times, became more honoured in the breach than in the observance.

The first of many rumblings against the new system can be found in a report in the *Birmingham Post* on 11 December 1968. It states, 'A Birmingham residents' association is to call for the reintroduction of foot patrols instead of Panda cars to combat prostitution. Councillor Charles Collet of the Anderton Park Residents' Association said last night, 'A Panda car driver has no chance of seeing what happens on the pavements or gardens'. He said a letter would be sent to the Chief Constable calling for the reintroduction of foot patrols in the Anderton Park area.' The debate between speed of response and contact with the public has continued ever since.

Robert Reiner, in his work, *The Politics of the Police* claims the idealistic nature of unit beat policing failed because of 'The unintended consequences of the ability of rank-and-file culture to frustrate managerial purposes. The constables' action packed perspective on policing was accentuated by the technology of fast cars, sirens and flashing blue lights. What was intended as professionalisation, ended up as the politicisation of relations with the public.' Reiner says the Police image changed from Dixon to Barlow, but perhaps his choice of a dramatic metaphor suggests that the reality is actually more complex than this.

The Changing Role of Policewomen

The role of policewomen also changed throughout the City of Birmingham Police in the 1960's. The establishment in 1960 stood at 107 officers. The actual strength was only 69. The difficulties of recruiting were also felt in this area of policing. The rank structure consisted of one superintendent, one chief inspector, three inspectors, 14 sergeants and 88 policewomen constables. It was a far cry from 1917 when the two Lock-Up matrons first patrolled the streets. The deficiency in numbers continued throughout the decade. This was so much so that in 1961, the Chief Constable was moved to write, 'I am convinced

The ubiquitous 'Panda' car at Tally Ho! in 1970

that much greater use could be made of the services of policewomen if they were available in sufficient number.' In 1965 the establishment had increased to 145 and the actual strength stood at 105.

The work of the Policewomen's Department in the early 1960's remained in the same areas. Their major preoccupation was control of traffic and especially road crossings, together with taking statements. In 1961 the department took Care and Protection Orders against 86 girls who frequented the City centre. It was the accepted fashion that such girls were responsible for encouraging young males to commit crime. The problem continued in 1962 with the girls, aged 12-15 years, being blamed for possessing 'restlessness and wanderlust.' By 1965 policewomen had branched out into other forms of work. They were employed in the Information Room, in Divisional Accident Enquiry Squads and eventually working beats. The fact that a very slow integration to full police duty was taking place in these years, can be found from the decision in 1961 to allow separate representation for policewomen on the Police Federation Joint Branch Board. It can also be found most conclusively in the 1966 re-organisation of the Policewomen's Department. Under this scheme policewomen were posted to divisions under the supervision of the divisional chief superintendent. They were no longer part of the Headquarters Division. The Superintendent of Policewomen, at that time Miss Pauline Wren, became an advisor to the Chief Constable on policewomen matters such as promotion, appointment, training and other matters. For this purpose she retained a small staff of policewomen in Headquarters.

Promotion of policewomen had been cause for concern as early as 1961 when the Chief Constable reported to the Watch Committee, 'Unfortunately there is a dearth of policewomen constables in Birmingham and elsewhere, who are qualified by examination for promotion to sergeant and at the end of the year there were eight vacancies.'

With the reorganisation the specialist skills of policewomen were to an extent lost. In 1968 a 'Policewomens Specialist Course' was established at the Tally Ho! Training Centre. This was a two week regionally based course for the Midlands, 'designed to cater for the more specialised work of policewomen.'

THE BUILDING OF TALLY HO!

The other major developments in the City Police at this time, revolved around the building programme. It must have seemed in 1960 that the plans of the Watch Committee to improve the conditions of the building stock were doomed when the City Council deferred plans to build five new police stations.

However, the building of the Tally Ho! training complex was completed. On 7 July 1960 the training and recreational part of the scheduled programme was opened by Sir Arthur Young, one time 1st ACC of Birmingham Police, Commissioner of the City of London Police. The remainder of the building was opened on 11 March 1964 by the Chief HMI Sir Edward Dodd, who as Chief Constable of Birmingham had overseen the planning and preparation of the building. An extract from the official opening guide reads, 'The Tally Ho! Centre provides residential accommodation in the form of study/bedrooms for 118 persons in an eight storey block. Teaching, recreational and staff facilities are round a system of landscaped courtyards. There are three classrooms, each capable of accommodating 30 students, which can if necessary be divided and three other classrooms each capable of accommodating 25 students. A lecture theatre provides permanent seating accommodation for 75 students with floor space for 65 additional seats should the need arise.'

The site also housed an indoor riding school and the combined Social and Athletic Club facilities.

The Home Office Detective Training School transferred from the No 4 District Training Centre at Ryton to Tally Ho! The other transfer that took place was that of the police library from Digbeth. The police library and reading room is worthy of mention. It was established at the Digbeth Training School in May 1957 after long pressure from the Birmingham Branch of the Police Federation. The Watch Committee had granted £200 for the purposes of the library and £170 was also contributed by members of the Force. Generous gifts of books were also made by members of the Force. The books purchased were of a technical nature only. There were to be no Zane Greys or Mickey Spillanes here! Advice was given by Mr D T Brett the Librarian of the Police College, at Bramshill House, as to the nature of required reading for policemen and the indexing and cataloguing of the books. In Police Orders for 1 May 1957 it is stated that, 'The object of the library is to make available for reference at a suitable centre, technical books of interest to the Police. It is hoped later to expand the service to include a lending section.' A committee of the 'Great and Good' of the City Police were appointed to manage the library. On the transfer of the library to the Tally Ho! seven years later over 1,500 books were held. This venture must be recognised as having the greatest ideals for the advancement of professionalism by the federated ranks of the Force. It is with some sadness that it must be reported that in an age when the value of the written word has drastically declined, the library stock has also been allowed to decline. The prohibitive cost of the modern book must bear the greatest blame for this. One section of the library which has grown however, is that concerning modern warfare and military matters. This section was a gift of a PC now deceased who was an avid reader of such works. It is said that his wife objected to these books and the interest they held to him. If true, her objection is a gain for the West Midlands Police.

The Digbeth school closed upon the opening of Tally Ho! With the closure of the school, a chapter of the history of the Birmingham Police also closed. No longer would the superintendent in charge of police training be referred to officially as 'The Schoolmaster,' and no longer would police officers be trained in the heart of the City. But the motto that was inscribed above the blackboard, 'It is what you learn after you know it all that counts', will be remembered by Birmingham policemen for many years.

New Police Stations

Irrespective of the City Council's veto on police building, plans were laid in 1962 for a police station in the Walsall Road area and at Weoley Castle. Since the closure of Bristol Street Police Station in 1946, there had been a pressing demand for a new police station in that area. Boundary changes in 1962 had seen the transfer of Speedwell Road Police Station from the 'F' Division to the 'B' Division, but this station proved inadequate for the purpose. A site for a new station was given much consideration and the final selection was made for Belgrave Road at the junction of Pershore Road. The building was finally completed and opened on 3 July 1964. It was said to, 'provide all the amenities needed in a modern police organisation.' Twenty five years later the building is cramped, unsuitable for modern purposes and isolated by the developed Belgrave Middleway to which it fronts. The *Birmingham Evening Mail* announced the closure of No. 4 Speedwell Road as a police station on the 11 June 1964 after 37 years service. The paper reported that Speedwell Road was the only Birmingham police station to have been burgled. In 1927 Mr Rafter, Mr Moriarty and another, had visited the vacant premises to view them. They had no keys, so Mr Moriarty had broken a rear window, gone through and opened the door for the others. Speedwell Road was demolished for new housing a short time after it was finally vacated.

On 4 August 1965 a new police station was also opened in Kings Norton at the junction of Wharf Lane and Masshouse Lane to replace the old building in Redditch Road. This old station had been inherited by the City in consequence of the City's expansion into Worcestershire in 1911.

At this time great plans were afoot to build new Police stations in Shenley Lane, Castle Bromwich, Kenyon Street, Coventry Road, Stechford, Selly Oak

Detective Sergeant Charles Elworthy lectures on the art of fingerprint identification

and to replace Bloomsbury Street Police Station, with a new station in Fowler Street, Nechells.

The next new building to open was the police station at Ladywood which replaced the older Ladywood Road station. This occurred on 7 October 1965. In the same year the death knell tolled for Victoria Road Police Station when the route and the construction of the Aston Expressway was announced. As a Learned Judge said after the Aston Riots, when Aston was policed by Warwickshire, which occurred in Aston Lower Ground in 1884, 'There should always be a strong Force on hand in Aston'. The search for a new Aston site began in order to comply with his instructions.

On 1 February 1968 the new police station at Walsall Road was opened as a sectional station. Initially a wing of the driving school was situated at this police station in order to cope with the increased training of drivers required for unit beat policing. At midnight on 31 March 1968 the police station in Lozells Road closed and the premises were handed over to the City Education Department. On 17 December the new police station at Nechells Green was officially opened to replace Bloomsbury Street Police Station which was demolished to make way for housing redevelopment.

On 23 October 1962 the Watch Committee took possession of Soho House, Soho Avenue, Handsworth. They had been approached by the City Council to do so, in order that the building could be preserved as a functional unit. The Watch Committee were pleased to do so and to use the building as single men's quarters. There can be no other police accommodation anywhere in the world which has such historical significance. In 1761 Matthew Boulton bought the lease of Soho Heath and together with his partner John Fothergill. erected a modern factory. The site was ideal for his purposes, having water power available from the Hockley Brook and coal brought from Wednesbury along the Holyhead Road. The foundation of Birmingham's industrial greatness were laid here. Boulton bought Soho Hall which stood on the land. Boulton as one of the founding members of the 'Lunar Society' held meetings of that august body in his home. Other members of the society included Erasmus Darwin, James Watt, Josiah Wedgwood, William Withering and Joseph Priestley. The Society took the title 'Lunar' for itself for the only reason that it could only meet at the time of the full moon when there was sufficient light at night for the members to make their way along the unlit paths and roads. Records also show that Benjamin Franklin, one of the Founding Fathers of the United States of America, also attended the meetings at Soho. The Lunar Society were instrumental in the parliamentary lobbying for the Bill to set up the Birmingham Assay Office and the founding of the Birmingham Mint.

Other notable visitors to Soho Hall at Boulton's time include Bosworth, Admiral Nelson and the admirable Lady Hamilton and no lesser a person than Catherine the Great, Czarina of all the Russias. The last lady planted a cherry tree in the grounds. Popular legend maintains that it was blasted by lightning at the time of the Bolshevik Revolution in Russia. Boulton died in 1809 and the hall was sold.

In 1896 the hall was used as a private school until the 1920's when it was rebuilt as a private hotel and finally as a residence for GEC apprentices. During that time the Adam fireplaces had been dismantled and sent to Australia and the remaining Boulton furniture had been sold to the Ford Museum in America. In 1968 an extension was built, completely out of character with the main building, to provide 18 additional rooms for quarters.

It is probably inevitable that a building steeped in such historical antiquity should have a ghost. Soho House is claimed to have such a spectre known as the 'Grey Lady'. In 1759 Boulton's first wife had drowned herself in Soho Pool when she had been distraught after repeatedly failing to conceive. Tradition maintains that her's is the ghost of a woman dressed in ankle length grey who passes silently through the walls. If so she is not alone as a Birmingham City police ghost. For years noises of movement and closing doors were heard at the old Stechford Police Station by office constables who knew full well they were on their own in the building. At least it kept them wide awake on night duty.

The last year of the decade, 1969, saw the first serious debate by the Watch Committee for a replacement Police Headquarters. At this stage a decision was reached that the best option would be to keep such a building in the 'legal precincts.'

MR DODD DEPARTS

The most significant change in the management of the Force took place on 1 September 1963 when Mr Dodd retired as Chief Constable to take up the position as Chief HMI. He had served the City of Birmingham Police for 22 years. Edward James Dodd was born in Reading in 1909 and was educated at Reading School and HMS Conway. He had served in the Royal Merchant Navy and the Naval Reserve from 1925 to 1931 and the Metropolitan Police from 1931 to 1941. He was the product of the Trenchard Scheme of the Metropolitan Police at Hendon Police College. In his own autobiography, 'In the Office of Constable,' Sir Robert Mark pays Mr Dodd the compliment of being one of the two most outstanding products of the scheme which guaranteed accelerated promotion and was regarded as producing an officer class for the police.

A sylvan setting for a Police Vespa, 1956

Mr William Derrick Capper, Chief Constable, September 1963 – August 1975

When asked in an interview, why he had become a policeman, Dodd replied, 'Mainly I suppose because of conditions at the time. I was in shipping and there was a shipping slump. I prefer service life to ordinary business life, so I joined the police force and have had no reason to regret it.' When asked 'Are the prospects of a career in the police force better than they were?' He replied, 'On the whole, yes! Provided that a man has a sound physique, a reasonably good standard of education, plenty of common sense, a good temper and a sense of humour, quite apart from such essentials as integrity, honesty and truthfulness, and is prepared to work hard, he can go a long way in the police service. We demand a high standard from our policemen and, generally speaking, we get it!'

The author finished his interview by commenting, 'Birmingham's Chief Constable is a popular personage. He knows his job. He has a keenly developed sense of humour, and at the same time maintains excellent discipline. Since, in this imperfect world, we must have a police force, we can congratulate ourselves that it is under the control of a very efficient public servant.'

Sir Robert Mark takes a different view of the equanimity of 'Ted' Dodd. When Mark was Chief Constable of Leicester that Force was in the same Chief Constables Regional organisation, which was known as, 'Dodd's Own Country.' Because Mark, correctly, believed that in policing relationships, Birmingham and Leicester have little in common in the geographical context, he states, 'Dodd, formed a profound dislike for me.' Sir Robert also points to Dodd as the hidden hand behind his failure to be appointed Chief Constable of Manchester.

THE APPOINTMENT OF MR CAPPER AND HIS DEPUTY

On 2 September 1963, William Derrick Capper was appointed as the last Chief Constable of the City of Birmingham Police. Derrick Capper came originally from Upton Magna, Shropshire and had been appointed Assistant Chief Constable in Birmingham in 1959. He also was a product of Trenchard's Hendon College having been a graduate of Birmingham University. He had seen wartime service in Nigeria and had been on the Directing Staff of the Police College.

Mr R E G Benbow was appointed Deputy Chief Constable on 3 November 1963. At the time of his appointment he had been the Chief Constable of Mid Wales. Mr Benbow had joined the City of Birmingham Police on 3 January 1928 and served until 1 April 1959. He had been Chief Superintendent of 'A' Division from September 1954. His return was seen as an asset by the Watch Committee.

CHERRYWOOD ATTENDANCE CENTRE

On 8 September 1962 an Attendance Centre was started at Cherrywood Road Secondary Modern School, Bordesley Green. The Centre was used as a sentencing option by the Magistrates Courts. Boys were sent to the attendance centre for training under a disciplined regime on alternate Saturdays. Boys between the ages of 10 and 16 years were sentenced to between 12 and 24 hours attendance, which would be worked off at two hourly attendances. The officer in charge of the centre was a police inspector who was aided by other police officers and members of the City Education Department. The miscreants were instructed in woodwork, PT, first aid, road safety, cycle maintenance, civic responsibility and, not least, personal cleanliness. Due to the numbers being sent by the local courts the centre was forced to open every Saturday. The attendance centre became the largest in the Country and the first officer in charge, who became a chief inspector, Mr Sidney Longcroft was awarded an MBE for his pioneering work at the Cherrywood Attendance Centre. The rate of recidivism amongst the graduates of Cherrywood was very low. The concept still remains good today; a very short sharp shock and then home to mum until next week.

THE ORIGINS OF THE SPECIAL PATROL GROUP

On Friday, 1 October 1966 the terrible tragedy occurred at Aberfan in South Wales. A mountain of coal slurry and waste moved and slipped down upon the village, burying the local primary school with great loss of life. By one of those fortunate coincidences of nature, an experimental police mobile column made up of local Midland forces was practising at Kingswood Camp near Wolverhampton. When the Chief Constable of Merthyr Tydfil and Cardiff asked for mutual aid, the contingent of 135 officers, with 31 vehicles was able to be at the scene within five hours. Out of that number, Birmingham City Police provided one superintendent, one chief inspector, four sergeants and 27 constables. They remained at Aberfan until eight days later, when they were relieved on Sunday, 11 October. Their vehicles and equipment were left for the use of their reliefs from other Welsh forces. The men from Birmingham, as did their colleagues, acquitted themselves well on this harrowing occasion.

Mobile columns had by this unfortunate tragedy, helped to prove the value of teams of police officers, highly mobile, able to respond to areas of demand. At the end of 1968 a Special Patrol Group was formed in Birmingham. The initial duties of the group were given as the control of crowds at football matches, processions and demonstrations, and the prevention and detection of crime, particularly robbery, theft and burglary. The SPG used J4 vans and radios and patrolled on foot in plain clothes or uniform as the occasion demanded. The group proved to be highly effective and by the end of 1969 they were supporting each of the divisions for a fortnight each month, as well as responding to particular occasions. At this time the SPG establishment consisted of one inspector, five sergeants, 40 constables and five detective constables. They were attached for 12 months and the tours of duty were 9 am – 5 pm and 9 pm – 5 am. The qualifications for entry were for young and active officers who were selected because of their noted ability and enthusiasm in practical police duty. A perusal of Force Orders from 1969 onwards, shows a large number of names who have gone on to achieve high rank.

The SPG were housed at first in cramped conditions, at Nechells Green Police Station. By the end of 1971 they had moved into converted police flats at the rear of Bradford Street Police Station. A flavour of the early work of the group can be found from the 1970 figures. These show that 767 arrests were made that year for crime in Birmingham and 47 for crime elsewhere. There were also 997 arrests for public order offences of drunkenness, disorderly behaviour and driving offences. The high arrest rate saw an increase in the SPG to two inspectors, six sergeants, 48 constables and six detective constables.

The large number of arrests for driving offences were due in the main to offences of driving whilst disqualified. Under the Road Safety Act 1967 this offence was made subject of a power of arrest. To cope with this a Disqualified Drivers Index was formed and maintained at Headquarters.

Improving Conditions in the 1960's

Conditions of service also underwent change throughout the 1960's. It is of interest to note that the Watch Committee was informed on 21 December 1960 that a majority of the Force was still being paid in cash fortnightly. The Chief Constable was dissatisfied with this as large sums of money were left in the possession of station officers, until individuals collected their wages. The question of cash versus cheque went to ballot at the insistence of the Police Federation, and the majority elected payment by cheque. Favourable terms were offered by the Birmingham Municipal Bank to officers who elected to open accounts with them.

In 1963 Police Regulations allowed for an extra rest day in order to make a shorter working week, based on 88 hours in every fortnight. In Birmingham, officers were still not receiving the rest day granted by the 1955 Regulations.

Faced with this new bonus, the Watch Committee was forced to approve the new rest day. Worse was to follow, for the management of the undermanned Birmingham Police, when acting under the Police Act 1964, the Home Office ordered the normal working week to be reduced to 42 hours by granting seven rest days, instead of six in each four weekly period. This additional rest day was authorised to be granted as overtime payment, when the need for manpower arose. In order to make effective use of the manpower available, the present four shift, 24 hour coverage, system was introduced. Officers were required to work a set pattern of seven night duties, seven second watches and seven first watches. The system was tried first as an experiment on one division in 1965 and imposed Force wide on 3 January 1966. By 5 November 1966, manpower limitations had been improved and for the first time the 42 hour week was properly experimented with.

But it wasn't all give by the Watch Committee. In 1965 they purchased 56 pedal cycles for use by the Force, thereby stopping payment of the cycle allowance to officers. The disgruntled owners of those large 'sit up and beg' machines must have cursed their bad luck.

The special course was first introduced at the Police College in October 1962. Under this scheme, specially selected officers are chosen, on success in the sergeants promotion examination, for training to the higher ranks. The City of Birmingham Police was successful in obtaining places for two officers, DC R 379 S J Perks and DC R 253 L V Stowe on the 1st Special Course. The search was on for talent. In the Force itself a new scheme of interview boards for promotion was introduced in 1963.

Following upon this, the requirement to pass an educational test as part of the promotion examination system was abandoned in 1967. This was not done, as the 'Old Sweats' believed, because of the inability of the 'Sprogs' to pass it, but simply because the educational standard of recruits had improved due to the benefits of the post-war education service. The reader may care to test his or her ability against the paper as shown at *Figs. XIV and XV*. In 1968, out of the male entrants to Birmingham City Police, three were university graduates, ten had one or more 'A' level GCE's, 87 had one or more 'O' levels, 29 had one or more other certificates and only 44 had no educational qualifications. That same year saw the introduction of the Graduate Entry Scheme to the British Police service. The Watch Committee encouraged members of the regular force and cadets to seek University Higher Training. One such who took their advice was one time Cadet P A J Waddington, who was given three years leave of absence to go up to University. He never came down. However, Birmingham City's loss was the gain of the police service in general. Dr Waddington is now one of

UNION OF EDUCATIONAL INSTITUTIONS.

SPECIAL EXAMINATION FOR CITY OF BIRMINGHAM POLICE FORCE, DECEMBER, 1946.

Time allowed - 1 hour. SERGEANTS AND CONSTABLES. Maximum marks - 100.

An additional ten minutes will be allowed to study this paper and during this period no writing will be permitted and no notes may be made.

Write your examination number at the top right-hand corner of each answer paper, but do not give your name, nor otherwise indicate your identity.

The number of each question attempted must be written in the left margin.

Answer question 1 first, and THREE others only.

....

GEOGRAPHY.

....

1. On the map of England and Wales supplied to you
    (a) Outline and name the Counties of Kent, Cornwall, Pembroke, Lincolnshire, and Warwickshire.
    (b) Indicate and name Yarmouth, Birmingham, Aberystwith, Carlisle and Bournemouth.
    (c) Shade and name Dartmoor, the North Downs, The Lake District, the Fens, and the Broads.
    (d) Draw and name the Thames, Severn, Tyne, Trent, and Great Ouse.

2. Describe fully the Holyhead Road between Birmingham and Shrewsbury with particular reference to the towns through which it passes, their industries, and the changing aspects of the countryside.

3. In considering the Relief of any country it is usual to divide it into Highland, Upland, and Lowland areas. Discuss the relief of England and Wales under these headings.

4. State accurately the positions of the following towns, their industries, and their railway communications with Birmingham:- Crewe, Sheffield, Northampton, Oxford, Bristol.

5. Describe the main differences between the agricultural industries of East Anglia and the counties on the Welsh Border, giving such reasons as you can to account for these differences.

6. Where in England and Wales are the chief centres for the production of dried fish, motor cars, cheese, hosiery, and china, and write a full account of any one of these.

Fig. XIV — Promotion examination educational test in Geography, 1946

UNION OF EDUCATIONAL INSTITUTIONS.

SPECIAL EXAMINATION FOR CITY OF BIRMINGHAM POLICE FORCE, DECEMBER, 1946.

Time allowed - 1 hour. SERGEANTS AND CONSTABLES.   Maximum marks- 100.

An additional ten minutes will be allowed to study this paper and during this period no writing will be permitted and no notes may be made.
Write your examination number at the top right-hand corner of each answer paper, but do not give your name, nor otherwise indicate your identity.
The number of each question attempted must be written in the left margin.
Answer four questions only.

....

GENERAL KNOWLEDGE

....

1. Define the following and give, in regard to ourselves during the recent war, one European example of each:-
Allied country; enemy country; ex-enemy country; neutral country; non-belligerent country.

2. In what connection or for what work are the following persons particularly well known?
Sir Pelham Warner; Mr. Jinnah; Dr. C. E. M. Joad; Gordon Richards; Viscount Alexander. Write a full account of any ONE of them.

3. Say who wrote the following and give a full account of any one of the writers:-
(a) A Midsummer Night's Dream.
(b) The Light that Failed.
(c) The Charge of the Light Brigade.
(d) Dombey and Son.
(e) Ivanhoe.

4. Answer briefly the following questions:-
(a) What is a Football Pool?
(b) How much is the inland postage on an ordinary sealed letter weighing 3½ ounces?
(c) What is a Preference Share?
(d) What is the difference between a microphone and a micrometer?
(e) Who, in the United Nations, are the "Big Three", the "Big Four", and the "Big Five"?

5. Where and what are:- The Gulf Stream, the Great Barrier Reef, the Rand, the Great Lakes, the North-West Passage?

6. What, in your opinion, are the main arguments for and against

(a) The 40 hour Week.
or
(b) Abolition of Price Controls.

Fig. XV — Educational test in general knowledge, 1946

the most erudite and knowledgeable commentators on policing in the United Kingdom.

In 1967 the first Force Planning Officer post was instituted to oversee the introduction of unit beat policing. The post was held by a chief superintendent. As a result of the success of UBP, force planning were engaged in the implementation of the Home Office recommendation of a change in the structure of the City Police. This occurred on 1 October 1968 when the number of sub-divisions was reduced from 17 to 12. Each Division was to be headed by a chief superintendent with a superintendent (class 1) as his deputy. The sub-divisions were led by a superintendent (class 1). This resulted, of course, in there being only two sub-divisions per division, a situation that did not remain for long. Twelve men were given promotions to fill the new vacancies.

Uniform also changed in the 1960's, for in 1961 a new style tunic was introduced with a fixed cloth belt and buckle. This year also saw the change of helmet fittings from black to silver. The police stores were responsible for stripping 1,500 helmets. The bands and plates were then cleaned and chrome plated by contractors. The Police Federation were involved in this change by suggesting to the Chief Constable that it would brighten the uniform and possibly aid recruiting.

As in all good feasts, it is best to keep the worst wine to the last. And so it is with the change of catering arrangements for the City Police in the 1960's. In 1969 station canteens were closed on divisions, with the exception of Duke Street, Digbeth and Steelhouse Lane. In their place came the marvel of the age 'Automatic Food and Beverage Vending Equipment' together with the new fangled microwave ovens. A central food production unit was situated first at Nechells Green and then at Digbeth Police Stations. The food was indescribably bad and boring. It was easy. If you wanted a baked potato that was no problem. You put your money in, the flap opened, you took the potato out, placed it in the microwave, set the microwave working by inserting the strip of black plastic that was provided with the humble spud, and waited for the cooking to end. But nobody ever gave instructions to remove the cling film wrapping from the potato. Plastic potato is not edible! In his report on the subject, the Chief Constable writes that, 'the arrangements appear to be working satisfactorily' — someone should have realised that policemen would eat any old 'rubbish' at three o'clock in the morning. After such a high investment in equipment, the vending machines took a long time dying. Fortunately, no members of the City Police died from poisoning or malnutrition.

G

7
'The Beginning of the End'

By the end of the 1960's the age of post-war reform was at its zenith. This was especially true in the reform of local government. Not only were the police unable to recruit and retain officers of potential and ability, but the same applied in the management of local affairs. In 1966 the Government decided that the time had come for a complete review of the structure of local government and appointed a Royal Commission under the chairmanship of Lord Redcliffe-Maud. The Commission reported in 1969 and the Conservative Government issued a White Paper on the matter in 1971. The death knell tolled for the City of Birmingham Police.

LOCAL GOVERNMENT REORGANISATION

In the major conurbations such as Birmingham, Manchester and Liverpool the proposal was for a two tier system of local authorities of District Councils and Metropolitan County Councils. The latter were to be responsible for strategic planning and provision of services, typically police and fire, which needed to be unified in larger geographical areas. The City of Birmingham Police were to be integrated into the West Midlands Metropolitan County. It was said that one purpose of reorganisation was to 'overcome the inertia of tradition.' Redcliffe-Maud had heard evidence, debated and delivered at the time of Wilson's, 'White heat of the technological revolution.' The modern idiom was that 'big' was 'good', and thus a large corporate size was the objective. The monolithic Department of Health and Social Security was the prime objective. A client who needed supplementary benefit would in all likelihood require free spectacles, medicines and other social benefits. One department could provide them all. Simple!

When the White Paper was published, the police were not slow off the mark in stating their opposition to the scheme. The police service in general had experienced amalgamations from the end of the war onwards. This was particularly true of those Forces; West Midlands Constabulary, Warwickshire and Coventry, Staffordshire and Stoke-on-Trent and West Mercia, which were to be part broken or absorbed with Birmingham for the proposed West Midlands Metropolitan Police. On 3 March 1971, the Birmingham Watch

Committee were presented with a report from the West Midlands Constabulary and its Chief Constable, Mr E Solomon, who suggested amongst other ideas, that there should be amalgamation of police authorities only. Mr Solomon and his committee stated, 'The West Midlands Constabulary finds it neither necessary nor desirable to undertake a further amalgamation of police forces in the West Midlands solely for the purposes of securing a single police unit for the Metropolitan area.' The West Midlands Constabulary had been in existence only since 1966, so the Chief Constable's stance is understandable.

However, Home Office Circular 65/71 was issued on 4 March 1971. Entitled 'Local Government Re-organisation in England: Police Areas' it made the message clear that the Home Secretary's view was that each new county should have its own Police Authority and Force. On 4 April 1971 Sir Derrick Capper, Chief Constable of Birmingham reported to his Watch Committee, 'In my opinion there will be only one police force for the Metropolitan area. There is no doubt that the Force to cover the area will be a very large police force. It is true that the Royal Commission in 1962, did state that a force in the region of 3,000 was the optimum size, although this had been departed from in the formation of both the Lancashire and the West Yorkshire Constabularies. I do not think that such a Force would be as easy to control as a Force of 3,000, and I do believe it would be unworkable. I suggest a combined Police Authority for the different sections. So far as Birmingham is concerned if the suggestion by the West Midlands were adopted we should come under an authority appointed by Birmingham District Council and therefore lose part of the present Birmingham districts but gain Sutton Coldfield, and part of the rural district of Meriden'. In the relevant issue of *Forward* magazine, it is reported that frequent discussions upon the subject of 'metropolitanisation' continue to take place between the Chief Officers of the three Forces, which it is anticipated will comprise the West Midlands Metropolitan Police Force. There was little however that could be done by the various Police Authorities and Watch Committees to prevent the inevitable.

Any consideration therefore of the historical development of the City of Birmingham Police in the early 1970's, must be seen as being overshadowed by the uncertainty of the unknown.

Hunting for a New Force Headquarters

This is particularly true of the search for a new Police Headquarters. The Chief Constable told the Watch Committee on 4 March 1970 that the need for a new Headquarters to replace those in Newton Street, had been recognised in 1962 and the City engineers had proposed such a new building in the area of the legal precincts of Steelhouse Lane. He stated that financial provision had been included in the 1968 police estimates for work, costing approximately £1,700,000, to begin in 1972. The committee were told that there was a pressing necessity to provide a new Headquarters for Police, not only because the present one was wholly inadequate, but also because a building should be available, capable of expansion to allow the City of Birmingham to play its proper part in the new Metropolitan Midland Region which would emerge with the implementation of the Redcliffe-Maud Report. The Watch Committee deferred a decision.

Sir Derrick Capper was obviously aware that time was running out for him and again broached the subject with the Watch Committee in the latter part of 1970. This time he pointed out the fragmented nature of the City Police Headquarters Department. He pointed out that the Traffic Department and Firearms Departments were situated in Steelhouse Lane Police Station. The Finance Department occupied converted flats in Newton Street, the motorways project was in the former Forensic Science Laboratory, Midland Criminal Records Office were in Lloyd House, the Regional Crime Squad were in a converted warehouse in Gooch Street and the Aliens Department in Colmore Row. He went on with the list showing that the Recruiting Department was at Tally Ho!, the Police Federation and the Central Property Office at Digbeth, the Special Patrol Group at Nechells Green, the Drugs Squad at Bridge Street West and the Special Investigation and Complaints Department were housed at Steelhouse Lane Police Station. The Chief Constable suggested that the site in Newton Street at Dale End, facing James Watt Ringway, should be permanently adopted for building. Failing this he proposed that consideration should be given to approaching the Calthorpe Estate to build upon the site of the zoo by the Tally Ho! The hunt was on for a new Headquarters.

The matter came before the Watch Committee again on 28 January 1971. It was reported to the Committee that a site had been considered by the Hockley Flyover, but the City Engineer had considered this to be very expensive to build. A site had also been found at College Road, Perry Barr, which 'would fulfil a great many requirements for a Police Headquarters.' The Chief Constable stated that his favoured site in Newton Street at Dale End had recently been examined by Home Office architects and surveyors, with a view to providing a new Magistrates Court. In his view therefore, it seemed that the site was lost. He was proved right as the site is now occupied by the Queen Elizabeth Crown Court. He correctly guessed this as the Courts Bill providing for Crown Courts had been published. A further site for a new Headquarters was also suggested at the General Post Office in Swallow Street and Hill Street, which would cost £1,300,000. Sir Derrick pressed urgency upon the Watch Committee. Alderman Lloyd told his fellow committee members that they must get a site allocated. Also that they could not afford any more delay and must therefore press for a site. He believed they should drop the Perry Barr site entirely, as the Headquarters ought to be in the middle of the City. They should pressurise the Council's General Purposes Committee. He pointed out that the site of the post office or perhaps on the site of the old Snow Hill station, should be adopted and even though they were expensive the committee should not forget that the Home Office were obliged to pay 50%. Councillor Lloyd's view was that the Snow Hill site should be the first choice, because it could provide adequate parking and Swallow Street Post Office site the second choice. Alderman Collet preached caution to his colleagues and all but accused Lloyd of acting on impulse. He believed that a central site was not necessary because of the regional nature of any Headquarters which would result from Redcliffe-Maud. He agreed to discuss the matter of the new Police Headquarters with the General Purposes Committee. The moment was lost.

It was not until a year later that the subject was again discussed in February 1972. The Watch Committee took notice of the fact that discussions had been held with City Wall Finance, the owners of Snow Hill, and the proposed rental of any new building would be £4 per square foot. Notwithstanding, a suggestion that there should be no fear of any debts incurred by the City of Birmingham Watch Committee, because they would become the responsibility of any new Metropolitan Police Authority, the Snow Hill site was dropped. The Watch Committee decided in favour of renting Lloyd House, at a rent of £140,000 per annum, from Messrs Stewart and Lloyds. The Ministry of the Environmemt were also showing an interest in renting the building and unfortunately the Watch Committee moved with haste on this occasion to secure the building.

Lloyd House Police Headquarters is a building singularly lacking in character, comfort or sense of continuity. As early as February 1970 the Watch Committee was informed that the heating of the Midland Criminal Record Office on the third floor was below the standard laid down and subsequently many complaints had been made. The owners admitted that there was nothing that could be done about the problem. In 1989 the problem still exists and not only on the third floor. The move of the City of Birmingham Police into its new headquarters was completed in the early part of 1973. The Force Control Room remained in Newton Street. A light hearted article in *Forward* says,

'Some problems will always be with us; the lightly mini-skirted females will continue to complain about draughts and the lack of heat, and at the same time their male colleagues will still protest about the stuffiness of the atmosphere and demand more fresh air!' The article continued, 'Chief office staff rapidly adapted themselves to their new home, but many in their glass and metal surroundings, reflect with nostalgia on their days at Newton Street where, cramped and inadequate though the building was, there was a character and dignity not to be found at Lloyd House.' Some people will never have the ability to overcome the 'inertia of tradition'!

THE FINAL BUILDING PROGRAMME

However, in all fairness to the City Watch Committee, this was the age when the programme of building new police stations went into forward gear. Kenyon Street Police Station, that relic of 1862 was still in use. No longer though did the building shake with the passage of 'Kings' and 'Castles' of the Great Western storming up out of Snow Hill station or braking hard on the descent. The last locomotives had pulled out in 1969 when the station closed. Time was now up for the police station in Kenyon Street. In February 1970 the Watch Committee resolved to lease space in the Vyse Street Flatted Factory for 21 years, to provide a police office for the Jewellery Quarter. In May 1972 the old station closed and the 'cop shop' in Warstone Lane opened. The last remaining relic of Kenyon Street is the station clock which hangs on the wall of the Tally Ho! Police Museum.

Plans had long been laid for a replacement of Washwood Heath Police Station, the building being in jeopardy due to road widening proposals. In February 1962 a site bounded by Washwood Heath Road, Wallbank Road and Church Walk was considered as a replacement for the existing station. Time and tide wait for no man and by 1967 it was realised that the new system of unit beat policing would require fewer police stations. Accordingly in that year a new site on the disused brick works in Bromford Lane at Fairholme Road, fronting the Outer Ring Road was selected. The Washwood Heath land was given over to the Fire Brigade. Building of Bromford Lane Police Station began in 1970 with the demolition of the brick works and kilns. The police station was formally opened by the Home Secretary, Mr Roy Jenkins in March 1974. Interestingly the contract was entered into for the building of the new Stechford Police Station in September 1973 and is identical to the Bromford Lane building plans. This was to be the model and every police station built after Bromford Lane was to be identical. A sensible idea when it is realised that savings would be made on professional fees and time taken to obtain Local Authority and Home Office planning consent.

In December 1970, agreement was also reached for the building of a new police station in Wilton Road, Erdington to replace the station then presently on the site. This building was completed and officially opened by Councillor Downey, Chairman of the Watch Committee, on 20 December 1973.

On 7 April 1971 the Chief Constable reminded the Watch Committee that in 1967 they had been informed by the Birmingham Corporation that the land on which the City Police garage and stores stood in Duke Street had been allocated to the University of Aston. The Police were still required to vacate the premises in due course. He told the Watch Committee that notwithstanding this the premises had become seriously overcrowded and suggested that they should consider the site at Perry Barr, that was an option for the new Police Headquarters, for a new police garage and stores. The committee deferred a decision until 6 October 1971. On this date they resolved to purchase a triangular site at Aston Expressway, Aston Road North and Park Lane to build the new garage. This was not completed until the early 1980's.

Motorway Policing

The only other major building project was for the Midland Links Motorway Group. There was never any problem with the siting of the building for policing the motorway. Obviously it had to have direct access onto the M6 or the M5. The site chosen was at Thornbridge Avenue, Perry Barr. What appears at first to be straight forward planning foundered though when problems arose when attempts were made to lay the foundations of the complex. Unforeseen problem with the make up of the structure of the site led to the shifting of the main building from its intended position. The centre was opened on 14 February 1971 and became operational on 1 April of that year. By that time the M6 was linked to the M5 at Ray Hall Interchange, West Bromwich. The Aston Expressway was opened to the public at 1300 hours, on 1 May 1972 and together with the final link of the M6 from Coleshill, formed the complete Midland link of motorways. A decision had been made by the Chief Constables of Birmingham, West Midlands, West Mercia, Staffordshire and Warwickshire in 1967 that the policing of the 'Mid-Links', as it became known should be based on a footing similar to the Regional Crime Squad. The Home Office agreed to this decision. The Chief Constable of Birmingham reported that, 'The policing of a motorway embraces two roles, firstly the enforcement of the law, particularly those aspects which relate to the efficient operation of the road system, and secondly the containment of emergencies to ensure the protection of life and property and, at time of accident, to take whatever action may be necessary to resolve the incident speedily'. In order to achieve this, the Midland Links Motorway Group was established to man the motorway control room and patrol the motorways. The strength of the unit comprised of a superintendent, one chief inspector, five inspectors, 12 sergeants and 80 constables. Birmingham's contribution based on a pro-rata figure of the miles of motorway actually running through the City, was one inspector, three sergeants and 21 constables. Attachment to the group was for a period of two years. The patrols had the use of Range Rovers and 4.2 litre Jaguar XJ6 cars. Because of its all round adaptability and greater load carrying capacity the Range Rover soon established itself as the best, and favourite, motorway vehicle.

POLICING CITY TRAFFIC

The Birmingham City Police Traffic Department were also changing and evaluating new vehicles at this time. In May 1971 the last of the Austin Mini Cooper 'S''s, Registration number LOL 542F, was sold, It had recorded over 25,000 miles and in the opinion of the Chief Constable they had not proved as successful as he had hoped. A white MGB sports car also met the same fate, failing to prove any capacity for patrol work in the City. In 1972, 11 Leyland Marina cars were purchased for comparison against the Austin 1100 as a UBP vehicle. After a fatality they were not taken up but the new Austin Allegro was bought instead in 1973. In the same year four Transit vans were purchased for use by the Special Patrol Group. Also in that year the lumbering 1800 saloon car was replaced by an equally lumbering 2200 saloon car for Traffic Patrol work, giving rise to the term 'Giant Panda'. The final change of vehicle was that of the BSA motor cycles to 750 cc Norton Interpol machines. The Norton was the only British made motor cycle then available. Birmingham had been the home of British motor cycle manufacture and the Force stayed loyal in the face of competition from German and Japanese imports.

In 1973 accident investigation courses were held for the first time on a Force wide basis. The courses were based on new techniques, devised in the United States, of investigating fatal and serious accidents by mathematical calculation. What generally appeared at first to be a complex system of evidence by calculation, soon became second nature and with the general introduction of cheap electronic calculators, simplicity itself.

The Recruiting Saga Continues

It is therefore obvious that the work of the Police was becoming more complex and demanding in Birmingham. It should have been hoped that the recruitment of men would match this transition of policing. It did not. The problems of the 1950's and 1960's carried on into the 1970's. In a report on Police pay to the Home Office on 28 January 1970 the Birmingham Watch Committee made their attitude and problems clear. They stated, 'The Birmingham City Watch Committee on 1 October 1969 expressed continuing concern about the number of resignations which had occurred in the Force. In spite of the increasing responsibilities in respect of public order, crowd control, crime, juveniles and other services to the public, the effective strength of the Force was still more than 500 below the establishment approved in 1968. Undermanning allowances are however no solution to the problem but only an expedient. The real issue is the recruiting and retention of trained men to maintain a Police Force of such size and sensibility as to ensure and preserve a society in a sufficiently stable state to adapt peacefully to changing conditions. The position on 31 December 1969, was that of a total male constable strength of 1,714, no less than 44.8% had under five years service. In the case of women constables, 67 out of 98 were in this service group'.

The Watch Committee went on to reveal that of the voluntary resignations in 1969, 47 officers had resigned for better pay and prospects, seven for dislike of Police work, seven for domestic reasons, four to emigrate and two transferred to other Forces.

The Committee had expressed their problems and fears concisely and objectively. The Home Office response was only an acknowledgement of the situation and the nationwide lifting of the previously mentioned recruiting restrictions. On 7 April 1970 the pay of a police constable aged 19 years was set at £900, anyone joining at 22 years was paid £1,025 and the maximum pay for the rank was £1,420. Policewomen were paid £810 on joining, or £925 at 22 years of age. Annual leave entitlement was raised for all ranks allowing constables with under 10 years service 15 days, over 10 years 18 days and over 17 years 20 days. Clearly very few officers stayed in the City Police to benefit from this change which only helped to compound the problem of undermanning.

In 1971 the television recruiting advertising was again shown in the Midland region. The Chief Constable had great hopes that the problem of unemployment that was besetting the industrial scene would bring more recruits. Unfortunately he had to report to the Watch Committee that the redundant workers were, on the whole, found to be unsuitable for police work.

In fact by 1972 he was reporting that, 'the level of unemployment has not been reflected in the numbers of applications for recruitment.' In 1973 only 16 men were gained over the numbers retiring or resigning. Sir Derrick was moved to write that the dearth of good recruits stemmed from the, 'lack of public acceptance that the role of Police in society now requires men and women of much greater sensibility and ability.' He laid most of the blame on careers masters at grammar schools and university appointments officers. In summing up his problem in Birmingham the Chief Constable offered the true wisdom that, 'Mere numbers will not bring any great improvement in the police service.'

The old stand-by for recruitment, The Police Cadet Corps also failed the Chief Constable. In 1970 for the first time since the scheme began in 1949 the Birmingham City Police were unable to fill all the boy cadet vacancies. The girls, however continued to be in competition for places and their standard was still found to be generally better than the boys.

A male chauvinist might claim that they were attracted by the new uniform introduced for policewomen on 6 June 1970. It was described as a semi fitted tunic without breast pockets and belt, and an 'A' line skirt with pleats at the rear. A new hat was also issued of the pill box style to replace the wedge shaped cap. On 12 July 1970 the Watch Committee agreed to purchase 20 dozen pairs of nylon tights as a sample for the policewomen, together with the normal order of black fully fashioned 30 denier nylon stockings. The elderly gentlemen agreed that the tights, if suitable, would provide extra warmth in the winter.

COMMUNITY RELATIONS

On a more practical note, in the same year a policewomen sergeant on each division was nominated to consult with the Birmingham Social Services Department and consultation was to be the keynote and this was true especially in the field on community relations.

At the end of 1969, consequent upon the divisional reorganisation of the Force, each sub-divisional chief inspector was made responsible for, 'maintaining close liaison with local communities and their special needs.' The problem was not new, for by then an officer had been a member of the Birmingham Community Relations committee. The City Police recognised that they had to go out to the immigrant communities and explain the role of Police in British society and the responsibility of the individual. On the 'C' Division, and particularly for Handsworth, a police sergeant was appointed for this important work. The year 1970 saw the publication of John Lambert's study of Birmingham Police, *Crime, Police and Race Relations*. In 1967 Lambert had been given unprecedented access to police files, and records and was allowed to accompany patrols on beats of his own choosing. For the purpose of his research, Lambert chose to investigate the 'F' Division centred on Kings Heath Police Station. The benefit of this 'open house' granted by the Chief Constable was that Birmingham Police received feed-back from John Lambert on matters he was discovering and in line with his recommendations, policies and practices were changed. When his report was published the more sensational revelations were seized upon by the public press. Amongst other things that he found were that the perception by Birmingham policemen of coloured immigrants was that they were prone to violence or crime, generally incomprehensible, suspicious and difficult to handle. The most striking result of his research that gave satisfaction to City police officers against their critics was that coloured immigrants were not arrested disproportionately to their numbers in the population. If the Birmingham Police were prejudiced then it could be expected that their use of their powers of discretion would have produced an opposite result.

Sir Derrick Capper was obviously satisfied with Lambert's research. He was moved to write, 'Our involvement in the day to day needs of policing makes it difficult for us to stand back sufficiently to examine our role in real depth and I am grateful for these contributions of research workers.'

By 1971 a chief inspector had been appointed as head of Community Relations. As a novel experiment 'surgeries' were held in police stations for people with police related problems. It soon became apparent however that those persons attending had a multiplicity of social problems which were in the province of other social agencies. Accordingly, the 'surgeries' were moved to the Neighbourhood Centre at Ladypool Road where they became known as 'The Police Consultation Service.'

The degree to which the Birmingham Police stressed the relatively new field of community relations is apparent, because from 1970 onwards, the topic was made the subject of a separate chapter in the Chief Constable's Annual Report. In 1972 a police sergeant was appointed on each division as a Divisional Community Relations Officer. A further 'Police Consultation Service' was opened at Villa Road Advice Centre, Handsworth. Senior officers of the Force attended two day seminars on the subject and, far ahead of the recommendations of Lord Scarman ten years later, all Birmingham police officers underwent a course in elementary sociology at Matthew Boulton Technical College as part of their initial training.

By the time of the amalgamation in 1974 the Force Community Relations staff consisted of a chief inspector, five sergeants and two constables and six policewomen, who were engaged part time on these duties. Youths selected by their headmasters in Handsworth and Winson Green were taken by the department, assisted by police cadets, to camps in Pembrokeshire. As a further initiative a Community Relations Office was opened in the surplus police house at 63 Holyhead Road, Handsworth. It was a success. Far in advance of any Lay Visiting Scheme a Councillor, who was on attendance at any time, could be called upon to give advice to any young person who had been arrested. A solid foundation was laid by the Birmingham Police in the early 1970's to tackle the problem of their relations with the immigrant population.

THE COMPUTER AGE

Perhaps the major technical innovation of the 1970's was the 'Birmingham Project'. This was a command and control system of resource management by electronic data processing. The scheme was launched by the Watch Committee and Home Office Police Scientific Development Branch in May 1970. Although other Police Forces were experimenting with computer system for general use, the 'Birmingham Project' was to be the first in Europe and another first for the City of Birmingham Police.

The last reorganisation of the Information Room had occurred in 1949 when it had been rehoused in a room on the top floor of Newton Street headquarters. The system of control had also been adapted at that time whereby the control desk had three positions where an operator channelled incoming telephone calls and radio by means of a telephone handset. In 1958 with the expansion of police duty and traffic, the number of positions was increased to six. A map of the City was fitted in the centre of the desk divided divisionally and showing patrol areas. Numbered markers were provided to place on the map, corresponding to patrol vehicles and coloured rings were placed over the markers to indicate availability. By the early 60's, three radio channels were in use by the information room. In 1969 a further radio set was installed in the room allowing two-way communication with Warwickshire, Staffordshire, West Mercia and the West Midlands Constabularies.

In 1958 the number of '999' calls received and despatched by the room was 22,912. In 1969 after the introduction of unit beat policing the '999' traffic had increased threefold to 69,697. The age of the abacus and moving markers about a map were doomed. Moves to modernise were already afoot in 1968 as Mr Philip Knights, one of the assistant chief constables, was granted three months leave of absence by the Watch Committee to undertake a sponsored tour of police forces in the United States. Mr Knights' main fields of study were 'The practical command and control of forces, communications training and the use of police operation and administration of the computer.' There is no record of Mr Knights returning to Birmingham and claiming, 'I have seen the future and it works,' but it would be fair to suspect that he did.

The first that constables on the beat noticed in the implementation of the new system was the fitting of tachograph devices to 'Panda' cars on the 'E' Division. These were fitted to collect data on response times to incidents. The fitting of tape recorders in the information room, coupled to the Post Office 'Tim' signal was also used to time the acceptance of a '999' call with the arrival of an officer at the scene of an incident. For the first time officers were obliged to radio their arrival to the control, a system which later became known as '+TA'. Records show that very few did and the accusation was made that perhaps the majority were being unco-operative. This was probably unfair. Most officers on arrival did, and still do, concentrate wholly on what they find.

COMMAND AND CONTROL

The computer went live for the 'A' and 'E' Divisions at 0600 on Sunday 6 February 1972. The first computer message to the new control room is recorded as;

001 CR5 06/02/72 0600
Received via — F or A Class (1) — Alarm
Location — D N Judge, Newsagent, 206 Streetly Road, Erdington
Informant — Auto Alarm

This was the father and mother of countless subsequent alarm messages. There is no record of the result of this message but it is fair to assume, having regard to the time it was received, that like its innumerable sibblings it was a false alarm.

By the end of April, Aston and Perry Barr Sub-Divisions had gone live with the 'B' Division following in July and the 'C' and 'F' Divisions taking up the rear. To the surprise of the uninitiated there were no problems with adaptability training of officers to operate the visual display units and the command and control system. Within a very short space of time the computer memory became inadequate and was replaced by a newer generation model of less than one micro second retrieval. One term the officers learned rapidly was 'crash' for when the system failed and went off line. This was very frequent in the early days and especially in the first few days when power failures caused by the 1972 miners strike brought the system to a standstill. Mr A G Wanklin who had been chief superintendent of the 'A' Division, had retired in 1969 and was a member of the 'Project' team. He had proudly informed the team, 'We have never yet had trouble with our power supply at Newton Street.' Mr Wanklin

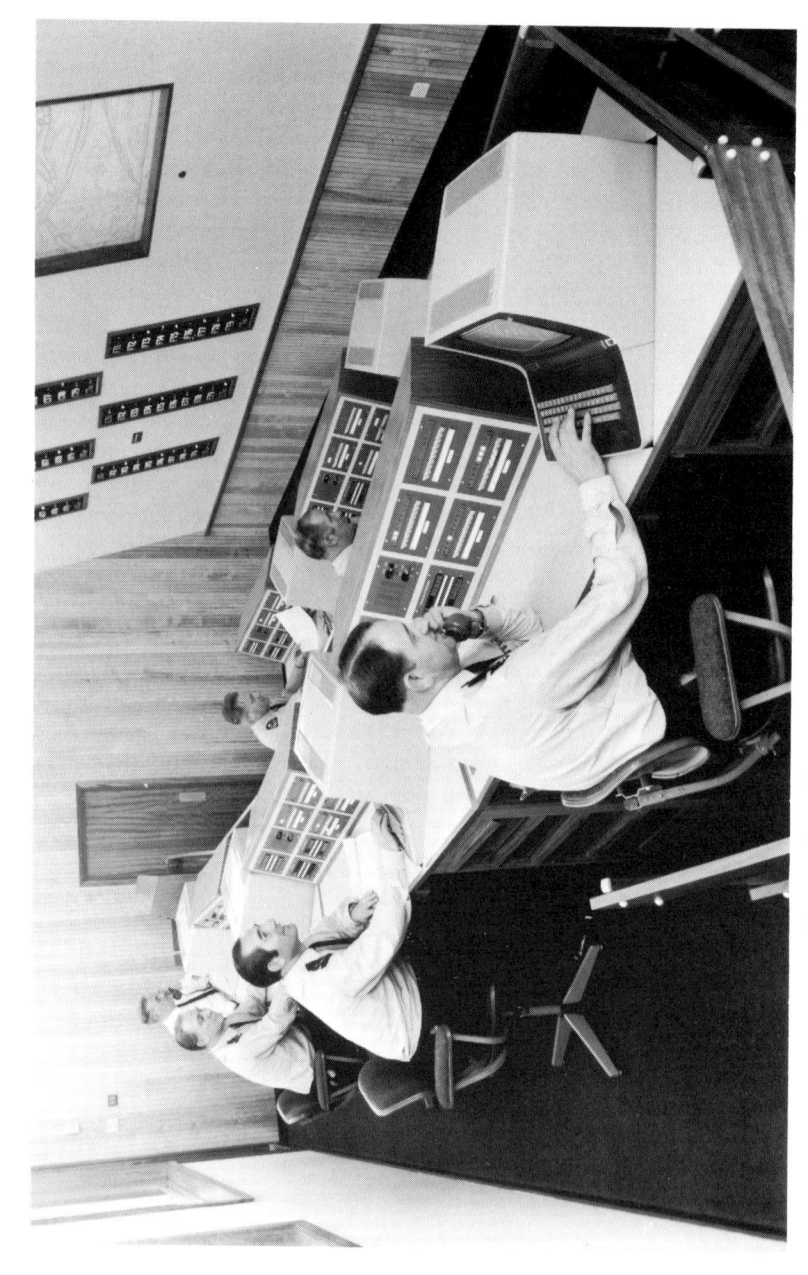

Command and Control goes live in the Information Room, 1972

reckoned without the 'Battle of Saltley Gate.'

THE MINERS' STRIKE OF 1972

In December 1983, Mr Arthur Scargill of the National Union of Mine Workers appeared on *TV-AM* to speak of the 'Three Magic Moments of My Life.' He said, 'The greatest moment of my life was in February 1972 during the miners' strike when I, and several thousand pickets, succeeded in closing Saltley Coke Works in Birmingham.' That was the cry of the victor. Michael Crick the author of *Scargill and the Miners* says that a complete account of Saltley may never be told. He rightly claims that it is tragic that we are unable to describe what happened only a few years ago in spite of the full spotlight of TV and the press. No full official record of what happened exists. The only record of the incident from the City of Birmingham Police is an interview with ex-Chief Superintendent Arthur Brannigan of the 'D' Division and the interview without verbatim quotes, by General Richard Clutterbuck, soldier turned academic, with Sir Derrick Capper for his book *Britain in Agony, The Growth of Political Violence*. Official City Police records are an absolute minimum. The Watch Committee minutes record only that the overtime bill for the dispute exceeded £25,000. Police orders only reveal that the dispute was declared a special occasion for overtime in accordance with police regulations. The Chief Constable's Annual Report speaks tersely of a number of industrial disputes in 1972 and says 'The most notable of these occasions was in connection with the National Coal Strike in February, when miners and others came from various parts of the country to picket the gas board premises at Saltley'. The images that do remain are of a triumphant Arthur Scargill marshalling his forces and a Chief Constable at the scene, in the wrong place and at the wrong time, hemmed in on all sides.

The history of the 'Battle of Saltley Gate' as part of the National miners' dispute in 1972 really starts from 3 February 1972. On that date a item appeared on page 13 of the *Birmingham Evening Mail*. Under a photograph and a by-line, 'The long, long queue to load with coal,' the story told of a mountain of 100,000 tons of coke at a Gas Board coking plant in Saltley, about a mile from the City centre. It was claimed that 30,000 tons had already been taken away by lorry, of which 650-700 were arriving each day at the depot to buy coke. The Mail rightly said that this was Britain's last major coke stock pile. The NUM had by then successfully picketed other stocks and the ports of East Anglia by use of the novel 'Flying Picket' system. When Scargill first got to Saltley he is quoted as saying, 'I've never seen anything like it in my life. It was the most gigantic stack of any colliery I had ever seen. It was estimated that there was a million tons. It was like a mountain. This was no coke depot in the accepted sense. It was an El Dorado of coke.'

When the newspaper story first broke it was brought to the attention of Mr Jack Lally, the Midlands Organiser of the NUM. He was a moderate and had easily come to arrangements with Police in other areas about coal movements. When he attempted to contact Sir Derrick Capper, the Chief Constable of Birmingham he got no response. Lally mounted an initial small picket at Saltley without success, almost being run over in the process himself.

On Friday 4 February, 596 lorries were counted being loaded at Saltley by pickets who had arrived from Hem Heath Colliery at Stoke. The following day the first scuffles broke out between the pickets and Police and the first two arrests were made. A police spokesman is reported in the press as saying, 'If the lorries wish to go in we have been given instructions that the entrance must be cleared. If the pickets bar the way they are causing obstruction.' The writing was upon the wall and battle lines were drawn up. At 4 pm on that Saturday, 5 February 1972 Scargill received a telephone call at his headquarters in Barnsley telling him of the situation. Within three hours he had 200 Yorkshire pickets in coaches on their way to Birmingham. Another 200 followed straight afterwards.

Scargill himself arrived in Birmingham at 3 am on Sunday 6 February. On that day the Police were on duty from 4 am and made a 'gentleman's agreement' with the NUM and the Gas Board to use only one of the two gates into the depot and to keep the other closed. Nevertheless lorries began to arrive and tempers flared.

Because of this the Gas Board management agreed to suspend the loading of coke until 10 am the following day.

THE BATTLE OF SALTLEY GATE

At 10 am on that Monday, 7 February 800 pickets were in Nechells Place and when the gates opened disorder immediately broke out. The arrests began. In order to stop the flow of traffic pickets crossed and recrossed Saltley Road. The action of all the pickets was successful as that day only 47 lorries were loaded and 44 turned away. Every lorry that got through had to be individually battled through by the Police against what grew to be 2,400 pickets. *The Times* for 8 February says, 'More than 500 miners pickets from the Midlands, Yorkshire and South Wales fought with the Police in Birmingham today in an attempt to blockade a convoy of lorries from all parts of Britain collecting coke from a Gas Board depot. The Police made 21 arrests. More than 100,000 tons of coke is

'The Battle of Saltley Gate' February 1972

stockpiled at the depot at Saltley. The trouble first arose last week when a few pickets asked drivers to turn back. The reinforcements today were matched by 300 policemen, two of whom were hurt. One had hospital treatment for rib injuries. The whole of the Birmingham force was put on two 12 hour shifts instead of the usual three shifts. In one incident pickets let down the tailboard of a loaded lorry and about three tons of coke poured on to the road. Policemen had to shovel it on to the lorry to clear the way. Other miners continually used pedestrian crossings to stop traffic. Bottles, stones, fruit and meat pies were thrown during the fighting. Some miners lay in front of lorries and were dragged clear by the Police, who eventually held back the men to allow lorries to enter or leave. Most of the lorries got away with loads'. On this day only 39 lorries got into the depot.

Arthur Scargill's moment was at hand. Using a loud hailer he marshalled and encouraged his men to heave one way against the Police cordon and then suddenly to apply pressure from another angle. When the pressure changed Police would rush in from the flanks to hold the line which would then be weakened at its extremities allowing Scargill to break the cordon. He exhorted his men by shouting, 'We've got them on the run lads, they can only last another half an hour.' Notwithstanding this he kept in contact with the Police trying to get them to close the gates of the depot but was always reluctant to meet any of their requests. At 10.20 am a lorry was driven through the Police cordon which broke. The driver being surrounded by miners panicked and accelerated injuring three police officers and two pickets. One of the officers, Chief Inspector Frank Shelley, received a broken thigh. The pickets parted like the Red Sea, to allow an ambulance through. As soon as the ambulance disappeared from sight towards Nechells the battle was re-engaged. It has been said, especially by Clutterbuck, that the pickets had little animosity towards the Police and especially towards those from the mining areas, but reserved their venom for the 'scab' lorry drivers. The reverse is probably true as when a collection was made for a miner killed at Keadby, a large number of Birmingham Police contributed to it.

On Wednesday, 9 February the battle continued with 2,400 pickets and 400 police with only 42 lorries achieving their goal. In *The Times* for 9 February, Sir Derrick Capper is quoted as saying that the number of pickets was illegal and tantamount to intimidation. He defended his 300 to 400 officers on the spot by saying that they were only maintaining law and order. This could have been the pattern for days but Scargill not wishing to lose the impetus had approached the TGWU and AUEW through the Birmingham Trades Council and asked for help. On that Wednesday, advertisements appeared in the *Birmingham Post* calling on trade unionists in Birmingham to support the strike.

Aware of this the Police had 800 officers on duty in and around Nechells Place on the Thursday. A march by workers from Drews Lane British Motor Corporation, and other factories. TGWU branches, formed up in Washwood Heath Road. They stated their intention to march past the scene of the picket to show solidarity with the miners. Led by Chief Superintendent Ronald Pickard they were orderly and well behaved and were allowed through two lines of Police barricade. On reaching Nechells Place the marchers unexpectedly joined the pickets. As a result by 10 a.m. there were 15,000 pickets blocking all roads to and from the depot.

At 10.45 am acting on the request of Sir Derrick Capper an official from the Gas Board walked across the yard, took the key from his pocket and padlocked the gates. The incessant cry of 'Close the gates, close the gates' died away. Arthur Scargill was asked to disperse the crowd. He agreed asking to use the Police public address system, saying, ''cos mine's knackered.' He climbed on top of the old brick built public urinal that still stands. He made the political speech of his life, like some latter day Lenin to the crowds in St Petersburg, and for the first time used the phrase, 'The Battle of Saltley Gate.' By 2 pm that day there were only two police officers left on the closed gates. Ex-Chief Superintendent Brannigan says, 'The Yorkshire Miners were in tears, they almost kissed us.'

On Friday, 11 February the gates remained closed to all but needy cases for fuel, such as hospitals, and only with the NUM's expressed permission.

Sir Robert Mark has said that in policing a democracy you win by appearing to lose. The question remains who did win at Saltley? The Battle of Saltley was fought on a gentleman's agreement to keep one of the gates closed. But was it fought between gentlemen? Arthur Scargill stated quite explicitly, 'We took the view that we were in a class war. We were not playing cricket on the village green like they did in 1926'. Sir Derrick Capper, a keen sportsman in his youth, played the game in an entirely different fashion. The site of the actual Battle of Saltley is in a natural depression at the junction of four roads, a difficult position to defend. But Scargill and the pickets were allowed to take the high ground by the Police. On the final day 800 police faced 15,000 pickets and in the view of Clutterbuck the total number of police available including those in reserve close by, was between 1,500 and 2,000. Intelligence must have been available to show that the support would have arrived on the final day. Where was the mutual aid from surrounding Forces? At Grosvenor Square, London in 1968, 9,000 police faced a similar number of demonstrators as at Saltley. Ex Chief Superintendent Brannigan is quoted as saying, 'They only closed the gates because no lorries wanted to go in that day. At the time I said there was no reason why the gates couldn't open again the following day. The unions could not have arranged the same kind of demonstration and we could have got more men there by then.' Indeed this was the Police tactic used at the Grunwick dispute in Willesden, London a few years later. In fact by the Friday, there was only 20,000 tons of coke left. Once it had all gone both sides could have appeared to win by losing. During the incident 30 people were injured and 180 pickets including Arthur Scargill were arrested. The decisions on policing were Sir Derrick Capper's alone.

There are those who at the time blamed the subsequent collapse of the Heath Government upon the Chief Constable. On that same week in February the nation was put on a three day working week and electricity cuts were instituted to preserve power. Eventually the miners' demands were met in full thereby destroying the Government's credibility when they went to the country for electoral support for their policies. Could it be true that the actions of the City of Birmingham Police had caused the fall of a Government? Douglas Hurd, the present Home Secretary was at that time Political Secretary to Edward Heath the Prime Minister. Hurd wrote in his diary for Friday, 11 February 1972, 'The Government wandering vainly over battlefields looking for someone to surrender to and being massacred all the time.'

One question that remains is that without the victory in the Battle of Saltley, could there have been a Grunwick, a Warrington or any pitched battles in the miners' strike of 1984-1985?

THE IRA RETURNS

Saltley was not the only battle fought on the streets of Birmingham in the 1970's for by 1973, 'The Sinn Fein boys in their yellow, white and green,' returned to wage war in the City. The IRA activity had been dormant since 1940 but with the upsurge of violence in Ulster from 1969 the bombing campaign returned to the mainland. On 30 August 1973 incendiary devices were placed in three City centre shops. Two were discovered but the third ignited and damaged the premises and stock of Freeman, Hardy and Willis by fire. By good fortune no one was injured. On 2 September an explosive device was found outside business premises in Sherlock Street and was rendered harmless by Army bomb disposal experts. The following day 3 September, six children found a bomb outside premises in Calthorpe Street, Edgbaston and dropped in into a bin. It too was rendered safe. On 17 September a device exploded outside a factory in Witton causing considerable damage, again no one was injured. On the same day Captain Roland Wilkinson of the Royal Army Ordnance Corps was fatally injured whilst dismantling a bomb at Bilton House in Highfield Road, Edgbaston. He died from his injuries on 23 September 1973. However these devices and explosions were only the overture to much worse, culminating in the night of carnage and horror on 21 November 1974 in Birmingham City centre.

THE END OF A SEPARATE BIRMINGHAM POLICE

Throughout this time the spectre of amalgamation hovered in the background. The Chief Constables of Birmingham, Warwickshire and the old West Midlands Constabulary formed a steering committee to direct and control the working parties and a planning unit was set up to smooth the transition into what was then called the West Midlands Metropolitan Police. The planning unit was formed on 1 September 1973 and was staffed by four officers, a superintendent from West Midlands, a chief inspector from Birmingham, an inspector from Warwickshire and Coventry Police and a sergeant from Birmingham. The work of planning was greatly eased on 23 August 1973, when it was announced that Sir Derrick Capper was to be the Chief Constable (Designate) of the new Force. The planning unit were tasked to identify problems which would require examination, to service the working parties with information, to undertake particular tasks set by the Chief Constables' Steering Committee, to maintain the progress of planning and importantly to keep all members of all Forces informed of any planned developments. In his first Report to the Police Authority for the West Midlands Metropolitan County on 15 October 1973, Sir Derrick stated that a realistic establishment for the new Force should be 7,295 men but accepted that the establishment should be the combined total of the constituent Forces which was 6,325 officers. In 1988 the establishment of the West Midlands Police was fixed at 6,754 officers, that is 540 short of the new Chief Constable (Designate)'s realistic number.

The new Force was to be made up of the Birmingham City Police, the West Midlands Constabulary, 1,033 men from Solihull, Chelmsley Wood and Sutton Coldfield Divisions of Warwickshire and Coventry Constabulary, 127 men from the Stourbridge Division of West Mercia Police and 97 men from Aldridge and Brownhills Sub-Division of Staffordshire and Stoke-on-Trent Police. The senior command of the new Force was set at a chief constable, a deputy chief constable and seven assistant chief constables. An examination of newspaper reports for the period would seem to suggest that the major concern of the working parties was which style of helmets would be worn in the Force.

The Federation favoured the style of the 'Combed' helmet as worn by the West Midlands Constabulary. However to cut cost the Police Authority selected the 'Metropolitan' helmet used by Birmingham Police and their Warwickshire and Coventry counterparts. They did however agree that all officers should wear a black and white diced headband on their caps, thereby bringing Birmingham into the same style as most of the rest of the country.

On Sunday, 24 June 1973 the last Annual Parade of the Birmingham City Police took place at Cannon Hill Park when contingents of the Force were inspected by the HMI Mr George Fenwick. The last church parade and service took place on Sunday, 14 October of that year at St Martins Parish Church in the Bull Ring. Roman Catholic members of the Force attended Mass at St Chads Cathedral. Both occasions had a long history in the City Police and were the few occasions when the Force appeared 'en masse'. In 1971 the Chief Constable, Sir Derrick Capper, held a referendum in the City Police with the aid of the Police Federation, to see whether the parades should continue. He pointed out that he was aware that they were not popular with the younger members of the Force but also recognised that the older men, especially those with military service, felt a sense of pleasurable achievement at the end of the parades. In asking the Force to vote in favour, Sir Derrick stressed the point that, 'a smart and cheerful turn-out in a body by the Police does much to establish a happy relationship with the public, upon whose goodwill we depend so much.' In conclusion he emphasised, 'Traditions should not be lightly discarded.' The referendum was in the Chief Constable's favour but it was moved that the parade through the City Centre at the time of the Annual Church Service should be discontinued. It was.

Sports and Social Activities

No history of Birmingham Police and policemen can be complete without reference to their 'extra-mural' or social activities and perhaps as an accompaniment the Birmingham Police Band should be mentioned first.

It was in 1864 that the Birmingham Police Band was first formed. The band finally ceased to exist in 1940 when wartime pressure on manpower forced its end. Early details of the band are obscure, but when Charles Haughton Rafter became Chief Constable in 1899 the City Police Band entered an official golden age. Rafter was a competent flute player and history can probably attribute the success of the band to this fact. Before the First War the band numbered about 30 officers and its conductors were all police officers. At this time the band would perform each Wednesday and Saturday evening in Victoria Square. It is said that if a piece was played which required an echo the instrumentalist would go to the balcony of the Council House to play the echo notes to give the effect of distance.

After the First World War the Watch Committee agreed to representations from Mr Rafter that they should support the band. Once done the band were free to spend their assets on new instruments. The Chief Constable took advice from the Army School of Music and the English philharmonic standard was adopted enabling the band to perform with the Town Hall organ and the City of Birmingham Orchestra. Once fully established eminent musicians such as Sir Adrian Boult conducted the band and composed pieces for it. One composition was known as Birmingham City Police March. Concerts were held in the Town Hall during the winter seasons and the moneys raised were given to charity.

The band broadcast on the radio from the BBC studios at Witton and in 1920 records were made of their performance but were never released for general sale. The City Police Band were fortunate in having specially adopted accommodation in the new Steelhouse Lane Police Station in 1933. Their last full performance was in the grounds of Birmingham Cathedral in 1940 in aid of the 'War Effort Weeks'. Afterwards the instruments were put into store until after hostilities when most were sold. The remainder were eventually donated to the Cannon Hill Arts Centre in the hope of aiding young musicians. The band's assets were distributed between the Police Dance Band, the Birmingham Police Choir and eventually the Birmingham Police Pipe Band.

In March of 1962 the Watch Committee gave approval for the formation of the Birmingham City Police Pipe Band. The band is still in existence and brings credit upon the Force. They wear the Prince Charles Edward Stuart tartan and have represented the Police at home and abroad. In 1963 the Chief Constable wrote 'There is a great deal of enthusiasm for this innovation among a small section of the Force, most of whom emanate from north of the border.' That is still true today.

In conjunction with the police band, the City Police Male Voice Choir was originally formed in 1928. As did the band, the choir gave performances throughout the City. Again, with the outbreak of hostilities in 1939 the choir was disbanded. It was not until August 1945 that a group of some 30 enthusiasts got together and reformed the choir. It continues as the West Midlands Police Male Voice Choir until this present time. The quote is often given that 'Practice makes perfect' and in the early days of the refounding of the choir they would meet weekly in what is now the dining room at Steelhouse Lane Police Station. In October 1956 they had reached such a high standard

An empty Selly Oak Police Station, 1976

that they were invited to take part in a concert at the Central Fire Station where they were accompanied by the band of Her Majesties Irish Guards. Over the years these concerts have taken place in the Town Hall and the bands have alternated between the Irish and the Coldstream guards.

Not only did the bands and the choir prove a positive force for the public image of the Birmingham Police but so did the Birmingham Police Sports Day. The origins of the sports day can be traced back into the last century and were solely at that time a Police Sports and Athletics Day held at different venues in the City. By the mid 1920's the Sports Days were at their zenith of success. They were a keenly awaited event which was given large coverage in local newspapers. The Sports Day was held at the Aston Villa Football Ground and all income, revenue and donations were given to Charity, in particular to the Birmingham Police Aided Association for Destitute Children.

Open invitations were given to all athletic clubs to take part and athletes and competitors travelled from different parts of the country to take part. A programme for the sports day on Whit Monday, 21st May 1923 shows members of Leeds Harriers, Bristol Athletic Club and Surrey Athletics Club amongst other visitors taking part. Of course the Birmingham clubs were well represented by Birchfield Harriers, Dunlop Athletic Club, Sparkhill Harriers and so forth.

A list of those who contributed money and donated prizes reads like a Who's Who and a Trade Directory of Birmingham, from Ansells to Webley-Scott they are all there. One prize donated by G Fletcher Esq. was a cup for the 100 yards boys flat handicap. The rules for this race, always the first of the day, were that it was, 'Open to boys under 15 years and over 10 years on the day of the sports, residing within five miles of the sports ground, or within the Greater Birmingham area.' In 1923 there were ten initial heats of this race of eight boys in each. There is no record of the achievement of Master H Taylor, aged 10 years and 6 months, and standing 4' 10", but he probably got the loudest cheer of the day. One other event that probably drew the greatest cheers of the day is billed as 'The Markets Tug-O'-War'. Four teams from the meat market, the Smithfield fruit and vegetable market and the fish market would annually 'Take up the strain' and heave against each other. With such ready access to high protein food it is a good bet who regularly won.

Competitors at the Police Sports Day were warned, 'No competitor shall be allowed to start unless he wears half sleeves and complete clothing from the shoulders to the knees, and the judges have the power to order off the track any competitor who is not decently attired.' Nonetheless a great day was had by all. The band was present and played such pieces as, the overture from Rossini's

'Tancredi', the march from 'Tannhauser' by Wagner, ballet music from Tchaikovsky's 'Sleeping Princess' and a selection from 'Iolanthe' by Gilbert and Sullivan, amongst many others. The programme also promises that, 'During the afternoon 'General' Handford, mounted on his fiery steed, 'Kaiser Bill' will give his inimitable humerous display.'

Were they all days of laughter, music, golden sunshine and sporting prowess? Let us hope so.

The Birmingham Police Tug-O-War Team were the Champions of All England in 1911. But this was in an age where there were few recreational facilities other than sports. However, if one takes the three major team games, soccer, cricket and rugby, it can be found that they were always well supported. Unfortunately in the case of soccer there were one or two lapses to this rule. The minutes for a meeting of the football section held at the City Police Social Club on Friday, 30 December 1927 tell a different tale. It was reported that the City Police team had been fined 11s 0d by the Birmingham Wednesday Amateur Football Association for failing to play a match against the RAF. Only eight policemen had turned up and they had no kit. The mitigation put forward by the Police was that due to ambulance 'turnouts' three of the players were delayed. As Murphy's Law dictates, one of them was responsible for the kit! On 2 May 1928 the team was also fined 5s 0d for failing to field a team in time for a match against the B'ham Trams 2nd XI. On this occasion 'E' Division members had been detained at Moseley Street Police Station for a clothing inspection.

However, all was not lost as the match against Birmingham Tramways became an annual fixture. The City Police versus Birmingham City Transport became a regular event in the City's sporting tradition and was held at St. Andrews, the home of Birmingham City Football Club. With the evolution of the West Midlands Passenger Transport Executive and a general decline in the prowess of the transport players, the fixture was abandoned. An annual fixture that has been held since 1951 is the match against Glasgow City, laterly the Strathclyde Police. The match is played alternately at Birmingham and Glasgow, the venues having been Aston Villa FC and Partick Thistle FC. Another regular fixture has been that against the Queen's Own Hussars, Birmingham's armoured regiment. The match is played for a silver trophy, which is the property of the sergeant's mess. This is a wise decision by the army officers as it is reported that in the 1960's a letter was regularly received from the regimental quartermaster asking if the trophy was still in Police possession and in good repair.

In the Police Amateur Athletic (PAA) competitions the Birmingham City

Police Football Team were always successful. Perhaps their greatest moment was on 1 May 1962 when they defeated Grimsby Borough Police 2-0. This was a sweet victory as the Chief Constable of that Force had a policy of recruiting ex-professional footballers. The victory was made even sweeter, as on that day they had fielded no less than nine such players. Mr Dodd, the Chief Constable, produced 12 bottles of champagne for the victorious Birmingham team. It should be recorded that the scorers of the Birmingham goals were Ron Brotherhood and Brian Boulton, a regular member of the British Police side.

Any account of rugby football concerning Birmingham Police officers must be overshadowed by the success and personality of PC E 137 Nigel E Horton. PC Horton was the only police officer from Birmingham to have received international honours for his country. The product of Wheelers Lane School and Birmingham Police Cadets, Nigel Horton progressed from playing for the City Police, Moseley Rugby Club and finally in 1968-1969 winning four consecutive caps for England. He won six caps in total whilst a member of Birmingham Police. Notwithstanding this he was also a recognised swimmer and water polo player.

The game of rugby was not played regularly by the Birmingham Police until 1938 when the first team was formed under the eye of the Chief Constable, Mr Moriarty, who had played as an international for Ireland when a member of the R.I.C. The first noted success for the Birmingham team came in 1953 when they achieved the first double over a Welsh Police side, defeating Cardiff City both home and away.

The Birmingham City Police Cricket Section probably has the longest established history of all the three major sports. However, it was not until 1942 with the appointment of Mr Dodd as Assistant Chief Constable, a very keen cricketer, that the game received 'official recognition'. No more would the team be treated as they were in 1935 and 1936 when an application for three new bats at 30s 0d was reduced to two and the 1936 expenditure restricted to a maximum of £6.

Annual fixtures were held against the R.U.C. and the Pembroke Cricket Club in Dublin. The cricketers also played regular matches against the Birmingham Trams and later Birmingham City Transport.

In other sporting fields, mention must be made of one other officer, and that is ex-Policewoman Sergeant Christine Coutts. Miss Coutts first came to notice from her expertise in table-tennis. From 1953 onwards she was the P.A.A. ladies champion for seven consecutive years. In the same period she was mixed doubles champion on five occasions. In 1954 Christine Coutts began playing competitive badminton and in that year was the PAA champion for that sport!

Together with another officer she was doubles champion at badminton on five occasions between 1954 and 1960.

So far the reader may agree that this is an admirable sporting record. However, it was in lawn tennis that she excelled. For seven consecutive years, from 1961 to 1967 she was both PAA ladies singles champion and together with Detective Constable Westwood, mixed doubles champion. Two further mixed doubles championships came in 1969 and 1970, together with the ladies doubles championship in that year! This is a memorable achievement by any amateur athlete. Miss Coutts is also remembered for entering the City Police Perpetual Tennis Challenge Trophy, an annual men's competition. By finding a loop hole in the rules, she caused consternation by entering. Either by bad luck or some face-saving 'jiggery-pokery' she found herself up against her old partner Mr Westwood and was closely defeated.

In the Chief Constable's Report before amalgamation, no fewer than 24 separate sections of sports and social activities are listed. There has been over the years: an amateur dramatics section, an art group, ballroom and Scottish country dancing sections, a judo section and a mountaineering club. All tastes were catered for and perhaps such a wide range of activities for off-duty time personifies the family atmosphere of a Police Force, such as that in Birmingham.

THE LAST DAYS

The last man to join the City of Birmingham Police was Police Constable Robert Duncan Wiltshire, who enrolled on 4 March 1974. The son of a serving Birmingham City Officer, PC Wiltshire was born in London and educated in Birmingham. He is presently serving as a police sergeant on the 'E' Division of the West Midlands Police.

The end of a separate City of Birmingham Police came quietly. A special commemorative 'last day' postal cover was issued by the Force and that was that. City of Birmingham cap badges, helmet plates and divisional letters lingered for a while. However, the Birmingham divisions formed the backbone of the new Force and took on that responsibility without question.

What can be said as a fitting epitaph for a Force that policed the second largest city in the nation for 135 years? Perhaps simply, that it was, 'Nulli Secundus.' Like the Coldstream Guards whose motto this is, the City of Birmingham Police may not have been the first Police Force in the Kingdom, but even though they are from the 'Second City' they were the equal to any others.

Postscript

'B' to 'F' Divisions West Midlands Police

Initially after amalgamation the policing of the Birmingham area continued very much as it had always done. The only notable change was the incorporation of the Royal Town of Sutton Coldfield into the 'D' Division. On the 1 April of 1974 control and responsibility for policing the mid-links motorways was transferred to the West Midlands Police. The dream of a Regional Traffic Squad never came to fruition. In May of 1974 building work commenced on the new Stechford Police Station. The building was completed and in occupation by 19 December 1975, being officially opened by the Home Secretary in May 1976. The police stations at Hay Mills and Coventry Road were silent and closed. The new police station at Bromford Lane had been officially opened by Mr Roy Jenkins MP, the Home Secretary on 20 September 1974. He was a fitting choice as for all of his parliamentary career he had been the Labour MP for Birmingham Stechford.

THE BOMBS BEGIN IN EARNEST

The new Force had barely established itself when on the evening of Saturday, 6 April 1974 the control room received a call claiming that three bombs had been planted in the City Centre. In view of the previous history of bombs in the City the Police plans by this time were to evacuate and seal off Birmingham City centre. Some people foolishly argued with the Police when their Saturday night-out was ruined. The arguments soon stopped when the first bomb exploded at the Lloyds Bank in the Rotunda building in New Street. A second bomb then exploded outside the British Rail signal box by Hill Street. A large amount of damage was caused by both bombs but luckily no one was seriously hurt. The third bomb was found at 6 am on the following day under a pile of rubbish in Stephenson Street, it was intact and had not been armed, either through forgetfulness or fear. It provided valuable forensic evidence. The bombs were made of either gelignite or weedkiller and sugar. On 27 April 1974 the bombing campaign in the West Midlands ended abruptly.

At the time of these explosions the leading IRA cell in the West Midlands was led by Martin Coughlin of Chelmsley Wood, together with Edward Byrne of the same area and a John Molloy. The author at that time was a young PC and takes the liberty of including a personal anecdote at this point. At 10.15 am Sunday, 17 March 1974 whilst patrolling the Chester Road, Castle Bromwich he had cause to stop a Ford Thames Van FNX 19C driving towards

Mr Philip D Knights, Chief Constable, August 1975 – April 1985

Birmingham. Inside the van was Edward Byrne and another man. The vehicle was found to have 17 different mechanical defects. The occupants could not provide any form of identification and the details provided by the driver proved to be false. He was arrested on suspicion of theft of the vehicle. A comedy of errors then commenced when the young PC was left to get on with the investigation on his own. The suspects having been released, the vehicle later reappeared as DOG 727C. Byrne was arrested by the author for suspicion of theft of the tax disc and released when it was clear that the two vehicles were a rebuild that had not been registered as such. Byrne and Molloy allowed the officer to search their railway viaduct lock-up in Viaduct Street, Nechells. However, they never took their eyes off him and Molloy was also arrested on suspicion of theft. When Byrne was arrested he struggled and fought on the doorstep of his home in Woodpecker Grove, Chelmsley Wood but suddenly without warning stopped and 'came quietly'. The answers to many strange questions were found when Byrne and Patrick Joseph Guilfoyle were injured as they were assembling bombs in Manchester. The author was patrolling on nights when told to report to Chelmsley Wood Police Station library. In that room sat twenty armed Special Branch and Crime Squad Officers and the story was recounted for them. All the papers concerning the arrests were taken away and that was that. My part in the war against the Birmingham Bombers came to an end. Fortunately, because where angels fear to tread the inexperienced will stride.

On Sunday, 14 July 1974 five bombs went off in quick succession in the City. The Rotunda was again attacked with gelignite causing extensive damage without loss of life or injury. Perhaps the biggest explosion occurred at Nechells Power Station. This caused a part of the City to be plunged into darkness. The other bombs failed to explode providing further fingerprint and forensic evidence for the Serious Crime Squad and the Bomb Squad. These bombings were followed by a three month lull until 5 November when James McDade and another man planted a bomb at the Conservative Party Offices in Edmund Street, which blew the building apart, and an incendiary device at the firm of Guidex Ltd in Constitution Hill. On 14 November an incendiary device was planted at a plywood firm in Ladywood but McDade was not responsible for this. He was in Coventry, and there part of his mortal remains stayed. He was killed when on arming a bomb, he had made himself, it blew him up. What was left of McDade was released for burial by the Coventry Coroner on Thursday, 21 November 1974.

At 8.18 pm and 8.20 pm on that night bombs exploded in the Mulberry Bush and the Tavern in the Town Public Houses in Birmingham. Twenty one people were killed and 168 injured. There are no adjectives in the English language which have not been used to describe the horror and futility of IRA activity. Within days Robert Gerard Hunter, Noel Richard McIlkenny, Paddy Joe Hill, Hugh Callaghan, William Power and John Francis Walker had been arrested and charged with the murder of Jane Davis a 16 year old victim of their bombs. They were later indicted with 21 counts of murder and found guilty by a jury of those offences.

SIR DERRICK CAPPER TAKES LEAVE OF THE FORCE

On 30 June 1975 Sir Derrick Capper resigned as Chief Constable having been the last Chief Constable of the City of Birmingham Police. He died less than a year later on 20 March 1976. An obituary in the *Police Journal* for July 1976 said, 'He had long been an outstanding figure in the service, rich in professional ability and in varied experience gained in Police duties at home and abroad. His relations with the public and with government at both levels were always excellent. His character and personality were immediately impressive. He tackled problems incisively and tersely, making his decisions with notable objectivity and cogency. Command came naturally to him and his qualities as a leader were never in doubt, enhanced as they were by his towering stature and his fine sporting record. He was generous to a fault and to be in his company was to share his huge love of life. . . His place in the memories of many people is secure. Rarely has a man inspired so much devotion or had such a large circle of friends.'

On 1 August 1975 Mr Philip Knights, the Chief Constable of South Yorkshire Police returned to Birmingham as Chief Constable of the West Midlands Police. He remained in post until Mr Geoffrey James Dear was appointed Chief Constable on 8 April 1985. There can be little doubt of Mr Knights' fondness for Birmingham, and Birmingham Police, for when he was raised to the peerage, the first ever police officer to be so graced, he took the title Lord Knights of Edgbaston.

THE MURDER OF POLICE CONSTABLE GREEN

One other notable event of 1975 was the murder of Police Constable David Christopher Green of the 'A' Division. At about 11 pm on 17 July, PC Green was on patrol in High Street, Birmingham. Outside the Rainbow Suite, a dance hall, he saw a group of youths, and one in particular who was seen to draw a knife from his pocket and place it in the waistband of his trousers. This youth, who answered to the unlikely name of David Charles Forskin, was approached by PC Green who intended to question him. He pushed the officer and ran off, only to be caught by PC Green a short distance away and relieved of the knife. On returning to the scene with his prisoner PC Green was attacked by Forskin's friends, by being punched and kicked. His helmet was knocked off and used as a football. Forskin escaped but PC Green arrested one of his own attackers, a Desmond Amos Wilson who had been born in Jamaica in 1955. A further struggle ensued until Wilson produced a knife and stabbed Police Constable Green fatally in the heart. Wilson was later arrested and sentenced to life imprisonment. Although it seems trite to say it, David Green gave his life in order that others may live, as Wilson and Forskin were armed with knives solely for the purpose of a revenge attack on other youths.

Old Buildings for New

On 22 December 1975 the Police Authority took possession of the Central Electricity Generating Board premises at Bournville Lane, Selly Oak in order to provide new Headquarters for the 'B' Division, replacing Cotteridge and Selly Oak Police Stations. Alterations to the building prevented occupation until April 1976. Eventually the Regional Crime Squad, Vehicle Squad, Drug Squad, Clothing Store and the Control Room were all situated at Bournville Lane. The move of the control room saw the breaking of the last remaining link with Newton Street for Birmingham Police.

Street Disorders

The years 1976 and 1977 are memorable in Birmingham for the violence experienced at political meetings and demonstrations. The first was at a demonstration at Winson Green prison on 15 May 1976 when a National Front demonstration was held to protest against the imprisonment of Robert Relf a well known right-wing agitator. The Anti-Fascist Committee hearing of this, decided to hold a counter-march and demonstration. Two very marginal groups decided to exercise a democratic right which if either ever gained power they would have denied to everyone else. As usual the Police played 'piggy in the middle.' The policing operation was a success in that the groups were kept away from the prison.

However, a concerted effort by 200 members of the Anti-Fascist Committee to reach the National Front group resulted in injuries to 69 police officers, two police horses and damage to police vehicles. The same circumstances arose

The old Stechford Police Station with the new building at the rear, 1975

again in the 1977 Ladywood disturbance. On 15 August 1977 a political meeting was held by the National Front at Boulton Road School. A by-election was to be held for the Ladywood Constituency on 18 August. This constituency has the highest coloured immigrant population in the United Kingdom. It was the ideal ground for the confrontation tactics of the National Front. This time their opponents were the Socialist Workers Party. When the NF supporters by-passed the demonstrators, by using a back door to the school, the SWP turned on the 400 police on duty with a variety of weapons, 58 police were injured, six of them seriously.

The problems didn't go away for on 18 February 1978 the worst and most serious outbreak of disorder occurred at a meeting of the Young National Front at Digbeth Civic Hall. For the first time in Birmingham, Police used shields and visors for protection. The Police cordon was subject to a prolonged attack by a barrage of missiles which caused severe injuries to several officers. Over 2,200 officers were on duty amongst whom were many from surrounding forces on mutual aid. For the first time a helicopter fitted with closed circuit television was used and the evidence gathered proved invaluable.

Restructuring and Reorganising

On 1 April 1978 the Birmingham Divisions were restructured and the number of divisions were reduced from six to five and the sub-divisions increased from 12 to 14. The Central Division of the Force ceased after 135 years to be known as the 'A' Division and became the 'F' Division. The same restructuring saw the introduction of First Response Vehicles or 'Zulus' to the City's streets. These vehicles are generally more powerful than unit beat pandas and by definition are the first vehicles to be sent to emergencies. Home Office approval was also given at this time for the building of a new central garage complex at Aston Road and Park Lane and advance planning was also undertaken to build a new police station at Woodbridge Road, Moseley.

In September 1979 extensions and alterations were made to Erdington Police Station in order to upgrade it to a third sub-division for the 'D' Division. The same year saw the very unwelcome return of terrorist activity to Birmingham when 13 letter bombs either exploded or were found at post offices in the Birmingham area. This necessitated the mammoth task of police officers checking every individual item of mail, and then re-checking it at the Central Post Office Sorting Depot in Royal Mail Street. It was a dirty and dangerous task carried out willingly in order to prevent injury or damage to others.

That same year found the Police Authority examining several sites for a new

Mr Geoffrey J Dear, Chief Constable, 8 April 1985

police station to replace Thornhill Road Police Station, Handsworth. The sites examined were found to be either unsuitable or unobtainable. In 1981 the pressure on Thornhill Road was as great as ever and in order to relieve this a third sub-division for the 'C' Division was planned. Negotiations were undertaken for a site in Rose Road, Harborne to build the new police station. This was a period of strong commitment to community policing on the 'C' Division led especially by Superintendent David Webb. The Lozells Project was initiated in 1979 with funds from the Inner City Project. The premises of the Wallace Lawlor Centre were used and the Police had the advantage of access to Holte School in Lozells. Valuable Police time and effort were put into the project in order to reach the young in the area. The Lozells Project ended in March 1985 when it became the Ladworth Project and grew to encompass Handsworth and Ladywood, hence 'Lad' – 'Worth'.

In 1981 a Central Process Department was introduced in Birmingham. The department was situated together with the Central Ticket Office in office buildings attached to Lloyd House. It replaced divisional process sections in Birmingham. This was not the only administrative innovation that year for a new Systime 6400 computer system was commissioned in the Central Lock-Up for the laborious task of the preparation of the daily Court List for Birmingham Magistrates Court. Both changes were a boon to officers hard pressed with the daily churn of paper work.

The following year of 1982 must be seen as a milestone in the policing of Birmingham as for the first time since the 1930's the actual establishment of the Force equalled the approved establishment. The approved establishment had not meanwhile kept pace with the increasing demands made upon the West Midlands Police, but that was perhaps no different from the rest of the country. The fact that recruiting and retention had reached such record levels must in no small measure be the result of the report of Lord Edmund Davies on police pay and conditions in late 1979. However, coupled to this there was economic uncertainty and mass unemployment in the nation. A decision was made in 1982 that the new police station being built at Woodbridge Road would be unsuitable as a new B3 sub-division. Investigations had revealed that in relation to boundaries and building locations it would not be suitable.

The first completed building of the West Midlands Police was the new Traffic Complex at Park Lane, Aston. It was completed in December 1983 and occupied after the Christmas holiday. On acceptance of the building it was found that structural problems existed in the multi-storey car park. This caused the retention of Duke Street garage for a short time longer, but temporary premises which had been used at the old Midland Red bus garage in Sheepcote

Street were relinquished. The structural problems were resolved in September 1984 and the long tradition joining Birmingham Police to Duke Street was finally ended. The first police station built by the West Midlands Police at Woodbridge Road was opened in April 1985. It was calculated at that time that the backlog of estate works for the Police stood at £5 million.

The demise of the West Midlands County Council was announced in 1985. 11 years after the new form of two-tier local government was introduced it was to be abolished. The very reason for the amalgamation of the City of Birmingham Police with surrounding Forces was to be removed. Again the proposed change caused a period of uncertainty. This was resolved when the new Joint Police Authority was proposed. Even though provision is made in the new legislation for deamalgamations no suggestions were made or have been proposed for any of the constituent forces of the West Midlands Police to go it alone.

Public disorder continued in 1985. On 11 May of that year the worst example of football disorder took place at St Andrews football ground, Small Heath when Birmingham played Leeds United. A riot took place when supporters of the teams spilled out onto the pitch. Outside the ground a wall collapsed from pressure by people and a 15 year old boy lost his life.

LOZELLS ROAD DISORDERS

There had been serious disorder and riots throughout the country in 1981 after disturbances at St Pauls in Bristol in 1980 and Brixton in London had erupted into street violence. Serious disorder had also occurred in the Soho Road of Handsworth at the same time but fortunately not on the same scale as in those other places. At the time this was attributed to the successful local initiatives in community policing. The report by John Brown of the Cranfield Institute entitled 'Shades of Grey' on policing in Handsworth had led to a greater use of foot patrol and permanent beat officers in that area. On the surface all had appeared well for several years until, at about 5.15 pm on 9 September 1985, a dispute arose between a traffic motor cyclist and a local resident over the issue of a parking ticket outside the Acapulco Cafe in Lozells Road. The officer requested assistance and on the arrival of other officers fighting broke out in which 11 officers were reported as injured. At 7.40 pm the Villa Cross Bingo Hall was set on fire. Fire Brigade units attending were obstructed by coloured youths and Police attended to assist the firemen. At 7.55 pm the first petrol bombs were thrown at the Police. By 9.00 pm the Lozells Road shops were being attacked, looted and set on fire. Burning barricades were placed across roads. The evening turned into an orgy of violence, damage and theft. During the course of this riot, that left scenes reminiscent of the war time blitz, two Asian men, Amirali and Kassamali Moledine suffocated to death in their post office that was being attacked in the Lozells Road by the mob, intent on stealing from it and firing it. Rioting continued the next day and when the Home Secretary arrived on the scene, stones were thrown and he was forced to make a speedy exit from Lozells. Over 290 persons were arrested for offences arising out of the riot, the vast majority of whom lived in the Handsworth area. The number of police officers injured was 79. There were also 35 members of the public injured, 83 premises and 23 vehicles were reported damaged. A total of nearly 400 offences were committed on 9 and 10 September.

The Continuity of Policing

Birmingham Borough Police was brought into existence at the time of the Chartist riots in the town. Its members dealt with serious disorder from time to time throughout its history and so did its successors the Birmingham City Police and the West Midlands Police. The evidence is that the fortitude and courage shown so often by their predecessors continues among those members of the West Midlands Police now responsible for peace and order in this great City.

Appendix

An extract from Moriarty's account of Birmingham Police in 1939:

The establishment includes 1 Chief Constable, 1 Assistant Chief Constable, 3 Chief Superintendents, 5 Superintendents, 18 Chief Inspectors, 63 Inspectors, 231 Sergeants and 1,565 Constables.

The five Police Divisions into which the area of the City is divided are known as the A B C D and E Divisions, and in addition there is a sixth Division termed the R Division, which includes the administrative and other departments and units of the Force.

This R Division contains the following branches of the service:

1 Chief Constable's Office in Newton Street, which deals administratively with all the work of the Force, and has an authorized strength of 16, with some female and boy clerks.

2 Criminal Investigation Department, which has, at the Detective Office in Newton Street, a clerical staff of 23, with some female and boy clerks, and an outdoor staff of 98 officers who are employed in dealing with criminal matters throughout the City, allocated amongst the five uniform Divisions. Superintendent F Baguley, assisted by Superintendent F Richardson is in charge of this Department.

3 Summoning and Warrant Department at the Victoria Courts, which takes charge of the Summary Courts and collects fines and fees to the amount of £80,472 in 1938. The staff serve summonses, 66,403 in 1938, and execute Court warrants, 14,131 in 1938, throughout the City. The establishment is 19 officers with some female and boy clerks.

4 The Lock-up in Steelhouse Lane, to which prisoners are brought from Police Stations. It is connected with the Victoria Courts and takes prisoners brought from HM Prisons for trial at Assizes or Sessions. The staff consists of 17 Police officers, with some matrons to take charge of female prisoners.

5 The Coroner's Department. Newton Street, which comprises 8 Police officers attached to the Coroner to make enquiries into sudden deaths throughout the City and prepare for inquests.

6 Public Carriage Department. Steelhouse Lane, which regulates taxicabs licensed by the Watch Committee, deals with lost property found in public vehicles, carries out enquiries concerning motor vehicles, and keeps records regarding street accidents. The strength is 15 with some female and boy clerks.

7 Explosives Department, Steelhouse Lane, consists of 6 Police officers who deal with the licensing and supervision of explosives, petroleum, carbide of calcium and cinematograph film.

8 Transport Department at Duke Street Police Station 'D' Division is responsible for the care and driving of the ambulances, 8 kept for street accidents, the prison vans 3, the Mortuary and other vans 5, and the motor cars kept for general Police transport purposes. Twenty-six Officers are employed in this Department.

9 Telephone Exchange at Headquarters which is manned night and day. The authorized strength is 8. The staff, in addition to dealing with any call on "Central 5000", which is the comprehensive Police number on which any Police Station can be obtained, control the multiphone broadcast system under which any officer can simultaneously speak to all the Police Stations from any telephone instrument. The street Police telephone pillars are also connected to this exchange.

10 Police Stores, in Steelhouse Lane Police Station, where uniform, equipment and articles for Police Stations are stored. Two Police officers are in charge and they are responsible for receipts and issues.

11 Instructional Staff. An establishment of 8 officers is allowed for instructional purposes.

The Police School, Digbeth, is known to the Police Services of many countries. Since its re-organisation in 1919, it has trained over 2,100 Birmingham Police recruits and over 3,500 recruits of other English and Welsh Police forces. It has also afforded training to many Police officers from the British Empire overseas and from foreign countries.

Training is given in Police duties, ambulance, swimming, drill, gymnastics, fire drill and anti-gas measures. Special courses for detective officers are periodically held, and the Home Office Forensic Science Laboratory in Newton Street is available for the assistance of the Police at any time.

A Police officer has to qualify in ambulance and anti-gas measures, and take a revision course every second year.

In addition to the above branches of the 'R' Division, the following units should be mentioned, as they are attached to the Headquarters of the Force:

1 Victoria Courts. The Curator of these premises is a Police Inspector and he controls the male and female staff necessary for the heating and cleaning of the building.

2 Women Police. Their office is in Steelhouse Lane, adjoining the Central

Police Station. The strength is 17 and the Police women work in uniform and plain clothes throughout the City. They also attend the Courts and assist with the female prisoners. Two of the number are attached to the Criminal Investigation Department as female enquiry officers.

3 Girls' Hostel, Newton Street, which is a building, with staff, maintained by the Watch Committee as an adjunct to the Women Police for the temporary reception of females.

4 Finance Department. An accountant, with male and female staff from the City Treasurer's Department, is attached to the Chief Constable's Office, Newton Street, to deal generally with pay and other financial matters.

5 Additional Police. These men are serving Police officers, lent to other Departments to assist in work of a Police nature, and they are paid for by the Departments concerned. One is the Curator of the Victoria Courts, two are engaged in the Lost Property Office, three are engaged in the Public Assistance Department, and 14 are at present, assisting in Air Raid Precautions work.

6 First Police Reserve. This reserve consists of pensioners, ex-servicemen, etc, registered as willing to be enrolled as Police Constables when required. Should the necessity arise, they would be medically examined, attested as Constables, supplied with Police uniform and equipment, and posted to Divisions for work as Constables, full time, with pay. They would be temporary Constables and their employment could be terminated when their services were no longer required.

Also mention should be made of:

a The Police Band, which has a strength of 48. The members of the band are Police officers attached to the five uniform Divisions, and they perform the usual Police duties on their Divisions.
When so required they form a band, with a civilian Director of Music, and as such are directed from the Chief Constable's Office, their band headquarters being in the Central Police Station in Steelhouse Lane.

b The Mounted Branch. The normal strength of this unit is 20 horses with 23 Police officers who are attached to the various uniform Divisions. Several horses are stabled at Duke Street, which is their headquarters, and the remainder are located in pairs or fours at other Police Stations.

c Police premises are numerous as will be evident from the particulars of Police Stations which follow. A Surveyor from the Public Works Department is attached to the Chief Constable's Office to assist in the care of Police buildings. Nearly 400 unmarried Constables reside in Police Stations, in which there is also accommodation for married superior officers in charge. There are over 300 houses built specially as residences for Police officers on the Corporation housing estates. Several of these houses are used as 'police cottages', to serve as Police centres in various localities.

The five Divisions may be given shortly as follows:

1. A Division (Central). Headquarters at Steelhouse Lane Police Station and a sub-station in Digbeth. Area 580 acres, with an ordinary population of about 27,000 but by day densely peopled and thronged by vehicles. The centre for business, shopping, trade, railways and the main activities of the City.
   There are 35 day beats with 17 traffic posts and 46 night beats.
   Chief Superintendent B Harrison is in charge and the total authorised Police establishment is 272.

2. B Division (South West). Headquarters at Ladywood, with sub-stations in Bristol Street and Speedwell Road.
   Sub-divisions at Harborne, with Police cottages in Quinton, Bartley Green, Stonehouse Hill, War Lane and West Boulevard; at Selly Oak with Police cottages in Northfield and Weoley Castle; at Longbridge Estate; and at Stirchley with a sub-station in King's Norton and Police cottages in West Heath and Cartland Road.
   Area 14,800 acres. Population 192,400.
   There are 57 day beats and 75 night beats.
   Superintendent W Talbot is in charge and the total Police establishment is 305.

3. C Division (West). Headquarters at Kenyon Street, with a sub-station in Bridge Street West.
   Sub-divisions at Dudley Road; at Lozells Road; at Thornhill Road with a sub-station in Holyhead Road and Police cottages in Handsworth Wood Road and Greenhill Road; at Canterbury Road with Police cottages in Perry Village and Walsall Road; and at Kingstanding with Police cottages in Kettlehouse Farm and Kingstanding Road.
   Area 9,376 acres. Population 270,300.
   There are 63 day beats with 2 traffic posts, and 80 night beats.
   Superintendent E Buckley is in charge. Total Police establishment is 351.

4. D Division (North East). Headquarters at Victoria Road, Aston, with a sub-station in Duke Street.
   Sub-divisions at Bloomsbury Street; at Erdington with Police cottages in Tyburn Road Marsh Hill and Marsh Lane; at Washwood Heath; at

Bordesley Green with Police cottages in Eastfield Road; and at Stechford with a Police cottage in Cole Hall Lane.
Area 12,660 acres. Population 246,000.
There are 58 day beats with 5 traffic posts, and 85 night beats.
Superintendent A Millington is in charge and the total Police establishment is 344.

5   E Division (South East). Headquarters at Moseley Street, with sub-stations in Edward Road and Coventry Road.
Sub-divisions at King's Heath with a sub-station in Woodbridge Road and Police cottages in Hauch Lane, Dane Grove and Hawkhurst Road; at Sparkhill with a sub-station in Billesley and Police cottages in Yardley Wood Road, Chinnbrook Road and Trittiford Road; at Acock's Green with a Police cottage in Dolphin Lane; at Hay Mills with Police cottages in Ravensdale Road, Fast Pits Road and Coventry Road, Sheldon; and at Robin Hood with Police cottages in Lakey Lane and Priory Road.
Area 13,731 acres. Population 311,700.
There are 67 day beats and 90 night beats.
Superintendent W Bloomer is in charge, and the total police estabishment is 369.

It will therefore be seen that in the City there are 24 sub-divisions with Inspectors in charge. In all there are 35 police stations, and there are 35 police cottages which have telephones available to the general public for communication with the nearest police station.

The A Division has one sub-division with 2 police stations; the B Division has 5 sub-divisions with 8 police stations and 12 cottages; and the C Division has 6 sub-divisions with 8 police stations and 6 cottages.

The D Division has 6 sub-divisions with 7 police stations and 5 cottages; and the E Division has 6 sub-divisions with 10 police stations and 12 cottages.

This brief record would not be complete without mention of a most useful adjunct to the Force, the Special Constabulary Reserve.

The Special Constable of early days was sworn in when needed, was untrained, was equipped with a truncheon, and was disbanded when no longer required.

Now there is a permanent Reserve whose members are afforded training, are supplied with uniform and equipment, are attached to police stations, and perform police duty as and when required.

This Force consists of citizens who have voluntarily enrolled to do duty as police in the event of any emergency. They are organised in a manner similar to the police system, with Divisional Commanders, Sub-Commanders and

Section Leaders, and they act with the regular police.

There are over 1,000 Special Constables enrolled for police work on foot.

In addition there are over 800 Special Constables of the Motor Section who are available with their motor vehicles when required. These motorists are also attached to police stations and have their own Commanders, Sub-Commanders and Section Leaders.

Also, over 40 Special Constables constituted the Observer Corps of the City, having been specially enrolled to act, in conjunction with the Royal Air Force.

Space does not permit of fuller mention of the organisation and activities of the Special Constabulary Reserve, which now numbers over 1,800 men, but tribute can be paid to their civic zeal and usefulness.

This Reserve is at the disposal of the Chief Constable, and many of its members are registered as willing to give whole time police service in a paid War Reserve.

In these modern days, provision is made in police life for athletics and recreation. The Police Sports Club deals generally with various branches of sport, including football, cricket, bowls and tennis, and there is a large pavilion in the Police Sports Ground at Tally Ho! on the Pershore Road. Each division also has its Athletic Club with its football and cricket teams.

The Social Club manages a canteen with dining facilities at Steelhouse Lane Police Station, and there is also another Registered Club in the Tally Ho! pavilion, where dances take place during the winter. There are billiard tables at several of the larger police stations. An Angling Club promotes fishing competitions during the season. All the clubs of the Force are managed by members of the Force, and the accounts of each club are duly audited by qualified accountants.

Bibliography

Rupert ALISON: *The Branch;* Martin Secker and Warburg 1983.
Harold J BLACK: *The History of the Corporation of Birmingham Vol VI, Part I and II;* Birmingham Corporation 1957.
W S BODEY: *Birmingham and its Civic Managers;* Standford and Mann, Birmingham 1928.
R BRAZIER and E STANDFORD: *Birmingham and the Great War 1914-1919;* Cornish Bros Ltd, Birmingham 1921.
J T BUNCE: *The History of Birmingham Vol I, Vol II;* Cornish Bros, Birmingham 1878.
R CLUTTERBUCK: *Britain in Agony;* Penguin Press, London 1980.
Michael CRICK: *Scargill and the Miners;* Harmondsworth, London 1985.
T A CRITCHLEY: *A History of Police in England and Wales 1900-1965;* Constable and Company, London 1967.
K DUNHAM: *The Constables Pistols;* Warwickshire and Worcestershire Magazine, Vol V, No 10, 1958.
E EDWARDS: *Personal Recollections of Birmingham and Birmingham Men;* Midland Educational Trading 1877.
Clive EMSLEY: *Policing and its Context 1750-1870;* The Macmillan Press 1983.
H HAWKES: *Murder on the A34,* 1970.
J T JONES: *The History of the Corporation of Birmingham Vol V;* Birmingham Corporation 1940.
J R LAMBERT: *Crime, Police and Race Relations;* Oxford University Press.
Sir Robert MARK: *In the Office of Constable;* William Collins and Son, London 1978.
C C H MORIARTY: *The Birmingham City Police Centenary 1939;* Birmingham City Police 1939.
R REINER: *Politics of the Police;* Wheatsheaf Books, Brighton 1985.
T Lloyd RENSHAW: *Birmingham, Its Rise and Progress, A Short History;* Cornish Brothers, Birmingham 1932.
G W REYNOLDS and A JUDGE: *The Night The Police Went on Strike;* Weidenfield, London 1968.
A V SELLWOOD: *Police Strike 1919;* W H Allen, London 1978.
Carolyn STEEDMAN: *Policing the Victorian Community;* Routlege, Keegan Paul 1984.
A SUTCLIFFE and R SMITH: *Birmingham 1939-1979;* Oxford University Press 1974.
Norman TIPTAFT: *My Contemporaries;* N Tiptaft Ltd, Birmingham 1952.
J T WILSON: *Diary and Reports;* Birmingham Central Reference Library.
C A VINCE: *The History of Birmingham Vol III, Vol IV,* Cornish Bros, Birmingham 1923.
City of Birmingham Police Magazine 1969-1974: *Forward.*
The Chief Constable's Reports:
  City of Birmingham 1839-1973.
  West Midlands Police 1974-1985.
City of Birmingham Police Force Orders 1839-1973.
The Minutes of the City of Birmingham Watch Committee 1868-1973.

Index

Aberfan, 176
Accident Prevention Squad, 149
Aided Association for Destitute Children, Birmingham Police, 42, *44*, 65, 205
Argyle, Michael V, MC, QC, 149
ATV, 147
Atkins, R, Superintendent, 17

Baguley, DS, 92
Baird, Stephanie, 136, 137, 138
Barrier, John, DC, 96, 113
Barrow-Cadbury, Harrison, Mrs, 65
Birmingham Assizes, 51, 78, 138, 149
Birmingham City Football Club, 156
Birmingham Daily Mail, 42, 43
Birmingham Evening Mail, 136, 153, 157, 162, 163, 169, 195, 196
Birmingham Mail, 78, 92
Bond, Edwin E, Major, 24, 34, 35
Boroughs and Counties Police Act, 19
Boulton, Matthew, 171, 172
Burgess, Francis, Chief Commissioner, 9, 11, 12, 14, 15, 16, 17
Byrne, Edward, 209, 211

Callaghan, Hugh, 212
Capewell, Arthur, PC, 78, 79
Capper, Sir William Derrick, Chief Constable, *174*, 175, 190, 191, 195, 198, 199, 200, 201, 202, 212
'Cappers Commandos', 149
Chartist Riots, 5, 16, 219
Cherrywood Attendance Centre, 176
Churchill, Winston, Prime Minister, 52, 113
'Constables Feast', 3
Coughlin, Martin, 209
Court Leet, 1, 4, 12
Coutts, Christine, PW Sergeant, 207, 208
Crime, Police and Race Relations, 190
Criminal Investigation Department, 16, 65, 66, 76, 78, 88, 125, 126, 127, 141, 149, 150, 151, 164
Critchley, T A, 4, 63, 71

Daily Herald, 75
Dear, Geoffrey James, Chief Constable, 212, 216
Defence of the Realm Act, 56, 60
Desborough Committee, 73, 74, 78, 115
Digbeth Police School, 117, 123, *131*, 169
Disqualified Drivers Index, 177

Dodd, Edward J, Chief Constable, 104, 108, *109*, 117, 126, 130, 133, 136, 143, 145, 151, 168, 172, 175, 207
Dunlea, Lawrence, 93

Eccles, George, 49
Edinburgh Award Scheme, Duke of, 159
Elizabeth, HRH Princess, 127
Employment of Chidren Act 1905, The, 50

Farndale, Joseph, Chief Constable, 35, 36, 40
Fenian Dynamiters, 36
Fenian Literature, 37
Fenian Terrorists, 37
Fenwick, George, 202
Fire & Ambulance Service, 68
First Police Reserve Auxiliary, 96, 98, 104, 113
Fishwick, Ivan, PC, 93
Ford, J, PC, 139
Forward, Birmingham City Police Magazine, 133, 183, 185

Gem, Charles, 11
George V, HM King, 50
Glossop, George, Sergeant, 18, 19, 21, 22, 23, 24, 39
Goddard, Frank 'Panto', Inspector, 102
Goodchild, Jack Frederick, PC, 102
Gready, Bertie, PC, 102
Green, David Christopher, PC, 212, 213
Guilfoyle, Patrick Joseph, 211

Harrison, Beaman, Chief Superintendent, 78, 104
Headborough, Office of, 1, 12
Heath, Edward, Prime Minister, 200
Hemlingford Hundred, 1, 7
Hendon Police College, 172, 175
Hill, Paddy Joe, 212
Hockley Brook Disaster, 79
Home Office, The, 189
Horse Police, 15, 16
Horton, Nigel E, PC, 207
Howick, George Anthony, 11
Hunter, Robert Gerard, 212
Hurd, Douglas, MP, 200
Hutton, Antiquarian, 3

IRA, 92, 93, 200, 209, 212

Jenkins, Roy, MP, 209
Johnson, William Clarence, Chief Constable, 104, *105*, 108
Judicial Sub-Committee, 74, 130

King's Police Medal for Gallantry, 50, 52, 53, 90
Knights, Philip, D, Chief Constable, 192, 193, *210*, 212

Lambert, John, 190, 191
Law, Gordon, PC, 162
Law, Jean, S, PW, 108
Library and Reading Room, Tally Ho!, 168
Licensing Justices, 83
Lipscombe, Rebecca, Mrs, 64, 65, 88
Lloyd-George, David, MP, 48, 71
Lloyd-George, Gwilym, MP, 143
Local Defence Volunteers, 98
Lock-Up Matrons, 64, 88, 165
London Gazette, 146
Lunar Society, The, 171

Mark, Sir Robert, 172, 175, 199
Matthew Boulton Technical College, 191
McDade, James, 211
McIlkenny, Noel Richard, 212
McMillan, Harold, Prime Minister, 136
Metropolitan Police, 5, 6, 9, 11, 12, 25, 63, 107, 110, 172
Metropolitan Police Act, 9
Miners Strike, 1984/5, 7
Mineworkers, National Union of, 195, 196, 199
Molloy, John, 211
Moriarty, Cecil, C H, Chief Constable, 90, *91*, 92, 95, 104, 169, 207
Moriarty's Police Law, 92
Motor Car Act 1903, The, 61
Mounted Branch, 77, 85, 126
Municipal Corporations Act of 1835, 4, 35
Murphy Riots, The, 21

National Front, 213, 215
Night Horse Patrol, 77
Night Watchmen, 3

Oaksey Committee, 115, 117, 129
O'Connor, Feargus, 5

Peto, DOG, Miss, 65,
Pickard, Ronald, Chief Superintendent, 199
Police Act 1890, The, 39
Police Act 1919, The, 63, 76, 77, 82
Police Auxiliary Messenger Service, 97
Police Band, 202

Police Bonus Scheme, 76
Police Cadet Clerks Scheme, 117
Police Cadet Corps, 158, 159, 160, 190
Police Dog Training School, 139
Police Federation of England & Wales, 71, 74, 76, 115, 135, 144, 164, 167, 168, 177, 181, 202
Police Force Museum, 21, 186
Police Headquarters
  Lloyd House, 61, 93, 184, 185, 186, 217
  Newton St, 40, 46, 77, 80, 85, 95, 102, 141, 183, 192, 213
Police Institute, 34
Police Male Voice Choir, 203
Police Manpower, Equipment & Efficiency, 162
Police Offices
  Bath Row, 12
  Beardsworth's Repository, 12, 13, 14, 15, 19
  Cardigan St, 12
  Crooked La, 12, 15, 16, 66
  Deritend, 15
  Nechells Pk Rd, 46
  New St, 18, 21
  Peck La, Prison Cells, 3
  Sandpits, 12, 14, 15, 36
  Staniforth St, 12, 14, 15
  Union St, 12
Police Pipe Band, 203
Police and Prison Officers, National Union of, 71, 73
Police Regulation 1920, 63, 76
Police Sports and Social Club, 21, 123, 168, 206
Police Staff College, Ryton, 117, 168
Police Stations
  Acocks Green, 45, 107, 116
  Alcester St, 19
  Belgrave Rd, 162, 169
  Billesley, 116
  Bloomsbury St, 46, *47*, 116, 140, 171
  Bordesley Grn, 46, 116
  Bournville La, 213
  Bradford St, 12, 141, 146, 171
  Bridge St West, 43, 79, 87, 107, 115, 142, 150, 184
  Bristol St, 116, 169
  Bromford La, 186, 209
  Canterbury Rd, 87, 116
  Chelmsley Wood, 211
  Corporation St, 46, 66
  Cotteridge, 213
  Coventry Rd, 24, 116, 162, 209
  Digbeth, *32*, 46, 68, 74, 102, 115, 154, 181
  Dudley Rd, 116
  Duke St, 18, 33, 46, 51, 68, 87, 115, 127, 140, 142, 181
  Edward Rd, 39, 116
  George Arthur Rd, 39
  Harborne, 116

Hay Mills, 45, 116, 209
Holyhead Rd, *10*, 116
Kenyon St, *20*, 34, 43, 49, 74, 85, 107, 116, 186
Kingstanding, 87, 107, 116
Kings Heath, 116, 140, 191
Kings Norton, 115, 169
Ladywood, 46, *55*, 116, 140, 171
Longbridge, 115
Lozells Rd, 116, 171
Moseley St, 19, 24, 107, 116, 141, 206
Nechells Grn, 171, 177, 181, 184
Quinton Rd West, 141
Robin Hood, 116
Selly Oak, 115, 140, *204*, 213
Shard End, 143
Sheldon, 142
Small Heath, 24
Sparkhill, 58, 116
Speedwell Rd, 116, 137, 169
Stechford, 87, 116, *215*
Steelhouse La, 34, *84*, 85, 92, 102, 115, 129, 137, 140, 142, 163, 181, 184, 203
Thornhill Rd, 45, 107, 116, 217
Victoria Rd, 45, 87, 116, 143, 171
Walsall Rd, 171
Warstone La, 186
Washwood Heath, 116, 186
Wilton Rd, 45, 116, 187
Woodbridge Rd, 83, 116, 215, 217, 218
Police UHF Wireless Communication Service, 107
Police War Reserve Auxiliary, 96, 113
Police 5, 147
Policewomen's Department, The, 82, 167
Politics of the Police, The, 165
Power, William, 212
Prevention of Crimes Act 1885, 73
Promotion Examinations, 85
Prosecution of Felons, Association for the, 3
Public Carriage Office, 61

Queens Police Medal, 108

Rafter, Sir Charles Haughton, 40, *41*, 52, 54, 56, 60, 71, 73, 75, 90, 169, 202, 203
Ramadha, Ralph, PC, 157
Redcliffe-Maud, Lord, 182, 184, 185
Relf, Robert, 213
Road Safety Act 1967, 177
Royal Army Ordnance Corps, 201
Royal Irish Constabulary, 40, 90, 104
Royal Navy, 52, 54
Royal Warwickshire Regiment, 52

St John's Ambulance Brigade, 68
St Martins Parish Church, 202
Scargill, Arthur, 195, 196, 198, 199
Scarman, Lord, 191

Scotland Yard, 50
Selleck, Mark William, DI, 102
Shades of Grey, 218
Snipe, George, PC, 42, 43
Soldiers and Sailors Club, 77
Sommerville, Thomas Bryce, PC, 136, 137
Special Constabulary, 54, 57, 58, 59, 60, 96, 113, *122*, 144
Special Crime Squad, 135, 149
Special Patrol Group, 176, 177, 184, 188
Special Protection Duty, 58, 59
Stephens, R A, Superintendent, 17, 18
Street Commissioners, 3, 4, 18
Street Keepers, 3

Tally Ho! Training Centre, 167, 168
Taylor, Edward, PC, 48, 74, 75
Times, The, 150, 196, 198
Total Abstinence Movement, 34
Town Hall Riot, The, 48, 143
Tozer, A B, 24
Trades Disputes Act 1906, 73
Traffic Department, 142
Traffic Wardens Corps, 154
Trenchard Scheme, 172
TV World, 164

Victoria, HM Queen, 25
Victoria Law Courts, 40, 46, 48, 66, 78, 102, 135, 140
Voluntary Womens Patrol, 63

Walker, John Francis, 212
Warwick Assizes, 7, 16, 22, 37
Watch Committee, 19, 22, 23, 24, 25, 33, 34, 35, 36, 39, 40, 42, 45, 49, 54, 56, 57, 61, 63, 64, 65, 66, 68, 71, 73, 74, 75, 76, 77, 79, 80, 81, 82, 83, 85, 88, 90, 95, 96, 97, 100, 104, 107, 108, 111, 113, 117, 123, 125, 126, 127, 130, 135, 139, 140, 141, 143, 144, 149, 154, 157, 167, 168, 171, 172, 178, 184, 185, 186, 189, 192, 203
Wellington, Duke of, 7
Wilkinson, Captain Roland, 201
Willink, Sir Henry, 130
Wilson, Charles Frederick, 147
Wilson, Harold, Prime Minister, 158
Wilson, John Thomas, 33
Wiltshire, Robert Duncan, PC, 208
Winson Green Prison, 147
Women's Auxiliary Police Corps, 96, 97, 113
Women's Co-operative Guard, 64
Women's Labour League, 64
Women's Police Department, *62*, 63
Women's Public Service, 63
Women's Royal Voluntary Service, 42
Women's Suffrage Movement, 63

Young, Arthur E, 104, 108, 168